Animal Messengers

"*Animal Messengers* not only reminds us that everything is inter-connected, but Regula Meyer illuminates the golden, invisible threads that weave between humans and animals. This book is an essential resource for everyone who has wondered: Why is this animal in my life? Why now? Take to heart the wisdom within its pages. It will fill you with gratitude for how lovingly animals are supporting your well-being, your dreams, and your spiritual growth."

ALLEN AND LINDA ANDERSON, FOUNDERS OF
ANGEL ANIMALS NETWORK AND
AUTHORS OF *A DOG NAMED LEAF, ANGEL DOGS,*
ANGEL CATS, AND *ANGEL HORSES*

Animal Messengers

*An A–Z Guide
to Signs and
Omens in the
Natural World*

REGULA MEYER
Translation by Ariel Godwin

Bear & Company
Rochester, Vermont • Toronto, Canada

Bear & Company
One Park Street
Rochester, Vermont 05767
www.BearandCompanyBooks.com

Bear & Company is a division of Inner Traditions International

Copyright © 2002 by Arun-Verlag
English translation copyright © 2015 by Inner Traditions International

Originally published in German under the title *Tierisch Gut: Tiere als Spiegel der Seele Die Symbolsprache der Tiere* by Arun-Verlag
First U.S. edition published in 2015 by Bear & Company

Library of Congress Cataloging-in-Publication Data
Meyer, Regula.
[Tierisch Gut. English]
 Animal messengers : an A-Z guide to signs and omens in the natural world / Regula Meyer ; translation by Ariel Godwin. — First U.S. edition.
     pages cm
Includes bibliographical references and index.
 Summary: "An animal-by-animal guide that reveals the meaning behind each encounter we have with animals"— Provided by publisher.
 ISBN 978-1-59143-161-9 (paperback) — ISBN 978-1-59143-832-8 (e-book)
 1. Animals—Symbolic aspects. 2. Human-animal relationships—Religious aspects. 3. Omens. I. Title.
 BL439.M4813 2015
 133'.259—dc23

                                                                    2014044606

Printed and bound in the United States

10 9 8 7 6 5 4 3

Text design by Virginia Scott Bowman and layout by Debbie Glogover
This book was typeset in Garamond Premier Pro with Gill Sans, Galliard, and Legacy Sans used as display typefaces

To send correspondence to the author of this book, mail a first-class letter to the author c/o Inner Traditions • Bear & Company, One Park Street, Rochester, VT 05767, and we will forward the communication, or contact the author directly at **www.regula-meyer.ch** or e-mail **regula.meyer@spin.ch**.

With great recognition to Basco, Brahma, Holly, Elai, Eyscha, Gina, Fenja, Laica, Diana, Ramon, Nora, Peterli, Kitty, Maudi, Vivian, Fofau, Cora, Dalina, Moni, Romi, Eli, Liane, Eric, Ramun, Emi, and whatever you all named yourselves . . .

◆ ◆ ◆

We probably enjoy observing animals so much because we learn a great deal about ourselves in doing so.

CHARLES BAUDELAIRE

CONTENTS

PART I
Mammals

PART II
Birds

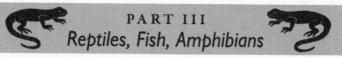

PART III
Reptiles, Fish, Amphibians

PART IV
Insects, Invertebrates

ACKNOWLEDGMENTS

This book took me about fifteen years to write. Many touching and joyful experiences with various animals motivated and inspired me to expand this project. First and foremost, I would like to thank those wonderful, fascinating, and wise messengers from the animal world who lived with me during this time, and continue to live with me, and all the animals I was able to encounter.

Special thanks are due to my parents, who gave me a rich childhood in a beautiful natural environment and showed great understanding and love for the way I was. Thanks to my siblings and the whole "clan" who have accompanied me faithfully and generously through my colorful life. Above all, my husband, Herbert Schönhart, who supported and motivated me, spent hours making corrections, made helpful connections to people, and who accepts me as I am unquestioningly, standing by my side in loving partnership. Thank you for your enormous commitment and your true enthusiasm for my book. I would like to thank my three wonderful sons, André, Roman, and Fabian, who are my life's greatest gift and who share my love of animals. My son André typed the book, helped me to find information for the descriptions, and continually improved the work with his wordplay and humor.

Great thanks go to my dear friend Susanna Rita Beck. She sat at the computer with me for hours and gave me suggestions. For almost ten years she was the second mother of the book. I would like to thank Fereidun Hyadarian and Terence McNamee for their confidence and generosity. Thanks to Heinrich Kössl and Monika Mitchell for hours and energy spent hunting down errors in language and spelling. Many thanks also to Gernot Kainz, who runs a hunting school in Austria and proofread the descriptions of the animals. I would like to thank Dr. Christoph Meier-Zwickly of Malans, Switzerland. He is a great bird enthusiast and advised me with regard to the descriptions of the birds. He is the author of the book *Vögel in Graubünden*.

Finally, I thank all the people who encourage me with their enthusiasm, who ask questions about the meanings of the animals, and who motivate me to keep writing and keep interpreting more animals in order to make my book a worthwhile source of advice.

I want to thank the people who made important contributions that made the book into what it now is. I would like to give my heartfelt gratitude to all of them. I would also like to thank my tireless proofreaders, Anita Juffinger, my mother Ann Suter, and Heinrich Kössl, for spending so much time giving the text a good final polishing.

HOW TO
USE THIS BOOK

This book is not a scientific work and is nowhere close to complete. It is left to the reader to decide whether, and to what extent, he or she will agree with my interpretations of the animals. Remember that animal encounters should be viewed as personal stimuli and not as psychological or ideological truths.

The messages of the animals come from my inner understanding of nature. The zoological descriptions were prepared from various sources with the help of Susanna Hasler-Beck and Herbert Schönhart. I will gladly accept reports of experiences and suggestions for the animals' messages via e-mail (**regula.meyer@spin.ch**). Readers are also encouraged to suggest further animals to be interpreted.

Information on my courses can be found at **www.regula-meyer.ch**.

In my life coaching practice I offer various courses and individual instruction regarding all topics in life. Consultations in person or via telephone can be booked with Urs and Beatrix Nipp in Balzers, Lichtenstein, at 00423–384 31 59.

Advice and courses are also available in Germany and Austria; further details are available from Herbert Schönhart at 0041–78 633 18 67.

Inquiries can also be directed to the publisher.

INTRODUCTION

YOUR INNER
AND OUTER WORLD

We often encounter animals. Not every animal encounter is an encounter that immediately signals something to us. Chiefly, those spontaneous, surprising contacts are the telling ones. It is also interesting to interpret the animals you encounter daily, or those you own as pets.

Perhaps I can give you an idea, perhaps I can help you to imagine how a chance encounter may have something to tell you.

Imagine that you are at the center of the universe. Everything that surrounds you is a reflection of your inner reality. Because everything that exists comes from the same energy source and also understands the same laws, one can thus assume that everything is interconnected. In your inner self, these energies are formulated into thoughts and feelings, which give rise externally to forms, colors, and spaces. What moves and touches you internally also shows itself on the outside. Your inner world is constantly enlivened by astonishing impulses and ideas. Your outer universe also shows these movements.

I believe that the outer world, as the individual experiences it, is an exact mirror of what takes place in the inner world. No two people on Earth ever take the same exact journey of perceptions through time and space. Even when two people spend a whole day together, they notice different details and react to different impulses. Perceptions are regulated by the "soul matrix"—the soul archetype. It is therefore the inner impulse that draws one's attention to something. You are the center of your universe, and your inner world changes, as if in a kaleidoscope, around the center of your perceptions. Thus your archetypes, dogmas, and life themes are always forming new, fascinating mandalas.

The outer world offers the natural counterpart for these mandalas, and our intuitively linked sensory perception is continually building bridges between the internal processes and the corresponding external processes. Because this happens unconsciously, we do not create any conscious connection between internal processes and external events. Thus one could also say that people create external experiences for themselves with the help of their inner worlds.

How Can an Animal Encounter Be Interpreted?

To interpret an encounter with a messenger from the animal world as precisely as possible, the process of this encounter should be observed as precisely as possible. For this, several factors are important.

1. Observe: What was I thinking about? What problem was I moved by at the moment? About whom was I musing? How did I feel when I saw the animal? Be very exact about this. What counts is not the loudest topic but the most important!
2. How did I perceive the encounter? Did I see, hear, feel, or smell the animal first? Was it a single animal or were there multiple animals?
3. How did the animal behave? Was it moving, did it hide, did it react to you, or was it simply going about its business?
4. Where did the animal come from; where was it located (above or below)? If it was moving, where did it come from and where was it going?
5. Note the various colors of the animals.
6. Note the sex.

7. Young animals, when they are clearly recognizable as such, speak to a certain level within the observer.
8. Dead animals also carry a message.
9. Animals in combination are interesting. For example, a dog chasing a cat; a deer in the cow pasture; and so forth.

All these factors should be seen as resources. They can help you to interpret an observation when the message is not yet clear. The mental clarification of an interpretation through the points given above often enhances the strength of the encounter's message. It is important, however, to arrive eventually at a point in your deliberation where you no longer analyze the message with your head. As soon as the first "Aha" moment arrives, follow your feelings, your impulses. Then ignore the external factors. The animal has brought you onto its trail. Just as the animal follows its instincts, you must follow your own.

Let us now discuss the nine points in more detail.

1. In most cases, you are not exactly aware of what has moved you inwardly when you have an unexpected encounter with an animal. Sometimes you are involved in conversation with another person, during which you have "background thoughts" entirely unconsciously. The animal encounter always speaks to the entire personal, inner world. It is a message for your innermost concerns, and it prompts you to contemplate the instantaneous present. The encounter is never about another person's concerns. Thus, if a cat runs in front of your feet while you are thinking about your partner's lack of sensuality, it is reminding you of your own sensuality and is in no way a justification for your complaint. Or if you are on the way to a difficult meeting and a fox runs across the street in front of you, it is not telling you to disguise yourself for the meeting but rather to take a step back, to observe yourself, without becoming so involved. Then you will be better aware of yourself and will later be able to appear confident and secure. The animal will only ever give you an answer about yourself. For this, it does not matter whether you engage with yourself consciously. Surely problems are

present in various areas of your life. Even if the connection is not clearly visible, these problems are mostly formulated from the same fundamental patterns in your thoughts and feelings. The animal gives you inspiring impulses for the flow of your perceptions and thereby also for your thought processes. The encounter draws attention to factors that need to be thought over and grappled with.

2. If you have a clear idea of what you were thinking about, or at least what problem was occupying your innermost thoughts at the moment of the encounter, then try to remember as many details as possible about the circumstances of the encounter. Above all, which of your senses did the encounter speak to? Did you first hear the animal, then see it, then only hear it again? Did you see it after you felt that you were being watched? Did you smell it, then hear it? Was it one animal, or a group of its species? The human senses can be associated with the four elements. Intuition and sight can be associated with the element Fire, smell and hearing with Air, perception and taste with Water, and touch with Earth. In humans, Fire corresponds to the spiritual aspect. The inner spiritual guidance belongs to this domain, as does spiritual development. Seeing an animal, then, is an encounter that was "planned" by your inner guidance in order to serve your development. Animal encounters during prayer are also associated with Fire. Air corresponds to the intuitive, creative, and philosophical domains. Ideas, and the fundamental energy for thoughts, arise from this element. Thought and contemplation make themselves heard through Water. An animal encounter primarily through hearing or smell should inspire us and encourage us to consider and philosophize about the topic of that animal.

Animal encounters in meditation belong to the element Air. The whole palette of feelings corresponds to Water. From the most tender sentiments to the hardest emotions and the agonized brain, everything is feeling. A heartfelt animal encounter takes place when, for example, a snake is nearby or a horse is at my side. Animals in dreams are also envoys for the element Water. An encounter through taste, however, should be disregarded. The Earth corresponds to the body, to health, and also to a person's material surroundings. The same goes for material belongings. Direct physical contact with an animal through stroking, holding, or a collision or an attack, is a message for this level of humanity.

3. The animal's message is clear above all when the animal enters directly and unambiguously into your life. The bee that alights on your hand, the bird that sits briefly next to you on the balcony railing—these are all clear messages. They have to do with you and are a command to engage with the problem. On the other hand, animals who share your living space and whom you therefore see every day, as well as house pets, are intensifiers of a problem, or of the energy for which they stand. When a pet falls ill, it is often translating its owner's blockages with regard to this problem into physical illness.

In the case of aggressive animals, you should be wary of exploring a subject too deeply or of misusing energy. Fleeing animals are prompting you to pursue a subject consciously. Hiding animals are telling you to observe the subject and draw insights from it. An encounter with an animal in which you see the animal but it pays no attention to you is an invitation to think of a problem, to relate it to other thoughts, or to become more conscious of this energy.

4. The cardinal directions can also be used for a more precise interpretation. This may make the message more understandable for you. The cardinal directions indicate tendencies.

The East

The light comes from the East. The sun rises in the East and brings the day. The East stands for the element Fire, and for the spiritual domain of humans. An animal encounter from the East is a message pointing to change, transformation, and energy. It means a new beginning, the awakening of an energy that should be embraced because it leads to change.

The North

The winds dwell in the North. It is the place of cold but also of clarity and purity. The wind moves things; it is the breath of life that can have a hard and cold touch but is also warm and friendly. Thus it is perpetually the embodiment of movement, liberation, and clarity. The North stands for the element Air, for the mental, creative domain of humans. The animal that comes from the North is a reminder of stalled energies, bringing clarity and movement into your life with its message.

The South

The South is warmth, the home of the vivacious life full of feelings, the inner child. Emotions, events, sadness and joy, love and life are energies of the South. It is the home of the element Water, and for people it stands for the world of feelings. If an animal comes from the South, it is telling you about your feelings. Its admonitions and messages point to the world of feelings, to the world of your consciousness, and not to your possessions. You cannot obey these messages by your actions but rather by becoming the energy of the animal.

The West

Darkness is in the West. The sun sets in the West, and night is born here. In the darkness of night, the day that has passed dissolves and the next day makes itself ready. Darkness gives life structure and order. The West stands for the element Earth, matter, the real physical world of people, the life narrative of which you are part and in which you pass each day. An animal in the West gives you indications of what you can realistically do and what you must pay attention to physically.

5. For most animal species, the individuals are more or less similarly colored. In mammals, above all, there are species with color variation. In these cases the coloration can be used for a more exact interpretation. The color shows you on what level of your consciousness you should approach the problem at hand.

Yellow colors correspond to the East and to Fire. Possible steps that may lead to insights relating to the problem indicated by the yellow-colored animal include prayer, letting yourself be led by your inner guidance, asking the angels for assistance, or seeking a conversation with a good spiritual teacher.

White belongs to the North, to Air. You can approach the problem with creativity, meditate upon it, read about it, gather information, or work on it through expressive therapy.

Red tones, fox red to red-brown, correspond to the South and to Water. These coat colors are telling you to think through and also feel through the problem symbolized by the animal. Relate the problem to the troubles and worries you feel. Talk about it with people who are close to you or involved with you.

Black is the color of the West and corresponds to the element Earth. Black animals tell you to take the energy they symbolize into yourself, to go around full of that energy, and to transfer it directly into your external life through your actions.

All mixed colors are derived from these four colors. Gray, for example, is a mixture of white and black. Dark brown comes from red and black, light brown can be a mixture of yellow and black or yellow and red. In the case of mixed colors, both primary colors serve as possibilities. In spotted animals, the background color applies, and whatever other colors are present apply in individual areas of the problem.

6. When it is possible, identifying the sex of the animal can be helpful for interpreting the message. Female animals speak to your intuitive, sensual, watery, passive, hidden, and repressed sides. Males, by contrast, speak to your active, visible, knowable sides and prompt you to action rather than emotion.

7. Young animals indicate an energy that will develop, a problem that needs care and attention, which can blossom into a gift or a strength only through your perseverance and loving devotion.

8. Dead animals signal the same message as the living ones. However,

you are encountering only the shell of the animal, the lifeless body. The message may be that the implied power of the animal is only a sham on your part. For example, a dead blackbird could mean that you set up boundaries and defend territory for yourself to which you have no claim. A dead fox can mean that you have disguised yourself too much and have therefore lost your place in your surroundings.

The message of a dead animal can also be that you have exhausted some energy too much, hurting yourself with it. If an animal has obviously died a natural death, then the problem that corresponds to it is simply over and should be consciously laid to rest. If, shortly thereafter, a living and animated example of the same species indicates to you that you should take up the bygone problem again, then this message also has validity.

9. Through observation, we often see how various animals encounter one another and what kind of tension there is in their relationship in these encounters. For example, dog and cat: the dog, representing the power of loyalty, drives away the cat, which represents the power of intensified perception, sensuality. This observation can be a mirror for you, showing you how you let inner energies work against you.

When you meet animals in "combination," interpret the message according to what you felt first of all—the first idea that came into your mind. In most cases you will be correct if you do this. Factors that may tell you a great deal are: Could aggressive behavior be observed on the part of one animal toward another? Was the encounter peaceful, or did it seem to be entirely meaningless for the animals?

PART 1

Mammals

BADGER

Aggression

Mixed and deciduous forests with soft earth, as well as large copses, are the typical habitat of the badger. The parks and gardens of many large cities also provide habitat for them. The badger is a solitary, gnarly fellow. By day he usually rests in his burrow. Unlike the fox, the badger is an accomplished builder. The badger's burrow is a labyrinth of passages and hollows, built at many levels underground and constantly expanding. The badger moves the displaced earth away from the exits, forming trenches around the holes. The typical badger's burrow has many entrances and is inhabited by a close family group.

Badgers probably mate for life. The family clans consist of between ten and twelve animals, which stake out very exact territories and defend them fervently. The family members live peaceably but very independently with one another. But they have fierce and vociferous battles with other members of their species. Any badger that is not identified as a family member through the scents that are released upon meeting will be considered an enemy and driven away.

If a young badger is raised by humans, it can become very tame and loyal to its owners. The badger eats almost everything that comes its way. Its diet includes small mammals, birds and their eggs, reptiles, frogs, insects, worms, snails as well as fruit, berries, nuts, grains, and mushrooms.

During the warmer months the badger accumulates a thick layer of fat on which it lives for the winter. However, it does not truly hibernate. It maintains its normal body temperatures and wakes up quickly when disturbed, ready to defend itself. It awakes likewise when warm weather comes, starting to look for food immediately. The badger is respectfully avoided by the other animals in the forest. It embraces its role as an aggressive and belligerent creature. Others give it as wide a berth as possible.

Message

If a badger crosses your path, it wants to confront you with your aggressiveness and belligerence. Aggressiveness is often a more or less unconscious attitude in humans that becomes a habit. It usually arises from feelings of worthlessness that are strongly suppressed for strategic reasons of survival. Feelings of worthlessness arise from memories of earlier harm that remain stuck in the subconscious like a thorn.

The existence of these wounds is rarely consciously known. Perhaps they are felt, and suppressed for that very reason. This behavior is comparable to that of a person suffering from an infected wound with a splinter still stuck in it. Any disturbance of this wound is enormously painful. The person protects the wound, even hiding it from view due to the great pain. His attentiveness to other things in life is greatly reduced, and he retreats more and more to his bed. But if the wounded person wants to heal, he must allow this wound to be seen and touched, and suffer the pain. Otherwise it may cost him his life. The message of the nocturnal badger comes from the depths of the subconscious. It says something like this: "Hello, human, you are gravely wounded, heal yourself, give yourself up to the pain so that you can know its origin." The badger is a healer, knowing more than any other the healing powers of nature, especially of roots. It tells you to explore the depths of your human existence, to find the roots of the illness, and then—however great the pain—to pull it out.

But the badger also tells you to rebuild yourself, to newly nourish and strengthen your weakened areas. Badger power is a fiery energy. It represents assertiveness, drive, decisiveness. Defend yourself when you are attacked; defend yourself when your boundaries are overstepped. Stop being an agreeable, nice person. Be yourself, then you will act and think with integrity. Be as solitary as the badger. Choose who to like and who not to like. You do not have to let everyone belong in your family or grant everyone entry into your life. Live with the people you choose, in the territory you choose! This is where you are at home and where you will find healing. If you are one of those people who are well disposed toward everyone and who make all others welcome, the badger's appearance is telling you to recognize the force that you sometimes exert upon yourself. Retreat deep into your burrow, and in the silence, for yourself alone, look for which of the many people around you are really part of your "family," find who has really built a community with you, find who really takes part in your life, and find those who take part in you and your life with a genuine human interest.

But perhaps you are someone who has developed into a true loner, hiding your wounds and showing them to no one. These people also can no longer distinguish whether someone else wants to heal the existing wounds or deal new wounds. The badger is telling you that it is time, high time, to show your wounds to someone and let them be soothed and healed. Look for someone in your burrow, just one person whose scent you can stand. Decide on one person and give yourself over to him or her. Do not bite the helping hand. You will probably feel great pain at first, but afterward you can be healed. Give yourself and your life this chance.

BAT

Rebirth

The bat is a very remarkable animal: the only order of mammal that can fly. Bats have exquisite hearing. In fact, they perceive their surroundings through their ears. Their vision seems to be adapted principally to cre-

puscular light levels. The species familiar to us are mainly insect eaters and night hunters. They orient themselves by means of a highly sophisticated echolocation system. Their prey is almost exclusively moths and other flying insects.

By day, bats hide away in caves and other hideouts, where they sleep hanging by their feet from the ceiling. Their young are born in this position. The mother lives in close connection with her pups. Mother and pup recognize each other by certain noises and stay connected by means of these throughout the young bat's juvenile stage. Bats are unsettling to many people. Their ghostly appearance, their presence in the twilight and the night, and their love of caves, abandoned ruins, and dark corners of houses have given these flying mammals a bad reputation.

Like the raven and the cat, the bat always seems to appear in connection with mysterious, creepy stories and the arrival of death. In many cultures it is a symbol for the death of the ego world and rebirth in the world of the healer. In Central America the bat is a symbol of rebirth in the literal sense.

Message

If a bat flitters into your life, it is time for you to let something die. A part of your life has done its duty. The bat tells you to let go and not obstruct your birth into a new chapter of your life. What were you thinking of when the encounter with the bat occurred? Consciously or unconsciously, you felt the need to seek out a new birth, a birth into a new chapter of life, a new theme for life, new virtues, new self-expression. As humans, we reach such points in our lives again and again. Experiences are had, knowledge integrated, and beliefs change in the living consciousness. Now is the moment for resurrection. New things want to make room for themselves in your life, to become actual parts of your being, to be born into reality. The bat announces a birth.

The bat appears to die every morning when it retreats to its cave to sleep, only to be reborn every evening at twilight. Your message should also be understood in this way. It speaks of the necessity for birth. But before something can be born, it must first die in its old form. Every mother must let go of her child inside herself, must go through a kind of death with him, so that he can be born into the outside world. And so you have nothing to fear in this birth; follow your inner rhythm.

Let yourself go, little by little, and trust in the good that will be born out of it. Perhaps a great spiritual birth will take place in your life, a birth into a new plane. But the bat also comes into your view when it is only a matter of letting go of old habits to allow a little more freedom, generosity, joy, empathy, and other such things to be born. The bat helps you tirelessly to drive forward the development of these domains of light. Night after night, it hunts out the fickle thoughts and scattered feelings (moths and nocturnal insects) that pepper our unconscious atmosphere. Thus, in the nighttime (the subconscious) it prepares for birth by day.

Meditate upon the areas in your life that you would like to hold fast. The bat also speaks of harmful things: traditions whose respect you must struggle for in your surroundings; ideas and opinions with which you clash and from which your fellow humans are distanced. Watch for signs in your life's mirror. If you encounter bats often it also shows that you are steadily moving forward in your evolution. You seem to be one of those people who can't be fooled by anything. But watch that this does not make you lose your joy in life, for it is a wonderful life rhythm to let go, and to be born, in order to let go again.

BEAR, BROWN BEAR
Birth, Origin

The bear, a fearless, majestic beast that appears in heraldry and motifs, was originally present all over Europe. However, it was driven out of our settled areas by humans. And yet, the bear has found its way into every child's room in the form of the teddy bear. Through individual migration and resettlement, this powerful animal has made a home for itself in the remote regions and mountain forests of the Alps. Discrete populations exist in the Pyrenees, in the Cantabria region of Spain, in the Austrian Alps, and in the Italian Apennines. Bears are considerably more common in northern and eastern Europe.

The bear is an omnivore, enjoying a diet rich in both meat and plants. It is a reclusive loner, going far out of the way to avoid encounters with humans. In winter bears retreat into hollows, where they hibernate. There, the female gives birth to at most two cubs. From spring to fall bears are always hungry and on the search for food. One of its favorite treats is the honey made by bees. It also often hunts large mammals, such as deer or sheep, and can cause considerable damage. Although often depicted as fearsome, bears are actually shy and normally flee long before approaching humans can see them.

Message

It is hardly likely that you will encounter a bear in the wild, but I would like to interpret bears in this book. The message of the bear, for modern people, is a reminder of roots for which one begins to yearn but which are almost lost. The bear is the connection to our primal roots. It reminds us of our earthly origin, shows us the way through the human life, and connects us to our human purpose. Stone altars with great piles of bear bones found in caves show us that humans, at the dawn of their history, revered the bear. Although modern people made sure to drive these noble animals out of our forests, we have left them to our progeny in the form of plush toys. It is as if we never wanted to entirely break the connection to our roots. Slowly, modern civilization has accepted the idea that the bear should be allowed to come back home, at least to more remote areas.

If the bear has "touched" you in one way or another, it wants to remind you of your roots. These are not the psychic, karmic roots but the human, genetic roots. You should have the courage to search for the sweetness of your earthly truth, for the tasty morsel of your true being, just as the bear has the courage to seek out and steal the honey of wild bees. The human soul, at the beginning of every life, searches for a fitting family that corresponds in its genetics to the theme of the chosen new life.

The hurdles of life, traversed by this individual member of the chosen family line, correspond exactly to the experience and desired development that a person intends to undergo in her life. From these genetically transferable fears, patterns, experiences, problems, and dramas, the new life creates the foundation for its own individual development. And it is only thanks to this genetic foundation that life and evolution, growth and being upon Earth, are even possible. Just as we have driven the bears out of our forests, so also we try to distance and liberate ourselves from our ancestors and their experiences. People must learn to live with the laws of nature and also to give internal and external predators their place. With the return of the bears, new recognition and respect for our ancestors will also return to the human consciousness.

Thus, if the bear is an animal that touches you, turn courageously and consciously back toward the strong and weak expressions of your own human roots. Dive back into the natural consciousness of the human existence. Let instinct, intuition, curiosity, and vitality be the tools that guide your hunger for life and allow you always to feel new joy and have new experiences. And watch out for the moment when it is time to sink into the deep, inner darkness to feed on your experiences in stillness and peace. These are the phases of processing, of digestion, a time that is given to you through the observation of your own self, for concluding and resolving topics and processes. And often, in this process, new things are born secretly and inconspicuously. In your life, too, the time will come again when a new hunger for experience draws you away from your inner self. Then you will recognize what powers are to accompany you through your new bear's summer.

BEAVER
Work

The beaver was once widespread in Europe, but due to hunting and the desire to take over its habitat it has been almost completely eradicated.

The beaver is an excellent swimmer and builder. It builds its home in the water and secures it by placing the entrance below the water level and constructing various escape routes. The beaver only builds dams when the water level is variable and jeopardizes the animal's safety by dropping. The beaver lives on young leaves, bark, and plants that grow at the water's edge—a meager diet for a creature weighing about sixty-five pounds. To maintain its energy balance, the beaver must keep searching for food all day long. To get the aforementioned tender leaves, it fells trees in the riparian forest with trunk diameters up to two feet. Thus it is an important link in the ecological chain. By feeling trees, the beaver brings light to the forest floor, without which the rich diversity of plants growing there could not survive.

Beavers live together in small family groups. Every member of this family works for the good of the collective. Great harmony and unity reigns within the families. But their territories are clearly defined with scent marks, and intruders are rigorously chased away. For humans, encounters with beavers are rare. But little by little, people are becoming aware of the significance of the animal world in their living space, and so great efforts are being made to restore nature, little by little, to its original state. The beaver is a creature that is returning in this manner.

We can tolerate its message once again, because through our very intensive, sometimes excessive approach to the topic of work, we have gone through an important learning process. Precisely because our approach to work has gradually gained new significance, as people's approach to it has become more mature, healthy, and natural, the beaver will once again find its place in our living space and be available to us individually as a teacher.

Message

If you encounter a beaver at work, it is directing your attention toward aspects of your own work. Perhaps it is advising you to finally put plans and ideas into action. But perhaps it is also important for you to grapple concretely with the work where it has accumulated, to look reality in the eye and to work, not just talk about working. The beaver does not plan for long; it acts. It sees what is needed and it sets about it immediately. There is no oversight, no risk analysis, but everything is done for the family. Thus, this is not a matter of strength or wealth but of work that serves the essential needs of life. The beaver works to eat, to live sheltered and concealed, and to give space to the relationships it chooses.

If you see a beaver eating with its family, you should think about your collaborative work. Strive for a harmonious professional climate; consider your coworkers but also yourself. Together many things are achieved, but only when all parties are comfortable can the best energies be released; then each individual can take and fulfill her place within the whole according to her abilities. As humans, work is the opportunity to have experiences in the real world, to exchange and combine creativity, knowledge, and strength, and together to reap new wisdom and experience from these things.

A beaver in flight or in danger advises you to not let yourself become pigeonholed professionally. Always keep a few possibilities open; leave yourself sufficient space for growth and expansion, for creativity and development. These are important ingredients for a harmonious work climate. Your work should be the foundation on which you, as a human, build the security that you need to strengthen your attitude to life without hindrance.

In general, the beaver also warns you against serving power with your work. The price you would pay for this is high. The person who works toward this goal loses access to her inner guidance, to her soul—and her living space becomes poorer and poorer.

CAT

Perception, Sensuality, Joy

When we speak of cats here we refer mainly to the domestic cat. The domestic cat is descended from the African wildcat and was domesticated in Egypt. From there, prized as a mouser and snake catcher, it spread throughout the world, transported by sailors. The wildcat

and bobcat are only distant relatives of the domestic cat. The ancient Romans are to be thanked for spreading the cat throughout Europe. Cats protect people's stored food, and with their playful, cuddly behavior they also impart security and happiness.

Cats are headstrong animals with a connection to the mystical, and they are especially comfortable with spiritual people. However, in the age of the Spanish Inquisition cats were persecuted because they were believed to be allied with the devil and animated by demons. Along with witches and wizards, they were tortured and burned in medieval Europe. Only when black rats came to Europe bringing the plague did the cat's reputation improve; then high sums were paid for fine specimens. The cat's excellent hearing, sharp eyes, and whiskers enable it to be a hunter, often nocturnal. The pupils of the eyes, which narrow to small slits in the daylight, open wider as it grows darker. Behind the retina of a cat's eye is a layer of reflective material that strengthens the cat's sensitivity to light. For this reason, the eyes can take in a great deal of light, even in darkness.

The cat's sense of smell is connected to the sense of taste through the vomeronasal, or Jacobson's, organ above the nose. This transfers the received impulses to the brain. The cat marks everything it owns with scent glands located on the cheeks, chin, and base of the tail. The cat's ears are also extraordinarily well constructed. When a cat lies, apparently sleeping, on the floor next to a mouse hole, its sense of hearing is actually giving it a precise idea of the mouse's movements inside the hole. The cat's ability to discern the position of sounds and hear high frequencies surpasses that of the dog. The whiskers constitute another sense organ worth mentioning. They are located above the eyes, around the nose, and on the chin. The whiskers of a cat are extremely sensitive. With their help, the cat can tell the size of any passageway and safely move its kittens to a new location.

This playful, affectionate animal, with its extraordinary senses, is widely distributed and loved throughout the world.

Message

Because the cat is probably the most popular pet in the world, it is no rarity to encounter one. You are immediately reminded of its sensuality: its ability to perceive with all senses, to devote itself to what it perceives so that it can inwardly picture the true nature of momentary situations.

Cats and spiritual people fit together, for they have sharp feelings. Sharp vision and sharp ears are not extrasensory perceptions. They are both sensory perceptions and trained senses. Observed sensuality lets the light of truth entirely into the heart and creates a grand, comprehensive picture. These images, which cannot be perceived by the eyes alone, contain the information of the moment. The subtle, invisible world opens itself to the heart of the sensual person.

The cat warns us not to fragment our senses. It encourages us to take seriously the information that comes into our consciousness by ways other than directly through our eyes. It is important for people to develop an alertness reaching from the head and eyes down into the belly. Only here can what is perceived be digested and pieced together into a complete picture. This grasping of the whole makes one alive and independent, gentle and strong. Then you can rely on yourself, evaluate yourself very accurately, and have a perfect knowledge of your personal limits.

Under these conditions, sensuality or affection experienced externally with someone else in a devoted give-and-take is a joy. Your soul will nuzzle up purring with affection for your fellow humans. Embrace the message of the cat. Joy, happiness, and pleasure are everywhere. Complete the picture in yourself, and you will find your way.

COW

Abundance

Cows are a relatively young species. They are ruminants and strict vegetarians. Cows were kept and raised by early humans later than goats and sheep. They serve as draft animals in agriculture and also provide meat, milk, leather, and horns. The good social order in cow herds makes the animals easy to control. In many cultures cows are holy animals. Calm and placid, they give us their strength, their milk, their bodies, and even their young.

If you see a cow chewing its cud in a meadow you will sense a great meditative energy emanating from it. It seems as if the animal were engaging in an inner dialogue with God. Chewing, it asks God for strength and plenty for itself, for its calves, and for the people it nourishes. The simple grass and hay it eats are transformed into delicious milk, rich meat, enormous bodily strength, and strong bones and horns.

Message

Cows remind us of the infinite wealth of creation. They teach us how, by unquestioningly accepting and admitting what life gives us, we can grow wealthy. Wealth is connected to abundance. Wealth is also connected to open receiving and generous giving. To live in plenty, one must first learn to accept with the whole heart.

Our hands are there so that we may give and take. But it is our heart that really gives and takes. Beat by beat, giving and taking forming an eternal rhythm. Open your heart wide and take this present moment, with all that it offers, into your heart. Let the essence of the moment circulate in the silent inner world of the heart, then breathe the love out from your heart and into your surroundings. In this way you will become a little wealthier.

The moment has filled you, and its essence has flowed from your full heart. You have let the moment into your heart and relayed its essence—that is wealth. Cows serve people not because they consider people to be needy. The cow lives in its abundance. In all cultures cows are revered for their great empathetic love. As humans, this unconditional giving of the abundance of nature has touched us since ancient times. The bison herds of North America nourished and supported humans, and many other beings, for thousands of years.

In India cows are revered as holy. The Germanic peoples worshipped Audhumla, the abundant, the primeval cow who came from fire and ice. She nursed and nourished the human being Buri. Buri begat Odin. For the Germanics, Audhumla was also a symbol of opulence. When we consider the way cows are kept in modern times, we must honestly ask ourselves whether we still practice respectful giving and taking, or whether it has become a form of greedy exploitation. The cow will accept what we give it, what life gives it. It will work that into itself and will give us back the result.

DEER

Dignity, Sexuality, Esteem

The deer is a very noble animal of great charm and radiance. The male proudly wears its mighty antlers and carries itself in a lordly manner. Its whole appearance radiates great harmony. The deer always behaves resolutely and reflectively. Within itself it unifies masculine vigor and strength with feminine gentleness and care. The deer is extremely alert and, despite its considerable size, very agile. Most deer live in small or large groups in sparse woods and open grasslands.

The deer's life is ruled by a constant rhythm. From March to August, the males grow their antlers. Around the beginning of June, the doe's thirty-six-week gestation period ends with the birth of a lightly spotted fawn. From July to August, the buck rubs off the velvet from the regrown antlers by scraping them on trees. Now the buck is ready for the rivalry of mating season, which lasts from September to October. The males invite their fellows to fight with angry hollow-sounding cries. In these duels the bucks adhere to strict rituals and rules. Injuries are generally avoided through dominant behavior. However, if two equally matched bucks come together, injuries may result. Only the strongest buck remains to mate.

The does are only fertile for a few days and are impregnated in succession by the dominant buck. From November to February deer retreat into the forest, though they sometimes winter in thick meadows or grasslands. The males usually leave the group at this point.

Message

If you encounter a deer, it wants to advise you to approach your life with precision but without pursuing rigid goals. Turn over the guidance of your life exclusively to your higher self and follow its impulses with a great deal of dynamic energy. There are certain times for certain steps in your life. Therefore, it is also important to note at what time of year the deer crossed your path. Because many people only rarely encounter deer, the message of this encounter should be taken seriously until a new encounter supersedes it. Thus, the message to "lay down your weapons" applies not only from March to August, but all the time, until your next encounter.

From March to August, the deer advises you to lay down your weapons and live life humbly, but with dignity.

In May and June the deer announces a new beginning. It tells you to examine yourself, to become conscious of your strength, and find a loving, gentle way to express that strength. Tone down your affectations a little; perhaps they are burying your natural dignity. Quietly stand by your gentle and caring sides, work on yourself and on what is important to you, and allow yourself to be affectionate.

If the encounter with the deer happens in July or August, it is now time to turn your dreams into reality. Act and take real steps in the visible world. Negotiate and make your mark through your deeds. Do things now that you have wanted to do for a long time, no matter whether they are small or great things. Those who only talk and never act lose credibility and respect. Turn your words into actions. Also, only speak in ways that you can back up with actions.

If you encounter a deer in September or October, it is calling to you to become aware of your strength, your creative power, your erotic energy. Accept your place in life and offer up your potential. In your relationships a strong dedication to your own sexuality is required. Make an offer to your partner, turn on your charm, signal your readiness for exchange. No matter on what level, you have potential; market that potential proudly and courageously. Seek out your opportunity and allow this universe to react to your offer. Sell yourself well and with self-confidence. You have value to be appraised.

Between October and February the deer advises you to save up your energy. Look for spaces and conditions in your life, relationships, and workplaces where you can relax. Perform no unnecessary acts of strength and no excessive effort. You do not have anything to prove and you do not need to fight. You will not lose your esteem and dignity if you let yourself rest.

In general: be quietly proud of yourself and of what you have achieved. Thus you will remain always open to the impulses of the higher self and be able to take the best steps in life. The deer is the bringer of wholeness, energy from light. He wears his antlers like a great crown on his head, into which he can receive the gifts of the universe. The deer, therefore, has brought this message to you. Open yourself to the universe; let the impulses from above into yourself and transfer them into your life. Thus you will keep control of your strength. You are no longer controlled from outside, and the gifts of the universe will be able to manifest in your life.

DOG

Loyalty

The dog is a domesticated animal. Its ancestry goes back to the wolf. Hardly any other animal has given itself over to humans so completely as the dog. From the ancestral wolf, through intentional breeding, an enormous population has arisen. For every dog lover a fitting companion is available, willing to place its entire being at his or her disposal.

The significance of the dog for humans can be illustrated by a story.

When Mother Earth was giving birth to the youngest child that she and Father Sun had together, all the older children came to the bed to greet and marvel at their new sibling. "It is called human," whispered Mother Earth to her children. "One day, it will deliver paradise to all of us, but first there are many things that it must learn, and it will bring many changes for us all. It needs help from each and every one of us in order that it may grow."

The children of the Earth were entranced by this new being, and all who were gathered there solemnly offered the child all their unique powers, placing themselves at its disposal as teachers and trainers. The rock spoke: "I will give the child a floor and a footing, it shall live on me and use me as its shelter and its dwelling. I will initiate it gradually into structure and form and will teach it to be stable and steadfast." The tree spoke: "I will teach it to unite the creative powers of heaven and Earth and will serve it well, body and soul, with my wood and fruits." The buffalo spoke: "I will nourish it with my body and give it strength and warmth, so that it may grow and thrive." The eagle opened its mighty wings and spoke: "I will draw its stare upward toward the light, so that it may look Father Sun in the face and aspire to be his likeness."

In this manner one being after another came to promise the child its help and knowledge, for they all loved it. Finally, at the end, came the old wolf. He looked at the young human for a long time, then spoke: "I will be a leader to it. I will show it how to assert itself in life and how to follow fate's plan wisely. But my teachings will come through over the course of many years, because at first it needs a friend who will help, comfort, and protect it, and teach it to love itself."

Then he turned around and looked, long and silent, at his pack. He summoned a playful, lively young wolf to his side and spoke: "You, my youngest son, will have the task of standing as a true friend by the side of this youngest child of our Mother Earth. Accompany it faithfully and watch out for it. It will cause us all plenty of anger with its curiosity and its sprightliness, and it will often injure itself. Then, my son, you must remind it of its goodness and rightness, you must show it that we, the older siblings, always love it and take joy in its growth." The young wolf looked at his father earnestly and nodded: "I will do that, Father." Then he turned around and looked at the human child. His eyes were gentle and meek, and his tail barely wagged. Mother Earth whispered to him softly: "Now, little wolf, you will always be under the spell of the human, and you will leave your own folk. You are no longer a wolf, from today onward you shall be called Dog, which means 'he who teaches true friendship.'"

The dog lay down happily beside the child's bed and sighed deeply. And since then he has never left that spot.

Message

The dog teaches us loyalty. Loyalty means faith in superiors, decorum, and honesty. The dog does not mean to teach us to be faithful outwardly, but mainly to be faithful to our innermost core. Deep in the heart, every human is guided by her divine plan, by her true self. This is the true guidance of the individual. The true self of a person is closely bound with every other true self and is charged with the task of making the truth of the whole possible, in its own individual place. Someone who obeys her true self is also obeying the higher plan for all of humanity. Loyalty to one's own self is in no way to be confused with egoism.

The multitude of breeds of dogs is as rich as the many sides of human individuality. The official worldwide list includes several hundred breeds. Beyond this there are countless variations and mixes. They are all expressions of the abundance of the individual missions of human beings. Dogs meet with us often, and they always remind us to be faithful to our true selves. One thing to take note of in your dog encounter is the fundamental idea that stands behind the dog's breed. For example, the hunting dog speaks to different areas in you than the guard dog. A small dog speaks to different areas than the large one. The color can also help you to discover in what domain you need to be true to yourself. Notice what unfamiliar dogs you encounter. Aggressive behavior indicates that you have lost your center. The dog perceives this as an infringement of energy into its owner's territory. Fear can also have a similar meaning for dogs, causing the dog to take a dimmer view of you and not trust you. Spontaneous contact from unfamiliar dogs, on the other hand, indicates that you are making your individuality perceptible and the dog likes what it perceives. In order to understand the message precisely it is also advantageous to have a basic knowledge of dog breeds. For the colors, as a rule of thumb: Black or very dark colors speak to the subconscious, feminine side in us, while light colors speak to the active, conscious, more masculine side. Red-brown shades stand for the world of feelings. The yellow dog (golden retriever) is related to the spiritual domains. If the colors are mixed, there is tension between these domains.

DOLPHIN

Breath of Life, Rhythm

Dolphins, like whales, belong to the cetacean order. They are mammals. The flat tailfin clearly distinguishes these mammals from fish. The snout is extended into a long beak. The body is perfectly streamlined in its construction. Dolphins are extremely fast swimmers, and with their mouths full of more than two hundred teeth, they are obvious predators. Dolphins live in all the seas surrounding Europe, and with a bit of luck they can be spotted. In earlier times dolphins were widely hunted

and, like whales, used for their blubber and meat. Today, dolphin hunting is not allowed in the Mediterranean or along any other European coast. Thus, since 1965 populations have rebounded.

Dolphins command a rich repertoire of specific vocal sounds, some of which are in the ultrasound range. They have an echolocation system. This system is used mainly to find great schools of fish. The dolphin's brain is also remarkable. Its mental abilities are entirely comparable to those of humans. What was long considered a seaman's yarn has been proved true: wild dolphins have quite often saved drowning people by pushing them up out of the water and bringing them to land. Sick dolphins are carried over the water by a group of their comrades so that they do not drown if they become unconscious. The dolphin's gestation period lasts eleven months. The young can swim by themselves immediately after birth, but the mother brings them up to the surface regularly so that they can breathe. Dolphins give birth to twins relatively frequently.

It is an impressive sight to observe a family of dolphins from the deck of a ship, swimming at high speed and taking great leaps out of the water in the ship's wake. For most of us, dolphins are most likely seen during a vacation or at a zoo, and yet these magnificent animals are deeply touching to humans. Since ancient times wonderful tales have been told about the dolphin in all cultures.

Message

If a dolphin enters your awareness you should consider the rhythm in your life. The dolphin stands for the rhythm between inhaling and exhaling, taking and giving, idea and perception. It advises us to let ourselves be inspired anew by the great plan before we dive back into our own feelings. Emotions can do us a great deal of harm. Every feeling we experience should be traced back to the clear, vast, airy essence of inspiration, the world of ideas, or indeed also to our spiritual guidance.

Life comes from the exchange between inhaling and exhaling. If we breathe in ideas and experience feelings in harmony, our life is full of energy and vigor. But it is possible that sometimes your focus is too much on one side of this natural pair of rhythms. Perhaps you are accustomed to giving a great deal of yourself and have forgotten that sometimes you need to breathe in as well? Or the flurry of material duties makes you fixate only upon receiving and taking, and you neglect the fact that giving is a requirement for taking? Everything in our world follows this wonderful rhythm that takes place with inhaling and exhaling, bringing fulfillment and nourishment. When you give, the previously filled space is cleaned out, ready to receive something new. Even the Earth, the sea, the land we live on knows this eternal rhythm, set in motion by the sun. With the sun's rays in summer, the warmed matter expands, takes the plan into itself from the light. When the days grow shorter and temperatures drop, matter contracts and breathes out its warmth. These movements are very subtle and fine, and almost imperceptible to our human senses. Every created being, when it inhales, takes in the energy of the world, the environment, and when it exhales it gives the energy of its own inner universe to the outer. Thus exhalation can be seen as a sort of repeating pattern in which every being and all matter participates. With renewed inhalation, this pattern, this information is taken in and thus connects us all closely to one another. The connection with the dolphin also tells you to balance the rhythm in all areas of your life. Give as much as you take! It is a spiritual order, and when one observes it, one feels one's best.

DONKEY

Will

The domestic donkey is descended from the wild African donkey and was used as a pack and draft animal in ancient times in the Middle East. Through crossbreeding of male horses with female donkeys, the hardier hinny is produced—and from the male donkey and female horse, the mule. These hybrids are sterile and cannot be bred further.

The wild donkey is an exquisite desert animal, able to live in very meager conditions. Herds are led by a single male. The males have their own territories to ensure reproduction with females that wander into the area. There appears not to be any close connection between the adult animals. Males are tolerant toward other males that enter their territory but prevent their having direct contact with the females. By day, large herds of up to fifty animals can form. In the evening these herds break up, and the animals return to smaller groups. Every morning new large herds form. The same social behavior is observed among domestic donkeys that have become feral. Donkeys react aggressively to an attack, as do, for example, horses. This may be connected to their slow running speed. These strong-willed animals can drive attackers away with well-aimed kicks and severe bites.

Message

The donkey reminds us of our will. There are various levels of will in us: the domain of the ego-will, the psyche's will, and the divine will. The will leads the motivation in the right direction. It is useless just to know something; you will reach your goal only through your will. Thus, the will is the beast of burden that carries the realization of knowledge along the roads of life into reality. If you encounter a donkey, you should consider your will in relation to your motivation. The ego-will represents the lesser energy, and its achievement is always of short duration.

Could it be that you set yourself up against your own intent (stubborn donkey)? Do not confuse motivation and intent with wishes, especially ego-wishes. The soul, with its will, always directs itself according to the divine plan. Motivation and intent are the inner way and should harmonize with a person's true knowledge and good conscience. If you really listen deeply to your heart you will be able to tell what is right and fitting. That is your road, your way, upon which you can live life positively and successfully. Keep this inner harmony always in your consciousness, and go along your road step by step. The will is the energy that makes the steps possible. Through emotion, we often steer our intent away from the harmony of the heart toward manipulations of our surroundings.

Your "donkey" will surely acquiesce to all these detours and take on all the burdens that he can carry. But the responsibility toward which you should direct your will is yours and yours alone. Thus, if someone has lost his way with his will and no longer knows his heart's harmony due to many manipulations, he will gradually lose the strength of his will. He will become manipulable, guided by his own and others' emotions, and with time he will entirely lose his personal radiance. The strength of the donkey, then, tells you to be entirely yourself and to follow your own road unwaveringly and with dignity. It does not matter whether the people around you understand this. When the donkey knows his way, he does not let himself be bothered. Calm and relaxed, he walks on. But if attacked, he can retaliate with vehemence and penetrating power. The message of the donkey lies therein: it is your duty to defend your will and with it your personal life's path. Like the donkey, the will is also highly sensitive and reacts rather stubbornly when mishandled. When everything in your life is running smoothly, you hear almost nothing from your will.

Only when you let yourself be overburdened, manipulated, or victimized will your will's true strength be known. Take it seriously when your subconscious gives rise to formulations such as "I don't want that anymore. It can't go on like this. I have to do that immediately." It is time to accompany your "donkey," with a great deal of intuition, back to the correct path.

FOX, RED FOX
Concealment

The fox, along with the wolf and raccoon dog, belongs to the family of doglike ground game and is found almost everywhere except Antarctica. It lives mainly on mice, but also will not turn down small birds, rabbits, earthworms, snails, insects, frogs, snakes, and ant eggs. In the fall it varies its diet with fruit and berries. It also preys on domestic birds when given the opportunity. It sneaks up skillfully on its prey, pouncing with lightning speed at the right moment.

The fox is mainly active at night. It spends the day sleeping in its den, consisting of one or more underground chambers, connected by tunnels. For safety, the fox digs multiple escape holes. This harmonious, beautiful animal is multifaceted and very adaptable. Its cunning, slyness, observant nature, ability to melt almost entirely into its surroundings, and ability to think and act quickly have not only saved the fox from extermination but have also enabled it to carve out a niche for itself, living in close quarters with humans. It lives with us clandestinely, almost unnoticed—even on the outskirts of big cities.

Message

If a fox slinks into your view it wants to tell you to examine your position in your life. You seem to want to express aspects of your life that would not be understandable to everyone in the society you live in. Therefore, create your own secret living space for yourself. This does not mean retreating into reclusion, but creating well-concealed spaces amid everyday life. Show only the sides of yourself that are understood by your surroundings. Give the other areas of your being time to develop and become strong. These are domains of your inner world, the feminine, nighttime side of your human self, which wants to bring new viewpoints into your consciousness.

Perhaps intuitive abilities will develop, perhaps old patterns will dissolve, or an external meeting is being prepared for your inner world. In any case, it is still too early to bring the notion to light. Most likely you yourself have not even noticed that something is in the works. It is important to hold yourself back somewhat. If you stay quiet and become invisible to your surroundings, you can hold back their influence and observe them in hiding. It is a great art to blend in with one's surroundings so much that one is not noticed. There are various reasons to want to observe life from a hiding place. But cunning, deliberateness, and falsehood can also turn on you and expose you. The fox encourages you to seek your own truth, to be genuine and effective in your life. But it also warns you against doing this too obviously. People who encounter foxes often should exercise diplomacy in all their forms of self-expression.

Train your observational abilities so that you can evaluate the people around you in terms of their behavior. There will be only a few people in your life to whom you can truly reveal yourself. Live a concealed life as a whole. Seek out friends suited to the various domains of your being, and share with them only what truly connects. Concealment in human life also requires a very great capacity for empathy with regard to others' right to the truth. Give other people this right. You do not need to take over their thoughts and mislead your own thoughts. Be aware that you should always recognize where you are retreating to. It is of no use to make yourself so invisible that you cannot even see yourself anymore.

Fox power is always closely connected with sensuality. Only experienced sensuality can lead to the ability to practice diplomacy and concealment. Your senses will show you when and where to practice concealment and when and where to become visible and act openly.

GOAT

Reputation

Goats were kept by humans beginning thousands of years ago. They were known as the "poor man's cow" or "railroad man's cow." Goats are not nearly as efficient as sheep. However, they are better suited for milking. With their hard, sharp-edged hooves, goats are excellent climbers. They are choosy about what they eat, which means that they do significantly less damage to mountain meadows than do sheep herds.

The goat's loud vocalization is known as bleating. Most billy goats have sickle-shaped horns. Some female goats also have horns. Grown billy goats emit an intense odor.

Message

The goat reminds us that our own quirks are the reason for our reputation. It is not telling you to watch out for your reputation but only advising you to live your real truth so that you can be known as you really are. Goats are headstrong animals in addition to being relatively stubborn.

This is no problem, because nothing other than that is expected of them. Being yourself does not mean fitting in. Being yourself means living with your own qualities so that they are seen by society. When one's reputation in society corresponds to the way one sees oneself, everything is fine. When this is not so, one feels misunderstood and excluded. If you encounter a goat, it is good to think about what reputation you have. It is time to ask friends or family members what they think of you. Do not totally ignore what others think of you.

People live in groups. To feel good we need to the acceptance and solidarity of a group. It doesn't matter what the whole town thinks of you, but you should know what the people who are important to you think of you. Perhaps now it is time to indulge in a bit of bleating about yourself. Such discussions not only give others the opportunity to voice something, they also give you a chance to explain yourself. Through discussions one can often get to the bottom of why the individual "I" cannot be expressed openly.

But perhaps the goat also wants to point out that you are worrying too much about your reputation with other people. As we have said, the whole "town" doesn't have to like you. Have the courage to test your reputation and to see through the eyes of others both what is lovable about you and what needs improving. Now is the time.

HAMSTER

Domestic Balance, Health

This approximately squirrel-size scrabbling rodent lives only in deep soils that are as stone-free as possible. Hamsters are loners, and outside of mating season they do not tolerate one another. They threaten and intimidate one another by standing up straight, hissing, squeaking, and chirping. The female gives birth to two or three litters a year, with four to twelve pups. By the time these are twenty-five days old they are independent, and after ten weeks they are sexually mature.

Many of the pups fall victim to natural predators such as owls, birds of prey, and foxes. The hamster is active mainly at night and lives on plants, insects, and small mammals. Seeds, however, are their preferred food. Hamsters hibernate from October to March, waking up only occasionally to eat.

In the fall they gather food stores, which they carry in their cheek pouches, specially adapted for that purpose. It is not unusual for each animal to store one hundred pounds of food each year. These provisions fuel the hamster, especially in the early spring when nothing is left to eat in the fields and the body fat is used up from hibernation. Due to this hoarding behavior, hamsters can be pests in the agricultural industry, and they are in danger of extinction in the wild due to targeted extermination.

Message

If the hamster has drawn your attention it wants to advise you to be thrifty in the use of your life energies. Perhaps you are overstraining your body and depriving it of the time it needs to regenerate. When was the last time you retreated into your entirely personal burrow?

Do not undermine your life energy with too many duties and social pressures; it could cost you your health. Observe the rhythm of time, seek out calm and repose, and set aside sufficient reserves for your well-being. Provisions are gathered in times of plenty. It is not very smart to push continually at the boundaries of your strength. The hamster decisively defends its personal living space, where it finds rest and relaxation. This is where the hamster's message for you is found. It is a matter of the physical and material domains of your existence.

If you have an exhausting time ahead of you, the hamster wants to advise you to build up your energies through good nutrition, enough sleep, and plenty of fresh air and sunlight. It is better to take preventive measures than to heal.

If you are the victim of a plague of hamsters, you have overdone your preparations. It is not necessary to exhaust your surroundings in order to prepare for every possible kind of strain on your energy. You do not need to stockpile, but instead live more in the flow of nature. Trust in your body's energies and manipulate them with neither excessive caution nor excessive strain. Eat when you are truly hungry. For this you need supplies that you can dig into. It makes no sense to eat unceasingly in order to avoid hunger.

HARE

Fear

The gray-brown field hare, up to twenty-eight inches long, lives alone in fields, meadows, and light forests throughout almost all of Europe. Its conspicuously long ears give it a very sharp sense of hearing. Unlike the rabbit, to which it is related, the hare is a loner. It has no fixed dwelling,

living in the open field where it has enough space for flight. When an enemy approaches hares usually remain undiscovered, squeezing themselves into holes and furrows in the ground.

Their coat color often saves them from being discovered. If someone comes too near, they jump up and flee, dealing blows. With their long back legs propelling them far from their starting point, they are able to reach speeds of more than thirty miles per hour. The female gives birth two to four times per year, delivering two to four juveniles, already covered with hair and able to see. Young hares are precocial, and as a defense from predators they have absolutely no scent. Their camouflage, sharp senses, fearfulness, speed, and maneuverability are their only weapons.

Message

The hare advises you to use your sensibilities, but increasingly to avoid unnecessary flight. Fear is an important component in human development. It protects us from the unknown, it restricts excessive curiosity, and it sharpens the senses. And yet, the goal of humanity is fearlessness. Do not allow your fear to agitate you and prey on you. Do not let yourself be life's prey, fleeing restlessly from one strategy to another.

If you encounter a hare, you need to grapple seriously with your fears. Go about this lovingly, but watch out. Could it be that a part of your soul is cowering in a trench of life, frozen by fear and no longer daring to move? Or are you running through life, dealing blows, terrified by some threat? However your fear is expressed, you must recognize it, keep it in check, and pay attention to the frightened part of yourself. Let your feelings become mellow and flexible again, and use all your senses to detect what you feel threatened by. Face life with the strength of your being.

Do not be a hare; instead, stand up, overcome fear, and use your senses to recognize threats early and meekly avoid them. The energy of fearful people is similar to that of the hare. Their ears are always perked up, eyes open wide looking all around, muscles tensed ready for flight, and a highly developed sense of touch, feeling every cool breeze.

If you recognize yourself in these images it is high time to find a resting place, to get to the heart of the matter, and to reopen your heart to the world. If you are no longer a victim, you will not be inviting any hunters to pursue you. Courage will return to your life, and generosity and tolerance toward others will once again be possible. Remember that fear has nothing to do with shyness.

HORSE
Life Force

The horse is one of the oldest domestic animals. The earliest records are from China. In 3468 BC, Fo Hi is said to have introduced domestic horses. They came to central Europe a couple of centuries later. This noble animal opened great possibilities for humans. It lent them its power and endurance and thus made them able to inhabit new spaces.

Many daily activities, as well as warlike activities, were made easier by the horse, and gradually the horse became an early status symbol for humans. Owning a good horse was synonymous with power and

wealth. It followed that horse theft was a great crime, punishable by death in most cultures.

The horse is a herd animal. It has an established hierarchy that was also conducive to its domestication. Like all herbivores, herds of wild horses were not safe from predators. Even early humans ate horse meat. However, horses have some very effective weapons: in addition to their endurance and speed, they also have their teeth and hard hooves. At best, a skillful pack of wolves would have a fighting chance at bringing down a weak horse.

Foals play games that involve movement. They gallop around their mothers, kick with their back legs, bite each other, then run away with great leaps and jumps. Young stallions also love to play fighting games. All the behavior of this animal is built upon strength and movement.

Message

The horse symbolizes strength. It is the life force, the power that represents movement, growth, and expression. If you encounter a horse, you should include its color in your interpretation.

A black horse symbolizes the energy that collects in darkness and strives toward light through growth. An encounter with a black horse tells you that it is time to activate the strength in your subconscious so that it may be expressed in the light. Could it be that you are searching for a new form of expression, but you do not trust in anything new?

In that case an encounter with a black horse means that you should sink into your inner emptiness and listen for the answer. All answers come from darkness, and if one cannot allow one's energy to rise up, these answers will never be heard. Perhaps it will take a bit of courage to rediscover confidence in your own energy and not to confuse emptiness with weakness.

The red horse speaks of the power of feelings. It advises you to give in to the playfulness, the wildness, the liveliness in your emotions. Do not let your feelings work like a draft horse, hauling the plow, plodding along in resignation. The strength of the horse is a living strength, and your world of feelings should be and remain just as lively. Be playful again, and lighten the work of your emotions with joy and humor. Consider that humor and play are more interesting to your fellow humans than deep, searching seriousness. For the fountain of your emotions to keep bubbling, expression, liveliness, and strength are indispensable. Much that you have to say and share in your world of feelings is blocked by seriousness, and then your life energy becomes restricted.

The white horse symbolizes the power of wisdom. The white horse shows you that wisdom belongs to your life expression. It also advises you, however, that every misuse of power can destroy your wisdom. Every human, as a tool of God, is in a position to serve the divine plan and to build mountains with his power. But be aware that when you encounter the white horse this encounter also contains the message that the power of wisdom is only truthful when the intent is pure and the humbleness genuine.

The yellow horse symbolizes the power of enlightenment. Perhaps a light has come on in your mind shortly before this encounter. The yellow horse does not want to point you toward the fullness of complete enlightenment but is telling you to take the light moments in your spirit seriously, to make room for this truth, and however small those "aha" moments in everyday life are, to be conscious of them, because they are the real building blocks of your growth. If there is an open question in your life, then in the yellow horse you are receiving a message that you have the strength to find answers for yourself. Take your enlightenment in earnest, for your answers will lead you in the right direction and steer you toward the final answer.

Encounters with horses in general always remind us to embrace our inner energies and bring them to expression. Give in to the life force in yourself and find the energy to manage all your problems in everyday life.

To change certain conditions may require endurance, submission within a hierarchy, and even teeth and hooves. The only thing that does not change anything is resignation. To stand still and wait for change to come from the outside is to betray your life force. You yourself have to sense where it is necessary to recognize, strengthen, and release the flow of your energies. In any case, do not linger on problems, because focusing on the problem itself will inhibit your life force more and more, and your view to a solution will also disappear.

The horse tells you to direct your view toward your strengths. Feel your strengths, live your strengths, and give your strengths real expression. It is a way for you to come closer to a solution to everyday problems.

There are so many possible ways in which you might encounter a horse. Is it running free in the meadow, harnessed to a wagon, carrying a rider, or standing in a transport vehicle? To understand the message of the horse precisely, it is very important to include the animal's exact situation in your interpretation. Empathize with the horse, and you will understand its message much more clearly.

LYNX

Mystery, Secrecy, Concealment

In the past two hundred years this largest European wild cat has been exterminated from western and central Europe. However, these secretive hunters live on thanks to resettlement in remote valleys and forests.

While the Eurasian lynx can reach a shoulder height of 2½ feet and a weight of eighty pounds, the European lynx is somewhat smaller, with a shoulder height of 1½ feet and a weight of forty pounds. The lynx is a skillful hunter, its prey including all animals in the region ranging in size from mice to half-grown deer.

In Europe the lynx mainly hunts deer. A full-grown deer can feed it for about two weeks. The lynx keeps returning to the remains of its prey day after day. Even in places where the lynx population has grown to match the old numbers, it is unlikely that you will encounter this gifted hunter. Lynxes are very secretive animals. A lynx's territory is at least two square miles, and only one animal lives there. The lynx avoids humans and is mainly active at night.

Message

Should you have the rare luck to encounter a lynx, you should consider this a highly significant message. The lynx is telling you to discover the great mysteries in yourself. Take this message very seriously, because the spiritual world is imparting an important communication to you. The lynx symbolizes the great knowledge of nature; it knows, and is silent. It will not entrust its secrets to anyone who is not worthy and whose time has not yet come.

Perhaps your thoughts are very often preoccupied by the lynx when you hike in natural areas. This constitutes a message to you to search for the mystery of life. You will not be able to trick this proud animal into telling you its secrets. With its constant smile, the lynx will keep touching your soul, slinking into your thoughts and memories, and not giving you any answers. It knows the magic of silence, and with this power it has unraveled the mysteries of nature. Be ready to open your senses and listen to the voice of nature. Like a wordless whisper, the voice of the world's great soul will flow into your consciousness. This voice will teach you, will allow you to grow more and more mature, and as you gain experience, you will also gradually gain knowledge. Then the knowing smile of the lynx will show upon your own face, and you will keep silent.

When one understands the wisdom of the lynx, it becomes clear why certain people are very afraid of this animal and are not yet ready to give it back its habitat. And yet it is not the guardian of wisdom; it is merely wise. Thus it is not the lynx that teaches or castigates you; it is a symbol representing the mysticism of knowledge. Invite this mysticism and this symbol into your life. And who knows, perhaps one day you will have one of those very rare, wonderful meetings with the lynx.

This will happen once you have learned from the lynx, once your outer silence speaks the language of your inner world, and you have turned real experience into wisdom.

MARMOT
Modesty

The Alpine marmot lives mainly in the western and central Alps, above the tree line, up to an elevation of ten thousand feet. Marmots hibernate for seven to eight months out of the year in deep hollows underground, where they live off the fat reserves that they pack on during the brief summer. Marmots live together in colonies. They are social animals and very playful.

The older animals protect the colony with great alertness. They warn of danger with shrill whistles that are audible at a far distance. It is not true, however, that they assign guard posts. Each mature animal is constantly alert and regularly monitors the sky and surroundings. Predators lie in wait everywhere for these cheerful rodents. They are a favorite prey for foxes, lynx, various birds of prey, and also humans. Humans have especially prized the fat of the marmot, which was made into an ointment for rheumatism.

Message

Marmots in the wild are found only high in the mountains, and only in the summer months. Therefore, if you encounter this messenger of the animal world, you are ready to find some distance from everyday life, and to find clarity, relaxation, or adventure. It is often good to turn your back on the everyday and look at your life from a distance. If, in the isolated mountains, you encounter one or even many marmots, then bow your head for a moment before the creator and give thanks for the wonder in your life.

Marmots live a frugal, dangerous life. But they live it intensively and happily. It is pleasantly touching to observe the joyous bustling of marmots. It reminds us of the free happiness of the simple life. The marmot encourages you to let go of your beliefs and give up all demands regarding the how, where, and when of life. You should withdraw all your claims to things on Earth and in heaven. Bow your head humbly and accept, without judgment, the primordial rhythm of giving and taking, day and night, winter and summer, life and death. Humbleness is a wonderful, beneficial power that arises from true meekness before the divine plan.

It takes some courage to be humble but no greater amount of courage to be modest. Present yourself consciously to God and give thanks for your current life situation. Do not ask for anything in your prayers. Do not give the creator any hints as to how your life could be made more comfortable. Turn your nose toward the wind, creep into the deep burrow of your real life, and recognize that it is your nest that you have made for yourself. Perhaps now it is spring and you can build a new nest. You can apply yourself to your duties with great attentiveness and care, be happily thankful for this new chance, and make preparations for the next winter. Have the courage to stand naked before the creator and give genuine thanks for all there is. Then you will feel the true joy in life that the marmot expresses.

What will happen next? You can go back, thankfully and alertly, to building your everyday life. You do not need to send any more requests to heaven, because through your humbleness you will experience constant fulfillment.

MOLE

Action

The mole spends practically all its life underground. In the course of evolution, its body and its functions have adapted entirely to this life. Its sight is almost completely atrophied, while its hearing has remained and its senses of touch and smell have improved a great deal. Its senses are adapted for detecting things at short distances.

The mole is an insectivore. It senses the insects and worms nearby

and digs to find them. With their strong, shovellike front feet, moles dig extensive underground labyrinths. Among the roots of bushes, near the surface, the female digs out a nest chamber for her young. There is one litter per year or, rarely, two, with four young. The nest chamber is separate from the other tunnels. The living chamber, lined with plant matter, is often built from soil that the moles bring up from strata lower down. Some cul-de-sacs in the burrow are used for storing food. In one such food chamber eighteen grubs and 1,280 earthworms were found, all made immobile by targeted head injuries.

The mole's extraordinary sense of direction helps it to find its way in its labyrinth. It knows the structure of the Earth like no other creature.

Message

If a mole digs its way into your life it is admonishing you to examine your real actions. Have you left the plane of reality, and can your ideas no longer be realized? Perhaps you are avoiding practical action by building castles in the air. Consider the fact that the mole has no chance of survival above ground. In exactly the same way, your actions cannot bring success if you depart from reality.

As humans, it is important to align our actions with the laws of nature. For this, a certain amount of vision can be useful. But when we lose ourselves in our visions, our life experiences are not nearly sufficient for us to find our way back to Earth without going through painful processes. The mole's medicine teaches us to live a life near the earth. In reality, endless possibilities are open for you, countless forms of expression and limitless space. But everything that takes place in your life must be realizable. Do not frivolously bypass the structures and forms of your life, moving events outside the framework of the real. No one expects you to understand everything, and it takes a good amount of courage to stand up to your own lack of understanding. If you encounter a mole, it also wants to remind you of what is right near you and entirely real.

There is a great deal of security in the reality of life. Perhaps now it will do you good to put yourself back into the arms of Mother Earth. Let yourself be calmly surrounded by the structures and laws of the Earth and have the courage to leave processes in other worlds to run their course. Because the mole only very seldom leaves its domain of the earth, it is recommended that you take this encounter very seriously. Consider what is graspable, real, and true in your life, and set your beliefs, visions, and ideas aside for the moment. Perhaps the worm is actually in your real life, and with all your vivid dreaming you have not even noticed it.

The mole may be blind, but its sense of touch is very highly developed. Therefore, feel the structures of your reality, and you will probably find a tasty worm. Often people find only the traces that moles leave behind, such as mole hills. Leave the little animal alone in its earthy home. You can be certain that if it has built its tunnels in your garden, all is in order in the structures of your life. The mole feels drawn to you because, like it, you have made the realm of Earth your trusty home.

MOOSE
Self-Awareness

The moose is the largest member of the Deer family living in Europe. Males can weigh up to 1,100 pounds. Today moose live mainly in

northern Europe. They prefer damp, light forests and open grasslands interspersed with bushes. They eat grasses, twigs, leaves, and often water plants. Moose are good swimmers, and with their long legs and broad hooves they can make their way well in both snow and swamps. In recent years one animal with an especially great wanderlust was reported roaming through the Czech Republic into Austria, across Poland, and even into Germany. Like all members of the Deer family, the males grow antlers for the rutting season. The moose's antlers are very large, mostly consisting of broad palmate surfaces. The organic effort required to grow these antlers is impressive. After the antler velvet has rubbed off and the antlers have matured, they often grow to meet in the middle. Then the various strong males engage in battle play. These games are different from true fighting, which is only done between equally matched males and often ends in injury. Female moose can be quite aggressive during the time of year when their calves are born. They can fight effectively with their heavy hooves and can even pose a problem for a pack of wolves. However, the cows like to linger with their calves in the vicinity of campgrounds, where there is little danger of wolf attacks. In winter moose break apart whole young trees for food, browsing on the twigs and bark. They then lie for whole days in protected places and lightly hibernate. They live off their fat reserves and the mineral salts in their bones. When spring comes and the southern slopes become free of snow and meager grasses grow, the moose defends these feeding grounds resolutely against other animals, and also against humans.

Message

The moose stands for self-awareness. It teaches us to be aware of ourselves. If you have an encounter with a moose, it means to tell you what areas of yourself, your gifts, and your strengths you are heedlessly neglecting. Our talents and attributes, as well as our energy and life force, are valuable tools for life. In the long term it is not good for a person to let her talents lie unused. We have talents and gifts because they have shown themselves to be applicable in our spiritual development and meaningful in the path we follow. Our life force and vitality come from what we have worked on all our lives, through effort and the will to express ourselves. If the moose—especially the female moose, and also calves—tells you to practice self-awareness, this mighty beast means to say that you have neglected your talents, leaving them sleeping and unused. It advises you to see whether that slowly vanishing thing is something that you really can easily relinquish. Certainly there are some talents that are no longer any use in modern times, or some that no longer fit with your spiritual growth and inner disposition. For example, unscrupulousness and ignorance may at one time have been a useful talent that would have helped you to survive. When that sort of talent atrophies, it is a good thing. Thus, the moose does not mean to indicate in general that you should preserve all your gifts but that you should be conscious of change and make decisions observantly. Ask yourself whether you really have use for a given talent. But do not ask yourself whether a talent of yours fits in with the opinions of contemporary society. If you encounter a bull moose, it is more an issue of the life force in general, of power. The moose tells you to use your strength and also train yourself. Have you perhaps become a little too comfortable, or have you begun, due to conscious boredom, to get used to a high level of inactivity, frittering away your time with senseless consumerist behavior? The moose, then, with its appearance, presents a very clear sign. Do not give away your life energy so freely. Retrain yourself by doing something active, and engage in something meaningful or instructive. It is not always necessary to accomplish something, and what you do does not have to be something amazing. Someone who just hangs around, repressing his energy and senses—for example, by watching television—not only loses his life force but also his joy and, above all, self-awareness.

MOUSE

Perfection

Mice belong to the enormous family of rodents. The family of true mice alone includes 120 genera and 460 species. This highly successful group of animals is one of the youngest on the planet. One of these 120 genera, the familiar house mouse, contains between thirty-five and forty species. Mice are spread throughout the whole world, but their origin is in Asia. The house mouse is an omnivore and prefers to live near, or even in, human food supplies. Most of these animals naturally restrict their range of action to a few square meters. The mouse moves through its habitat by running, jumping, climbing, and even swimming.

With its finely tuned sense of touch, its exceptionally fine sense of hearing, and its excellent sense of smell, the mouse perceives every tiny change in its familiar environment. It is surely due to their perfection and unassuming nature that mice have even been able to raise their young in frozen meat in walk-in freezers at temperatures of fifteen degrees Fahrenheit.

Mice live together in small groups. They identify their territory and food with intensive scent marks. If a population grows too large, a sort of birth control takes place. Many of the growing females become infertile. The origin of this birth control lies likewise in the great sensitivity of this animal. When groups are too large, stress appears to create a hormonal reaction that causes infertility.

The bustling movements of mice also attract a great variety of predators. As widely sought-after prey, the mouse continues to develop its senses and alertness. Exactitude and perfection are the strengths of the mouse.

Message

Are you one of those people who are afraid of mice, or one of those who find their little paws, black button eyes, and pink noses wonderfully cute? Either way, you will always encounter the mouse when your attention needs to be drawn to the small and invisible things in life. The great, marvelous plans that are made in human lives often shatter when examined in detail.

The mouse tells you to check the details precisely at this moment. Put your thoughts, feelings, and finances in order, concentrate on important and significant things, and avoid great excesses. If it is a matter of the financial and material parts of your life, you are more likely to find the mouse in your pantry. If it is a matter of your feelings, you are more likely to encounter the mouse in the natural environment.

If the mouse is an animal that disgusts you, then either you are extraordinarily finicky and are overstraining your mouse power, or you are refusing to be precise with yourself, your thoughts, your emotions, or your material environment. The mouse also brings you the message of order. This is not so much about finding the perfect place for every object as it is about attentiveness and alertness in your handling of things. Bring order to your whole life: in your relationships, in your financial matters, in the social sphere, and also to your material possessions. Make your world manageable, because where it is manageable for you, you will feel secure. If mice are daily companions in your life, beware of becoming too finicky. Perfection can grow into hysteria in certain people.

Keep in mind that the mouse is a small animal, low on the food chain, and thus serves many larger powers with its life. Precision serves wisdom (the owl), sensuality (the cat), and transformation (the snake). Finickiness, however, is not a form of nourishment for these energies, only a hindrance.

MUSKRAT
Settlement of feelings

The original home of the muskrat is North America, where it was hunted for its pelt. In 1906 it was introduced to Bohemia, in Europe, for pelts, and from there its population radiated outward. The muskrat lives on the water and is very well adapted to the wet element. Its hind feet are webbed and the edges of the toes have clefts for swimming. The animal is approximately one foot long. Its tail is hairless, covered with scales, and serves as a rudder for swimming. It builds its home, like the beaver, in sheltered places at the water's edge. When threatened, adult and juvenile muskrats flee into the water. They can stay underwater for up to twelve minutes.

The muskrat is an example of a "great experiment" to see what happens when an alien animal with a high fertility rate and no natural predators propagates itself in a free biotope. Dams, flood control systems, and other water structures are threatened by muskrats.

Message

If you encounter a muskrat while walking by a river, you are being called upon to test the familiar course of your emotional life. Could a suppressed fear or an unconscious problem have crept in and be nagging at your self-assurance and well-being? Stay awake and try to observe the truth in your life neutrally. Let all dreams go for this moment. Only in this way will you be able to tell whether your visions of happiness can be built upon the existing reality at all. In any case, it is now time to determine your position and finally decide to make a new riverbed for the flow of your feelings. In our densely populated civilization we view the muskrat as a pest because it threatens the natural function of our man-made environment.

We humans have strengthened riverbeds artificially, but when undisturbed, rivers continually seek new courses. This hardworking rodent helps the great river to establish its course anew. Obviously this quality of the animal cannot be appreciated in modern times. But in your inner environment, you should preserve the natural quality of change. Floods of feelings and droughts, changes in riverbeds are exhilarating and they foster your growth. Fears build high dams in the river of emotions; when the muskrat shows itself to you, quietly let your inner dams overflow a little.

OTTER

Femininity, Love

The otter, besides the badger, is the largest member of the Marten family. Evolution has adapted its body and fur to a life on the water. It inhabits stagnant and flowing water, salt and fresh. Otters exist in many different sizes, from the six-foot-long giant otter native to South America to the Asian dwarf otter, about two feet long. In Europe there is only one species.

The European otter, about three feet long, weighs about twenty pounds. Because of its great appetite for fish, it was mercilessly hunted in Europe. Later these animals became protected under the Washington Convention. Slowly, populations rebounded in eastern Europe, Spain, France, and England. Central Europe is not yet ready for a resettlement of these magnificent animals. Many rivers have been straightened, lakes thickly settled, and various river power stations pose great danger to these playful, friendly creatures. Since the 1980s environmental protection organizations have devoted themselves to the restoration of bodies of water. But even today it has not yet been possible to start any large-scale resettlement program. The otter needs a large territory. To support a small population of fifty to one hundred individuals, three hundred to six hundred miles of riverbanks or lakeshores must be available, with minimal development.

To meet its body's high energy requirements, a grown otter needs up to three pounds of fish each day. But the otter does not live on fish alone. It also eats all sorts of amphibians, aquatic birds, water rats, crabs, shellfish, and dragonflies. Therefore, it experiences hardly any seasonal periods of scarce food. This is probably why the otter has no fixed breeding season. When a female meets the right partner, it appears as if ovulation occurs spontaneously. After mating, the animals separate immediately. After two months' gestation, up to three young are born in a specially built chamber on the riverbank. When otters are kept in pairs in captivity, the male's constant presence works almost like a contraceptive.

The otter's den has entrances from land and from under the water. Otters are very playful animals. Their movements on both water and land are lithe and graceful. It is endlessly fascinating to watch playful young otters. They tumble and run, ball themselves up, twist their flexible bodies together, race along the riverbank, and hardly seem to get tired in the water.

It is noteworthy that there is no more room available for this symbol of femininity in our world that has become so masculine.

Message

Because encountering an otter in the wild is hardly possible anymore, we must make room for these animals in films, zoos, fantasies, and dreams. If you encounter an otter, it wants to seduce you. It invites you to play with it, lose your inhibitions, be light and free like a child, and glide through the realm of sensuality without prejudice.

Release your control for a moment, and allow yourself to flirt with life and everything in it. Trust in yourself and remain unbiased and guileless before everything that comes your way. The otter is a very feminine power—femininity in its complete form. It is friendly, naive, unprejudiced, loving, light, and playful.

The otter teaches us to open our hearts wide and accept the life that is all around us without questioning, without jealousy, envy, or conflict. Everything is good. Femininity is gentle and flowing like water. Flowing, warm femininity does not break apart on impact. It moves aside, gives way, and closes wounds seamlessly. Surrender to your femininity and be permeable and touchable. The softer you are, the more invulnerable you will be. Now is not the time to fight, it is time to flirt. Whatever may be the topic at hand in your life, let yourself be carried by the flow of your own emotions and embrace this free, light way of being. Seductively, playfully, coquettishly, and without judgment, seize the moment and all that it offers you. Let those who want to fight do so. For your part, you will jump into the gentle water without leaving a trace. To each his own.

It may be that this animal frightens you and seems threatening to you in this particular moment when you are perhaps afflicted with fear and anxiety. In cold emotional times it is especially important to let your inner warmth flow. Love is the sun that melts the frozen emotions in us—emotions frozen by shock and sorrow. Learn from the otter; let a smile be conjured in your soul by its playful, naive ways. This brings your own love back to you.

PIG, WILD PIG

Instinct

The wild pig and the domestic pig are closely related. More than five thousand years ago wild pigs were domesticated and raised for their meat. Pigs walk on the tips of their toes; they are cloven hoofed, like cows. The pig's long snout has a round tip. With this, pigs root through leaves and loose earth in search of food. Their extremely well-developed senses of smell and touch help them in this search.

The male wild pig, also known as the boar, breaks up hard soil with his tusks. Pigs are omnivores; like humans, their jaws and stomachs are adapted to eat both plants and animals. Sows are excellent mothers. Up to twelve piglets are delivered each year and raised with love. Wild pigs prefer large forests with thick undergrowth. Their thick, bristly hide

protects them from thorns and branches. They like damp, swampy areas, where they dig mud holes to wallow in. After a mud bath, they let the mud dry on their hide, protecting them from sunlight and insects. They prefer to sleep during the day.

At twilight wild pigs become active and leave the protective forest to search for food in fields, to the distress of farmers. The males defend their herds viciously. An angry boar is a dangerous opponent for a human or a dog. Pigs are also highly intelligent. When raised by humans and accustomed to them from an early age, they can be more trainable than many dogs. In homes they can be trained to be hygienic. In many places, pigs are used to hunt for truffles.

The pig is revered in many cultures as a symbol of good luck and fertility. "Having a pig" means having good luck. When something works out well, one has "had a pig." The pig symbolizes fertility, opulence, and potency.

Message

If you meet a pig, this animal symbol wants to help you to awaken your primal instincts and show you how to mobilize those energies that lie at the root of your yin-yang principle. The male pig reminds you of potency, abundant creative energy, generative power, fierce protectiveness, and possessiveness; the female pig reminds you of primal feminine instincts like nourishing motherhood, solicitousness, herding instinct, and the power of seduction. These powers are primal instincts of our human nature. They are easily dismissed, but in order to reach lofty goals or even master everyday life we must grapple with these energies.

Whereas the wild pig symbolizes uninhibited primal energies, the domestic pig corresponds to their regulated forms. To be a pig, colloquially, means being an unrestrained, uninhibited person. The encounter with the pig does not mean you should be this way, but it tells you not to dismiss your deep human instincts. Usually it is enough to consider how you would react if you yourself were a pig. With this trick, you can gain many important insights about your inner truth, your hidden feelings, and your reactions that have grown lethargic through your upbringing. It is wrong to suppress the primal qualities of our humanness—both masculine and feminine—to the point where we are ashamed of them.

It is right, however, to allow your primal emotions to emerge inside yourself and then follow these instincts in a diplomatic and sensible manner. In this way neither masculine potency nor the feminine nesting urge becomes an agonizing pitfall. Become proudly conscious of your piggish side. You will recognize that it is completely human and normal, and once you are conscious of this you will know the right direction in which to steer your emotions. Pigs are very sensible animals, and sensibility is an important strength that is necessary for obeying one's animalistic feelings in a prudent manner.

RABBIT

Fertility

The rabbit found its way into human settlements early on. Many medieval manuscripts include information regarding rabbits. Its original homeland was southwestern Europe, especially Spain, where rabbits live in large colonies.

These originally very timid animals were initially cultivated by humans for their great fertility and tender meat. Today there are countless breeds, colors, and sizes, and the rabbit is one of the most common house pets. The rabbit is just as good a pet for small child as for a retired hobbyist. Rabbits, in extreme cases, can produce up to eleven litters a year, each with six to eight young.

Message

If a rabbit hops into your life, it brings you the message of fertility. In the rarest cases, this is meant in the sense of physical proliferation. The rabbit offers the medicine of expansion. It tells you to expand your human essence, to remain fertile, to open yourself to divine impulses, and to let them multiply. When spring comes and the sun's light awakens the Earth, the rabbit begins to expand its existence, perpetuating its colonies with new life. The rabbit turns light into life. This is what the rabbit you encounter wants to show you.

Consider the message of the rabbit on all levels, for as a human you are capable of letting moments full of light expand, spreading joy and happiness. Sadness and sorrow can also multiply, then the sky above your life will be covered with thick clouds. Children also express the wish to have rabbits as pets, because their souls yearn for light. Wild rabbits are not found everywhere in Europe. But pet rabbits have the power to appear in your life when you need them.

When this happens, fundamentally examine your attitude toward life. Are you ready to let light into your life, to radiate joy and happiness, and thereby to courageously support the expansion of your being? Every year in spring, around Easter, rabbits are widespread. This announces to people that they should awaken from the winter sleep and begin taking part in life again. It also reminds you to consciously nurture the seeds sown at the winter solstice and support them in their growth. You can no longer choose what grows there, but it is your duty to accept life attentively and consciously and to learn how to yield new seeds from the harvest at the end of the cosmic Earth's year.

RACCOON

Egoism

The raccoon is a member of the Procyonidae family. It comes from North America but has become established in Europe since the twentieth century. The raccoon is an omnivore and highly skilled thief. It can even plunder nests on high branches. It is also very adroit in the water. This approximately badger-size animal, with black face markings, long-fingered hands, and a dark-ringed tail, lives mainly in forests and floodplains near ponds, lakes, and rivers. Raccoons usually make their nests and winter hideaways in hollows in old trees. When these cannot be found, hollows in rocks and well-hidden niches in buildings are possible hideouts. According to recent observations, the behavior of dipping objects in the water has nothing to do with the cleaning or moistening of food. This behavior is a kind of stress relief. In the wild, raccoons live to be six to eight years old. At one year old the females are able to breed, and each year, after two months' gestation, they give birth to four young. The mother takes care of her young with courage and devotion. Raccoons are very playful, curious, and fairly solitary.

Message

The raccoon tells you to live in harmony with yourself in relation to your world. Connect yourself to your life plan and use it to your benefit. Alertness and outward attentiveness are recommended, directed toward yourself. The raccoon stands for our human ego. It is the personal "I" whose task is to claim our space in the outside world. The ego, as it were, is the cell of humanity, which unites us to the Earth, nature, and also our human essence. If one observes humanity as a whole, as a creation—as a child of the Earth, so to speak—the level of human development seems like that of a six-year-old child. Every ego of every person, viewed independently, corresponds in its spiritual development to this six-year-old child. Our human ego needs loving but clear guidance from our inner consciousness. The ego is not a monster but a part of one's self, deserving of love. The encounter with the raccoon clearly tells you to observe your own ego, maturely and empathetically. Watch the games it plays, try to understand its motivation, and if you do not like what you see, then deflection is a better strategy than appealing to the intellect. There is no way to get rid of this ego along the path of your development. Its guidance and accompaniment are part of our task on Earth. Besides, a beloved child is a wonderful guide in the outside world. You need a connection to your ego so that you can live and exist in the external world. Quietly become a little more egoistic. Give your human world what you need to give it. If you guide your ego lovingly it will not behave like a bull in a china shop. Otherwise it may do considerable damage to your social standing. The raccoon is not telling you to steamroll your ego but rather to take on the task and use your ego, in an attentive and understanding manner, as a bridge to your own inner world.

RAT

Repression

The brown rat and the Norway rat have spread practically over the whole world. Brown rats are somewhat smaller than Norway rats, but their tails are longer in relation to their bodies. The brown rat prefers drier, warmer climates. In nature it often lives in the trees, and in human settlements it lives in attics and lives mostly on plant matter. Also, it does not breed as prolifically as the Norway rat.

The Norway rat prefers damps areas: cellars, garbage dumps, and drainage ditches are its haunts. In the natural environment it lives in moist areas and digs long tunnels. The Norway rat is a great omnivore, especially fond of carrion. Norway rats can reproduce in uncanny quantities. In a good situation with ample food, a female can give birth four times per year, producing up to twenty young. Almost nothing can stop rats from expanding. They learn very fast and are extremely cautious. With their sharp incisors they are completely able to gnaw through metal and concrete to get to food sources. They test unknown food at first in small quantities. They quickly become familiar with poison pellets, which are then avoided by the entire rat population. Traps also lose their effectiveness very quickly. Once a trap has snapped shut once or twice, no other rat will go near it.

In the Middle Ages the Norway rat brought the plague to Europe, and today rats are still feared spreaders of epidemics in third-world countries, where they also do great damage to harvests. However, there are always young people who keep a rat as a pet around the time of puberty. The rat is carried close to the body and moves under the clothing. Through their exceptional social bonding, a rat handled in this way can become a faithful and clean companion.

Message

If a rat scuttles across your path, it is drawing your attention to the repressed sewers of your astral body. Admittedly, this is not a pleasant thought. But every human produces waste along with her emotions. Emotionality has a sunny side and a shadowy side. It is very important to deal consciously with our daily feelings. Purifying the astral body of emotional detritus is as important a part of human hygiene as bathing and brushing one's teeth. Emotions and feelings that arise from the present moment and are only expressed in relation to themselves can cause major changes in the natural system of the world of feelings.

Compare the world of feelings with the plant world and the flow of water. A healthy system with good water produces good plants, and when these die, they become nourishment for other plants. The ecosystem becomes polluted by aggressive emotions. It does not matter whether the aggression is against someone else or against oneself. Everything that angers us or makes us sick has its origin somewhere in our own behavior.

The rat shows us the repressed dirty feelings and thoughts that are in us and warns us not to keep wandering into the same traps or blindly continuing to eat the poisoned bait. Start to accept that your emotional behavior as victim or perpetrator is, above all, polluting your inner being.

Practice discipline with happiness; practice generosity and tolerance with yourself and others. When practicing discipline with happiness, always be aware of the happiness in the moment. No one is better than you, but also no one is worse. It is not for you to judge other people. It is no wonder that in big cities, where fewer rising conflicts are directly expressed due to anonymity, enormous plagues of rats exist. Where the accumulated load of uncontrolled emotions is let loose, rats find vast amounts of nourishment. Dive in to your repressed, hidden feelings, clean them out, and cleanse your conscience. You will be the one who profits from it, for the health of your inner world will be restored.

SEAL

Emotion, Indulgence

The seal inhabits North Atlantic coasts from Portugal to Iceland. It does not live in the actual polar regions. Like all pinnipeds, seals have an excellent sense of hearing. Their sense of smell, however, is weaker, and their eyesight best serves them underwater. Seals have been used by humans for a long time for their meat and their fat. Sealskin can be tanned to produce soft and durable clothing. Interestingly, pinnipeds' blood lacks the ability to clot, and their thick skin is their only protection against bleeding to death when they are injured. Sometimes, an individual seal will chase salmon up a river far inland, even reaching inland cities in Germany such as Magdeburg.

Seals live happily in groups and seek out large sandbanks or shingles on the coasts, where they relax. In the water their movements are elegant and sleek. They can dive a long way and are exceptionally trainable and playful. Most females give birth to their young along the North Sea coasts. Unlike the ringed seal, the common seal is not born with a thick white pelt. The young common seal can very soon follow its mother in the water. This is very important for them because of the movement of the tides; they must be able to swim from birth. In the first weeks the mother stays close by her helpless pup. The young seal cannot yet fight the strong waves. If a mother seal has twins she must choose one of the two and abandon the other. The abandoned pups drift along the coast, crying loudly, and are known to fishermen as "howlers." Many are captured and raised in zoos by bottle-feeding.

Message

The seal tells you to immerse yourself in the depths of your inner sentiments. Dive into your own heart. Meet with yourself, your sensuality, your strength, but also your hunger for love, your yearning for affection, and the sadness that comes from rejection. You are a being full of sentiments, a being who searches for an expression for all these sentiments. The seal reminds you of the sentiments that sleep, not yet experienced, begging for fulfillment. Take a look at these sides of your being. Cry a couple of tears when your heart opens and comfort radiates out from your inner center. It is often a kind of homesickness that radiates within us when the depths of the heart are touched. It is a homesickness that hurts, but when the tears are allowed to flow, it also heals. The seal leads you back to the depths of your senses, those that are primal in humans. Humans are intensive beings. We want to live, perceive, give, take, and experience intensively. Every restriction hurts in some way. Perhaps the seal encounter indicates that you should simply let yourself overflow and give in to the depth of your feelings to your heart's content. Enjoy it with enthusiasm, boundless and reveling. It will do you good.

SHEEP, MOUFLON
Sacrifice, Assertiveness

Sheep originally lived in mountains. With their thick wool, cloven hooves, and well-proportioned, muscular bodies, they are adapted to a life in a harsh climate.

The sheep was domesticated around nine thousand years ago. From the various breeds of wild sheep, at first in central and western Asia, sheep with better wool and more meat were bred, the main result being the mouflon. The sheep was highly prized as a sacrificial animal in many cultures. Besides their religious significance, they were also useful for their wool, hide, meat, and horns—all products that were important for people's livelihood in days of yore. As herd animals, sheep can be cared for easily with the aid of a couple of sheepdogs.

Sheep are unpretentious domestic animals. Even in high, dry steppes and deserts, herds of sheep still find enough food, and they can also reproduce without a problem under difficult conditions. Their relatively fatty milk allows lambs to grow plump quickly. And if a mother sheep has only one lamb, there is enough milk left over for her human owners.

Rams are brave and assertive. The size of their curved horns predicts their rank in the flock. Rams with the same horn size tend to invite each other to fight repeatedly. They face each other, rise up on their hind legs, and slam their heads and horns together.

Message

The sheep reminds us of our sacrificial role. For sure, devotion, readiness to help, and considerateness are wonderful qualities. But how easy it is to fall into the position of the gentle blackmailer, slipping silently and secretly into victimhood, stamping the recipient of our gifts with the label of wrongdoer!

To be noble, many people force themselves to be much more magnanimous than they really are, overstrain themselves, and end up with a deficit of energy. Those who lay themselves gracefully on the sacrificial stone and give their "blood" in the service of the divine end up honored but also sapped. Out of helplessness they then unconsciously ascribe guilt to their surroundings. Surely you yourself have experienced how hard it is to recognize this attitude and stand by it. The sheep tells us, in all areas of life in which there are wrongdoers, to recognize our own attitude of victimhood, examine the extent of our devotion and dedication, and set ourselves back in line with our true nature. In this manner the domestic sheep transforms back into the wild sheep. The latter is also a prey animal whose hide, horns, and flesh are readily available, but first it must be hunted down. The wild sheep never lets itself be placed on the altar as a material commodity.

The ram is the symbol of the wrongdoer. The roles of victim and wrongdoer are always very closely connected. If your attention is drawn to a ram, then for a moment you should pull away entirely from your external life. Consider whether there are people around you on whom you are definitely forcing your will. Many forms of abuse make one into a wrongdoer. Bashing your head against a wall may not be any problem for you. If your opponent is of the same power and has the same assertive strength as you, then everything is fine.

But consider that a ram only fights with one of equal strength to his own. He never invites a weaker or stronger ram to fight. Don't be hotheaded; don't try to get your way with violence. Especially not when the weaker one is looking for a wrongdoer. Always avoid power struggles when you cannot battle fairly and with completely worthy opponents. Relationships between men and women, and relationships between parents and children, are not the right areas in which to use force. Even though it sometimes takes some nerve to avoid it, one cannot raise children or preserve love and friendship by the methods of the unruly ram.

SHREW

Activity, Concentration

The shrew family contains many species that live all over the world and in very diverse habitats. They are insect eaters, and some species are among the smallest mammals in the world. The dwarf shrew, living in Europe, is only two inches long, not counting its tail, and weighs between .09 and .21 ounce. The Etruscan shrew is even smaller, with a body length of 1.4 to 2.1 inches and a weight of .04 to .08 ounce. The females give birth two to eight times per year, producing two to seven young. The dwarf shrew has a birth weight of .011 ounce and the Etruscan shrew .007 ounce. The latter, when newborn, are smaller and lighter than a coffee bean. There are also large shrews, the longest of which measures about eight inches. The shrew's metabolism is one of its amazing qualities. It is a wonder that such a tiny body can correctly perform all life's functions. During the winter months shrews are active by day and by night, searching constantly for food. Their bodies are too small for them to gather sufficient fat reserves to take longer breaks from eating, let alone to live on all winter long. Every day, in relation to their body weight, they devour huge amounts of animal protein. Consequently, shrews are very useful for controlling unwanted snails and insects. These tiny animals are very agile and extraordinarily active. They do not dig their own burrows. They use the holes and tunnels made by mice, or else natural chinks and cracks between stones. Little is known about how abundant the various shrew species are. It is tricky to observe these tiny, nimble, secretive, pointy-nosed animals.

Message

If you encounter a shrew it means that you should spit on your hands and get to work. It relates to a current topic that you often think of. In the message of the shrew, it is important to understand that this is not a matter of direct work as such, but of the thousand steps and decisions that must be made in order that actual work can be done. The shrew instructs you to set aside all passivity and to be effective, diligent, ambitious, and decisive. Maybe this is in relation to a real project, such as a building project, writing a book, or preparing for a party. In these projects, it is now time to take care of the core requirements, to plan precisely, to prepare seriously, to delegate optimally, and during the work to check everything carefully. Be alert, concentrated, and above all, present. The shrew is an insectivore, and therefore it is also showing you that you must take care to avoid all mistakes through vigilance. Not only your mistakes but also those of other people taking part in the project can be avoided in this way, thus preventing possible harm. Do not be afraid—it is not the big things that must be watched. It is the small details, which even a person without expert knowledge can notice. In building, the architect's work hardly needs to be supervised, but the unstable board that is no longer properly covering the pit must be discovered. The shrew is not an animal that, in general, warns us; rather it should be understood that with this encounter, we receive the message that we should do more, be more alert, and use our talents and strengths, even and especially where we seem to ourselves to be weak and useless.

Perhaps at the present time you are also preoccupied with an emotional topic. In that case you should interrogate yourself on all levels. Do not seek clarifying explanations, instead try to find the areas within yourself that cause problems. Often your own beliefs and established patterns hinder you from seeing things in a more liberating way and thus also hinder solutions to the problems. The shrew advises you to let go of all the principles you may have in relation to this topic—consciously and unconsciously—and to accept the possibility that there may be ways that you have not yet been able to imagine. Also, become active in relation to emotional themes. Make important steps forward in your awareness, and observe how your surroundings react to what you are secretly doing. Remember, though, our first movements in our surroundings are often not what we hope for. For example, if we seek more harmony and realize internally that we must suspend the idea that our harmony must also be that of others, then it is entirely possible for things to seem dissonant in the first moments, before the new insights can become established.

SQUIRREL
Preparation, Collecting

The squirrel is a very agile, extraordinarily clever, restless little animal, always moving, acrobatic and fast. Its movements are spontaneous, unpredictable, and lively. It springs feather-light from tree to tree. It is an animal that prepares, that creates security, in order to enjoy its life to the fullest. So, for example, it builds multiple nests high up in the crowns of trees, where it spends the greater part of its life.

The squirrel gathers a surplus of supplies for the winter and bur-ies them in various places in the woods. Squirrels crack nuts with their sharp teeth, holding them in their forepaws. They live according to a precise rhythm, yet the conditions in their lives are constantly changing. It is often not easy for a pine marten or hawk to catch a squirrel. The squirrel is provident, yet also carefree. They sometimes hide their provi-sions so well that they cannot find them at all. In this manner they help tree and bush species to spread.

Message

The squirrel tells you to stock up on provisions. Gather the fruits of life in the moment, when they are plentifully available. This means not only material provisions but also vitality, joy, friendships, relaxation, and security. But in the message of the squirrel there is also a message of lightness, movement, and spontaneity. The gathering of energies should be done with enjoyment and fascination.

Consider that in every person's life plan the means for the fulfillment of that plan are always abundantly available. However, great alertness and affirmation of life are necessary in order to harvest these fruits that will provide the energy for the next step. The squirrel advises you to gather supplies in the times when it is easy for you to do so. Work, then, when the work is there, celebrate when there are parties, and rest when your fascination for outward things abates. Be spontaneous, avoid entrenched patterns, and open yourself to all possibilities for enrichment that the river of life offers you. The flow of life leads us through highs and lows.

The art of preparation is to be able to take in the surplus of the moment and also to give it out freely in the same moment. It is not necessary to deny one's enjoyment of good times out of worry for the future. The squirrel gathers nuts and buries them in preparation. In this manner it puts the fruit back into the natural cycle and consciously stores up its supplies. If it gets hungry in the winter it will remember the location of sufficient supplies, and the forgotten provisions will, over time, grow into new food sources. You will have to consider your stored provisions, in two senses: Are you ready to really take everything that life offers you, and are you also ready, at the same time, to let it go? Whether the energy of matter, the energy of feelings, creativity, or spirituality, everything is abundantly available to you at the appropriate time.

When it is there, you can create out of the fullness. Take in abundantly, and let go, and trust that your cupboards will be full. However, the squirrel warns you not to hoard your supplies. If this agile animal were to weigh itself down with its own supplies, it would be easy prey. Encounters with squirrels are also moments when you should think of letting go. Perhaps your cupboards are overflowing with useless stuff that can finally be given back into the natural flow of matter. Or events and thoughts from long ago are stored up in the flow of your emotions, hindering you from freely expressing your essence and feelings of the moment. Perhaps you have also hoarded ideas that can never come to fruition and now only hinder your spirit from flying to new heights. Spiritual truths and lessons can also be hoarded, standing in the way of new steps forward and new realizations.

To recognize what domain this animal encounter corresponds to, it may be useful to determine from what direction the squirrel came. Any kind of hoarding of energies hinders your movement and slowly causes the flow of energies to stagnate. Set yourself free and accept your freedom. But do not forget the joys of life, airiness, and pleasure. You need to take responsibility for the flow of your energies. You know the game of taking and giving from all areas of your life. It is like breathing, eating, or drinking. Decide what tastes good. And your system will decide what can be let go.

VOLE, FIELD MOUSE
Deficiencies

Voles, or field mice, are a subfamily of mice, more closely related to hamsters and lemmings than to the house mouse. The vole is closely connected to its system of burrows and tunnels. It lives mainly on roots and plants and is very damaging to agriculture. When the snow first melts on a big meadow the extent of these small animals' activity can easily be seen. About every three hours, day and night, winter or summer, the vole digs deeper, looking for food. Only the roots and plants that it digs into are eaten. Heaps of earth are pushed up all along the vole's tunnel. Unlike the vole, the insect-eating mole normally makes only one molehill above its burrow. The vole does not notice plants growing to the sides of the tunnel. Voles live in colonies in meadows and fields. They avoid dense woods and hollows liable to flood. Five or six young are born in each litter. Gestation is only sixteen to twenty-four days, depending on the season. The young are born in ball-shaped grass nests and nursed for seventeen to twenty days. At only thirteen days—while still being nursed—the young are sexually mature and fur covered. About five adult females and one male live together in a colony. In the wild voles only live to be about five months old. They are food for many predators.

Message

The vole wants to draw our attention to deficiencies. It is part of human nature always to be deficient in some regard. The times during which we feel entirely happy and content with our surroundings are brief. Some sort of hunger always reappears, a hunger for challenges and emotions that promise satisfaction, then we get back to the search. Humans are emotional beings, and it is part of our nature to always be searching on all levels. We often connect our positive feelings with objects, people, or outward circumstances and try to re-create these outward conditions in order to regain these feelings.

Like the mole/vole that kills the plant (corresponding to the feelings) by eating its roots, we destroy the magic of feelings by focusing on possession. In order that our emotions may develop free and unfettered we cannot be chained to reasons or conditions. The garden of our emotions grows mainly on the gift of our inner imagination. Even if you can speak from memory about how open your heart was when you met a certain person, you cannot expect your heart to open in the same way in connection with this person, nor can you expect your heart to react in the same way at every meeting with this person. The vole invites you to remember the beautiful, uplifting moments in life but also advises you to release these feelings from the past and let them shine upon your everyday life. Indisputably, it is possible to experience great happiness, contentment, or, in the broadest sense, love, from an event, an acquisition, or a gift. But it is your inner capacity that makes you able to feel this happiness. Happy conditions awakened it. The vole teaches you to perceive happy feelings in yourself and project them strongly onto all areas of your life. Do not allow the search for emotions to draw you away from yourself and turn into dependency, for this will only wilt the flowers in your spiritual garden.

WEASEL, STOAT

Spying, Concealment

The family of weasels includes the short-tailed weasel, also known as the stoat or ermine, and the least weasel. They are secretive animals, adept at blending in with their surroundings.

The stoat's fur color changes with the seasons: the winter coat is white. Both the summer and winter coats have a black stripe. Weasels are hunters, mainly preying on mice, other small mammals up to the size of hares, small birds, and insects. Ermine pelts were used to decorate royal robes.

Message

If a weasel scurries across your path, it wants to advise you to be vigilant. Perhaps envy is working against you on some level. Be alert, and watch what emotions your presence awakens in others. The weasel does not imply bad feelings necessarily, but as a spy, it informs you that you have set something in motion.

Use your senses to tell what your competitors are up to. Competitors can be coworkers, friends, siblings. Do not panic; this is not a warning in itself but a reminder to watch out. A weasel appears in your life when your stage of growth is recognized and others are consequently forced to make room for you.

Keep going along strongly, but keep an eye on your opponents. It is dangerous to underestimate your strength and that of others.

Take care not to reveal your confidential thoughts, ideas, and plans to your surroundings. The encounter with the stoat means above all that your position as monarch in your own life is being questioned.

WOLF

Leader, Teacher

Although the wolf has been exterminated from many parts of Europe, it is still a powerfully omnipresent animal. This is not only because it lives on as the ancestor of our dogs but also because it remains extant in language and in the human consciousness. The wolf is an animal that loves freedom and needs wide, wild areas with plenty of space to hide. Wolves live together in highly differentiated social structures.

Within the pack, clear ranks are established, and every animal must stick to its assigned place. The wolf is a clever, sensible animal. The individual packs are very adaptable, and they develop remarkable tactics to bring down prey.

Because the social order of the wolf pack closely mirrored the order of early humans, and because both humans and wolves followed the great animal herds on their wanderings, wolves and people had contact very early on. It is believed that wolf packs served early humans as a model for hunting techniques.

Abandoned wolf pups and injured wolves were sometimes adopted and raised by humans. Wolf pups often imprinted on humans because they were nursed by women. There are also stories of humans being raised by wolves. Gradually, through careful selection and breeding, thanks to their adaptability and usefulness to humans, wolves became beloved helpers in the human pack.

Message

In the wild this primal ancestor of the dog is only rarely encountered. Now and then, an individual will make headlines, and many spiritual people feel very connected to these proud, freedom-loving animals. The wolf is the teacher. It guides us through the rules of being human. It encourages us to live with and train our strengths. It encourages us to develop our instincts. It teaches us to come to terms with ourselves as individuals, to take our places as part of a group, and to fulfill this role according to our own abilities.

The wolf is a mystic teacher that accompanies us through the world of our own subconscious so that we may find our innermost, holiest place. But the wolf also tells us to seek our spiritual family. Thanks to the song of our soul, we find people who harmonize with our essence. We feel understood by them, have the same interests and visions as them, and speak the same "language of the heart." The wolf shows us how to bear our teeth and defend against intrusion from strangers who do not speak our spiritual language.

When a person has found her pack, the wolf teaches her to take her proper place. It teaches her to conform to social structures, be sociable and affectionate, and to remain independent and free. Within the pack wolves are loving and respectful to one another, but with intruders they are very wary, suspicious, and when someone does not fit in, they are merciless. When the wolf touches you, it wants to guide and teach you. Be open to its guidance.

Let your instincts and intuition out of their cage and see whether your generosity and magnanimity truly show themselves in your spiritual family pack. The wolf admonishes you not to exhaust your spiritual companions so that you may also remain generous to the outside world.

WOLVERINE

Decisiveness

The wolverine is a member of the Marten family. It is a robust hairy predator, about 1½ feet tall and weighing sixty pounds. It is especially strong and aggressive. Although it is not very large, the wolverine's favorite prey are young moose and reindeer. But it will gladly prey on anything it can hunt. Like the bear, the wolverine eats berries, tender plants, and roots. Wolverines live in the northern, thickly forested parts of Europe, Asia, and North America. The wolverine is a typical loner. It walks around its enormous territory, which may be as large as 750 square miles, and marks its borders with feces and urine. Because of the long summer days and long winter nights in its habitat range, the wolverine does not specialize in night or day. Every couple of hours it rests, then continues on the hunt for food. In the snow it has a considerable advantage with its large, almost flipperlike paws, and it can overcome large prey. The wolverine's only nemesis is the wolf pack.

Wolverines do not hibernate. One might almost think that they are more adapted to winter than to summer. They glide over the snow almost without a sound, surprising every animal they can prey on. Unlike other members of the Marten family, wolverines only kill as much as they can eat. In February or March the female gives birth to between two and four young, which are born naked and blind. Around ten weeks, the young ones are fed previously chewed food along with milk. After three months, they are fully grown, but they remain with their mother until the second year of their lives.

Message

If a wolverine prowls across your path, it is touching the primal energy in you. It reminds you that you must be entirely open to yourself in order to stand up decisively for yourself with your own strength. Consider your everyday life with its challenges. Trust your energy and your instincts and stand up decisively for your beliefs, for your life and all that comes with it. What were you thinking of at the time of the encounter? Perhaps you are too unassertive about this topic? Perhaps you are confused because so many well-meaning people are offering advice as to how you should change? The wolverine does not ask for others' opinions. It follows its path. It relies only on itself. You are, in yourself, a divine being and should follow your path with precisely this level of self-assuredness. Seek out the places that correspond to encounters with the wolverine, even if you are not entirely comfortable in these locations. This is likely, because encounters with wolverines are not a daily occurrence. You are also advised to choose an unaccustomed way of behaving in order to achieve what you now have to achieve. Assert yourself. Do so energetically and mercilessly. Follow your way, even if you have to wait for a long time to be celebrated for your behavior.

PART 2

Birds

BITTERN
Opening

The great bittern, along with its smaller relative the little bittern, belongs to the Heron family. They live well hidden in the reeds. Although the great bittern grows to a stately height of 2½ feet, it is much more likely to make itself known with its foghornlike mating call than by actually showing its face. However, if you make the effort and have the patience to observe a reedy area quietly for a long time, perhaps this well-camouflaged bird will briefly fly out of the reeds, only to disappear again right away. The little bittern is also very secretive. With a bit of luck and very careful observation of a reed bed, you might see one at the edge of the reeds spreading its cream-colored, black-edged wings for a typical short flight or climbing up to a high point to observe the area. If something appears suspicious, the bird punctiliously disappears from view. In mild winters when fish, amphibians, or water insects are plentiful, bitterns may stay for the winter in their breeding grounds. But when the ground and swamp water freezes, they fly south.

Message
If you have a meeting with one of these very shy birds it is time to turn your innermost self outward and openly and honestly "out" yourself.

This is not a matter of superficialities but truly of what is most hidden. Try to remember exactly what you were thinking about when the encounter took place. Perhaps, indeed, it was a well-guarded secret in your life that you have entrusted to no one. But now it is time to do this. Seek out someone you trust and talk about the subject from the heart. It does not matter whether this is a problem, a wish, or an idea. If the matter to which the encounter points does not consciously occur to you, then think of what in your life would be most embarrassing to you if someone—perhaps only one specific person—were to discover it. It is important to consider that the bittern is not telling you necessarily to air the secret to someone who has something to do with it, but simply to tell it to *someone*. If you are having a secret love affair, this is not an admonition to tell your spouse but to seek out someone trustworthy whom you can tell. A neutral person is often recommended for this, such as a life coach or a psychologist. Talk about the secret from your heart, and try to figure out what frightens you so much about the circumstance that you keep it secret. Certainly, it is possible that you have no idea what the encounter means for you. Perhaps you are really aware of nothing that you are keeping hidden. In this case, the great bittern is advising you to engage with fundamental taboo themes, topics that are normally not aired or discussed. The little bittern, on the other hand, is advising you to grapple with your fears and their origins.

BLACKBIRD
Boundaries

The blackbird is a widespread bird. Males and females are easy to tell apart. For the interpretation of the blackbird's message, this means that the male speaks for the active, masculine side, the outer world of the person, while the female speaks for the passive feminine side, the inner world. The male is a gifted singer. He has a large repertoire of sounds; the ones he makes during everyday life could be described as shrill. But during the evening chorus of birds, to define his territory to the others,

he perches on the most exposed spot possible and sings his beautiful song in a voice that can be heard a long way off. The song ends with a dulcet piping that sounds like a gentle hum.

This song of the blackbird is admired by bird enthusiasts even more than that of the nightingale. But if a blackbird family is faced with danger in their well-defined territory, they sound the alarm with nervous, clamoring shrieks. Both blackbird parents care devotedly for their young. The young birds often exit the nest before they can fly. During this dangerous time the parents care for them and defend them.

Message

If a blackbird casts its spell on you, you are advised to consider the boundaries in your life. The male stands for the external boundaries, for protecting your own vulnerability and the space that you must create for your existence. If the bird is loudly defending its territory, it may be that people have intruded in a harmful way upon your territory.

Consider precisely where and with whom things are going well for you, and have the courage to defend your truth and your living space very clearly. Do not forget always to speak lovingly about what you feel, think, want, and can do. The male blackbird's evening song should remind you that every evening you should also contemplate yourself and broadcast your own being, brightly and lovingly, to the world. Be active!

Say loudly and clearly who you are, what you like, who and what you want to let into your life. In other words, express your boundaries. But choose a loving tone for this. Be aware that every person has, and must have, her inner and outer borders. In order for your fellow humans to keep to these borders, they first must be created.

The female blackbird, on the other hand, tells you to be aware of your inner qualities and inner boundaries. Often enough, feelings of duty, fears, and traditions force us to use our life force recklessly, depleting ourselves. Begin again to listen for soft voices on the inside, voices that lovingly urge you to create a light-filled garden of joy from your life. The female blackbird also reminds us that our duty on Earth is not to achieve integrity with respect to society but to create God's domain on Earth, which means creating joy, light-filled life, sensuous togetherness, and happiness for people.

You above all must keep to your inner boundaries. To recognize these you should learn to take your wishes and dreams seriously in order to trace your way from them to your inner needs. Consider that you are the creator of your life. The external and the internal are simply mirror images of one another.

BLACK GROUSE
Sacred Center

The black grouse lives on moors and heaths in northern Europe and in the Alps around the edges of forests. Due to increases in human population density, the black grouse population, like that of other grouses, has declined. The black grouse prefers to live in open stands of trees ringed by heaths or moors. Its courtship behavior, known as lekking, is noteworthy. For this, a courtship location is chosen at which many cocks gather, and each one marks out its own territory with its dance.

The red caps on their heads are fluffed up, and their lyre-shaped tails are spread out so that the white feathers stand out on the black background. At the edges of each grouse's territory, between dances

either symbolic or real fighting takes place. The dance is accompanied acoustically with hollow-sounding vocalizations. The hens sit during the lekking and observe the process with interest. They mate with the victor, and in secluded nests, hidden under bushes, they incubate six to ten eggs. The hen, unlike the cock, is well camouflaged. Her feathers are speckled with shades of brown and black. If she sits quietly in the bushes she can hardly be seen at all.

In winter black grouses make tunnels in the snow, the entrances hidden by fallen or drifted snow. When the warm weather comes they dig their way out and eat the needles of fir trees.

Message

It is an extraordinary event to encounter a black grouse. It is a symbol that shows you are called upon to embark on a great search. The time has come for you to inwardly pursue the deep questions of spirituality. A higher power is calling to you and wants to guide and teach you.

Life is a sacred dance, a dance on many planes. The powerful brashness of the ego, with its territories and boundaries, must be experienced just as much as the meditative way, which leads in a spiral to the center of your inner being, to the place where question and answer form a single unity. Open yourself and see whether, somewhere within you, there is a center around which your life moves, dancing.

When the black grouse enters your life, it is time to go on a great search for your innermost center. The search should not take place in absolute silence and deep meditation upon emptiness, on the contrary— the black grouse connects silence and loudness, ego with spirit, frugality with bounty. You do not need to separate from yourself to find your spiritual center, you only need to find your rhythm and understand your own dance around the center.

Then you can enter into the center of light, live silently and peacefully in your center, and look calmly out at the bustling of the external world.

BULLFINCH

Vulnerability

The strikingly colored bullfinch is a year-round resident in most of Europe. It lives on seeds, berries, plants, and also tree buds when other foods are scarce. This makes humans not exactly friendly with it, so it is no wonder that the bullfinch is a shy bird, retreating immediately from people. In the wild, the song of this beautiful bird is rather humble. But when kept by humans in a cage the bullfinch quickly begins to learn all manner of songs. Unlike most other small birds, bullfinch couples remain together through the winter. During the summer months the female builds a nest of twigs, moss, and lichen, usually in a fir tree, where she lays and incubates four to six eggs. The male helps devotedly to raise the offspring. In good years a pair can breed twice. If the nest is threatened by a predator, the bullfinch becomes an actor. It pretends to be sick or injured, luring the predator away from the nest.

Message

The bullfinch has sought you out to make you aware of your vulnerability. People are most vulnerable during transitions. Something in your life is putting out new buds. An upheaval growing in your inner self has remained hidden from the external consciousness for a long time. In everyday life this means that we unconsciously collect all the impulses and information necessary, which can include those of restless, unstable, and troubled times. Then, when all is collected, everything goes haywire. The impulses and information merge with existing experiences and knowledge into a new form of expression. Such processes take place again and again unnoticed on other levels of our being until this new form begins to inconspicuously weave its way into our lives. During this time what is new is vulnerable and sensitive. But for the affected person it is hardly even formulated, and it cannot be protected through one's own experiences and strengths, nor does it take the form of an attempt at a new, undefined possibility. It could be that a career change has led a new form of self-expression to emerge in you, or new aspects of give-and-take have emerged in your relationships. It is also possible that you have opened new existential ways, which are slowly taking visible form. Perhaps it is a spiritual realization, slowly making old behavior patterns obsolete.

In any case, the bullfinch advises you to pay great attention to discovering what is new in yourself and to protectively support its development. Consider very precisely what mode of self-expression feels right to you. Give yourself enough space to experience yourself. Get to know your own quirks and their meaning in your life. Carefully protect those idiosyncrasies that serve you appropriately and meaningfully in your life. Stand by yourself and guard against distraction from well-intentioned advice and criticism. Possibly, not all the people around you will be thrilled when you change. It could have uncomfortable consequences for some people. But you must not worry about this. Take the bull-finch's warning seriously. Protect your buds, lest they be quickly nipped by the requirements of other people.

BUZZARD

Evolution

The buzzard is a widespread bird of prey. In winter it leaves the north and returns to central Europe, and the buzzards that live in central Europe return to the Mediterranean. In milder climates it remains at its inherited territory the whole year round. It is an excellent flier, swooping in spiral patterns above its territory. As it circles the proud bird scans its whole living space. If it spots prey—usually mice or other small mammals—it swoops down vertically from a great height to the ground.

More rarely, the buzzard can be seen nesting. This large bird of prey builds its nest in tall trees in the forest. Both parents share in building the nest, incubating the eggs, and raising the two or three chicks. For hunting, buzzards prefer open fields with freestanding structures to sit on. They are often seen on fence posts along highways.

Message

If a buzzard dives into your consciousness, it is advising you to become conscious of the power of your evolution. Evolution is development, and development is the greatest gift every person has. We also revolve in great circles around the patterns of experience on Earth, thus collecting divine truth, piece by piece. It is not necessary to understand the whole pattern and see it all the first time you circle around. The buzzard often flies in the same circle for hours to find food in its territory. It is advising you to keep patrolling your life from whatever distance is necessary and to build your own evolution upon the knowledge and abilities that are currently available. It also reminds you to maintain the necessary distance and be observant.

Perhaps now is the time in your life to circle broadly over your memory, allowing you to draw new knowledge from your own past experiences. Let things happen, be alert and observant, and remain free emotionally. Many things will come together without you having to interfere with your own human thoughts and actions.

Whether you see the buzzard circling or sitting still on some high point, it always wants to remind you that your life is taking place at your own center. There, at the center of your being, the experiences of body, soul, and spirit are united into a great whole, which projects life situations into your outer world in a magical way.

Externally, you cannot bring about any changes. However, through precise observation, perception, and knowledge, you can influence the inner world that this outer world has created.

Evolution is an eternal process without beginning or end. There is no time constraint and no goal that you must reach. Altercations between buzzards and crows (symbolizing law) can often be observed. This reminds us that the true divine laws, the rules of nature, dictate our evolution and steer it along their paths, and instilled or self-inflicted forces can cause our development to veer off its natural track. Consider that it is always your own thought-magic that disturbs your evolution. More precisely, it is the vociferous thoughts of the ego, thoughts that are nourished by the ideas of society.

In reality, the buzzard cannot be dangerous to the crow, no more than you, with your development, can be dangerous to the divine rules or laws of society. And yet the reaction of the crow is similar to that of society. Be like the buzzard: sidestep society's rules of behavior calmly and with dignity, and climb to high cosmic altitudes where you can return to the paths of true laws and get the best view of your life's pattern.

The buzzard, with its yearning reputation, often wants to conjure you up to its high altitude to remind you that the fulfillment of your longing resides in your own heights. And only those whose circles fit with your own belong as a part of your evolutionary plan.

CHICKEN
New Beginnings

The chicken is a very well-known bird. With its short, truncated wings, it can only fly for a short time and for short distances. Chickens live mainly on the ground and have developed a notable ability to run, augmented by short spurts of flight. The sexes are clearly different. The rooster is larger, has more colorful plumage, and can also be distinguished from the hen by his crowing.

A flock of chickens spends more or less the whole day searching for food on the ground, establishing their pecking order, and taking generous dust baths. In the wild, chickens fly up into trees in the evenings, where they sleep with their heads under their wings. The new day is announced by the rooster with a loud "cock-a-doodle-do." Then the birds leave their roosting place and return to the search for food. They eat seeds, grains, worms, caterpillars, beetles, and other small animals. During the summer months, mature hens lay an egg almost every day in a nest where they accumulate. Thus, a flock can raise multiple broods each year. The chicks hatch after twenty-one days, and the hen takes care of them all the rest of the summer. A mother hen leads up to fifteen chicks and enjoys a high rank in the pecking order. This order is established with pecks and blows with the spurs of the feet.

Fights between rival chickens can lead to serious injuries. Because of their good egg-laying capacity and tender meat, humans domesticated chickens early on. The clear day-and-night rhythm of these birds fits very well with the lives of people. People used to go to bed with the chickens and get up when the rooster crowed.

Message

Whether it is the hen or rooster that comes into your awareness, both stand for new beginnings. With its loud crowing, the rooster greets the new day each morning. Then life begins in the chicken coop. The life of the chicken flock is well structured and follows precise rules. But these rules are never rigid in the lives of these fowl. They are always being renewed, improved, and redefined. Peck by peck, boundaries are set and strengths tested. In this way the rules are being reformulated continuously, in every moment.

Each member of the flock gains or loses rank depending on momentary strength or weakness. With the help of these well-structured power games, the chickens also decide which hen in the colony will brood and lead the chicks. Therefore, the chicken urges you to let in new beginnings in every part of your life, to react to strengths and weaknesses, to recognize change, and to accept the rules of the moment. Tell yourself "that's how it is" about the moment, and try to grow and learn from it.

It is of no use to remain fixated on the eventuality of the past or future.

The only time that counts is the present, and out of it a new present will be born. Anyone who observes chickens knows that these animals are very alert, searching the ground for food with great attentiveness, commenting loudly at each finding, and missing almost nothing. Therefore, in your life, pay attention not only to the inner changes but also to what comes at you from outside. Consider the applicability of every encounter, and do not forget to give your full attention to how it is expressed. As humans, we live in a society that can function only when the expression is correct.

The message of the chicken tells people to proclaim their own perceptions, unaltered and honestly. All these perceptions then come together into a new whole. This whole gently changes so that the ideas of individual people develop. The chicken does not take the pecks of the others personally. It accepts them as the rule, grows stronger from them, and takes on a position of power where appropriate.

Although the chicken's message speaks to the plane of the ego, it also requires very great psychic tolerance and an understanding of polarity. Consider, in your life, whether you are able to support your opinions and deal out the appropriate pecks without judging or needing to retreat in a huff. The pecking order of a flock of chickens is the natural norm in the ego plane of human life.

CORMORANT

Unknown Feelings

The cormorant is a large aquatic bird weighing about six pounds with a wingspan of about nine feet. Because they live mainly on fish, they have long been persecuted by humans as competitors, and their nests destroyed. Today populations have recovered, even on large inland bodies of water. Cormorants prefer to nest in colonies in trees and on cliffs.

Both parents build the nests, incubate the eggs, and raise the chicks. The birds mainly retreat inland in the winter. When swimming, the

cormorant lies low in the water and holds its head and beak straight up. Before diving it squeezes the air out of its feathers and lets them fill with water. Under water, it is fast and agile. It brings its prey up to the surface and swallows it whole there. To dry out its wet feathers, it sits on a stone or pole and spreads its wings.

Message

The cormorant is an aquatic bird and therefore speaks to the world of feelings. Do you have a question or a prayer deep inside you that you are not articulating? Is there a feeling in you that cannot develop into a conscious thought because then something would have to change, or you would have to change something? The things that are repressed within us begin to ferment and cause pain. We often do not know what is repressed; often they are feelings that cannot turn into thoughts because we were too young when they originated, and we did not have the language in our thinking.

Fermenting feelings are the cause behind many unexplainable behaviors and fears, unexplainable sadness and depression. Added to this, it takes energy to keep something bottled up, even when it is unconscious. If your attention is drawn to a cormorant, it is time to work on your sadness. For this you do not need to know any history, or to trace any pain to its roots. If you saw the bird on a tree or in flight, it is advising you to give expression to the shadows through creativity, dive into your innermost consciousness, and surrender to this nameless shadowy feeling.

Breathe in this blackness and lighten it in your heart with your own light, your love for yourself! Paint pictures of the shadows, write stories, whittle and hammer, but let something happen when you do so. The expression, not the end product, is what counts.

If you see a cormorant drying its feathers in its prayerlike position, it is inviting you to open yourself to yourself, look inward into your own deepest being, to the place where the divine enters the human realm through the powers of creation. Turn in prayer toward the unknown. Pray for answers, guidance, help, and strength.

CRANE
Concentration, Initiation

These wonderful, elegant birds can be seen on moors and remote lakes in northern and eastern Europe in the summer and in the Mediterranean in the winter. During breeding season cranes are scattered very inconspicuously throughout damp forests and swampy areas. Cranes are monogamous and raise their young together. For migration, they gather together in large groups in the wide fields. Cranes fly in a typical V-formation.

They are excellent gliders, using updrafts skillfully. The body position in flight is similar to that of the stork. Both the neck and the legs are outstretched. The crane behaves as quietly and collectedly in the air as on land. With deliberate steps, it moves carefully through shallow water, on swampy meadows, and on the forest floor, looking for frogs, slowworms, mice, nests, and also seeds, fruits, berries, and tubers. Motionless and concentrating, it waits for moving prey. This observant bird hardly misses a thing. Even in their unusual spring dance rituals, for which a group of mostly young cranes will gather, these majestic birds remain concentrated and dignified. The dancing ritual takes place at traditional locations. When dancing, the birds spring high in the air, flap their wings, walk around each other with wings spread and head hanging, bow to each other, throw pieces of wood or stones in the air, and stand in rigid, outstretched, upright postures, ending by shaking strongly all over.

Message

An encounter with a crane has a great deal of significance. Destiny means well for you. Now, in your life, there will be a trial to undergo, a task to solve. Do not expect this task to come from the outside, from your life's narrative. The test relates to your inner world. The crane invites you to follow your inner guidance in the depths of your consciousness, and there, in humble submission, step before the old, wise "I." There, ask the question, "Who am I?" for as long as it takes, until the answer no longer has anything to do with names, professions, credit cards, clichés, character traits, or status. Do not let your head seek the answer, because your head will find a form. Seek with your heart. The heart finds many-layered, all-encompassing answers that you will perceive as an idea. Concentrate on this idea and consider over and over whether the image it shows of you is related to what you are for other people, or to what energy you are made of. To be ready for such an initiation you need a great capacity for concentration and the strength to confront yourself. It does not matter what spiritual knowledge you have accumulated thus far, or in which esoteric or religious camp your beliefs fall. Let go of everything you know in your head and follow the crane into your inner self. In ancient mythologies the crane is sometimes depicted as the companion for the journey into the world of the dead. It is the bird that brings people into the hereafter, and as the stork, it brings them into life again. Thus, it accompanies people through time. Concentrate very deeply on that which is eternal, outside of time—or, if one views time as a wheel, inside of time. That is where the answer lies.

CROW

Law, Norm

Birds of the Crow family are widespread and divided into three types: ravens, rooks, and crows. The crows include carrion crows and hooded crows. Hooded crows are easily recognized by their gray "hoods." Rooks have no feathers at the base of the beak, where their light-gray skin is visible. The carrion crow looks most similar to the raven, which is about eight inches taller, approaching the size of a buzzard. The raven is distinguished not only by its deep, sonorous calls but also by its wide repertoire of sounds.

Members of the Crow family will gladly eat garbage and carrion. They are omnivores, also eating insects, worms, snails, grains, seeds, and fruits. They often rob the nests of smaller birds. As agricultural pests, they have long been persecuted, but this has made no significant dent in their population. Crows are social birds, mostly gathering in small groups and going together to seek food. In the farming areas around villages, food supplies are fairly plentiful. In rural areas, crows are often associated with life and death.

It is said that whenever someone is born or dies, a flock of crows can be seen in the vicinity of the house.

Message

In the symbolic language of animals, the crow signifies law. Of course this does not mean the laws made by humans, but the laws of nature. The laws of nature are the norm from which normalcy is derived. Birth and death are natural laws; they are normal. Like the raven, the crow is a border-crosser between worlds. Its black plumage is a reminder of the darkness of night.

The origin of the law is in the place where the creative power still rests undisturbed. The processes of creation take place with immeasurable precision, on an infinite number of planes of the known and unknown, as long as the creator gives its will to this nothingness. As humans we can only understand and identify a very small part of this. But the crow, when it appears, reminds us of these laws. It tells you to follow your inner nature, tells you of the great and precise interconnectedness that has led to the present moment.

And it makes clear to you that everything you do, feel, and think will bear fruit in the universe in accordance with these eternal laws. It is normal for things to go badly for you, even when, from your point of view, only other people are responsible for that. It is normal for you to feel fit, happy, and self-confident without any external event being responsible for it. "It is normal" means that events are following their natural norm. How we bring things about, and which of our old and new deeds, thoughts, and feelings combine into causes that lead to effects, is impossible for human understanding to grasp. But that is how it is.

Everything, absolutely everything, is a manifestation of this eternal law, and we are a part of its expression, whether or not we like it, and whether or not we know it. The crow is not telling you "You're guilty!" No, instead it is urging you to relax. Be calm in yourself and look into your deep, inner nature. Be natural, be normal. If you encounter crows often, you should calm down in general and remember your own most fundamental normalcy. The crow also advises you to give careful consideration to your behavior.

Have you tried or trained yourself to achieve something in your life? Your most fundamental truth is your being just as you are. This being is the law given to you by the creator, and when you are as you are, then you are normal. Consider how much of your fundamental truth you actually live, and how much of it is buried beneath instilled traditions and goal-oriented behavior.

CUCKOO

Wealth

Who does not know the touching call of the courting male cuckoo? It is as much part of the spring as the flowers, the fresh light-green leaves on the trees, and the warm sun rays. The cuckoo is a migrant, spending its winters in Africa and its summers all over Europe and Asia. The cuckoo is a brood parasite. This means that it lays its eggs in the nests of other songbirds. The unwilling stepparents are left to raise the cuckoo chicks. The female cuckoo keeps careful track of when songbirds build their nests and lay their first eggs. Most songbirds lay an egg every morning until they begin to incubate.

When the songbirds are away in the afternoon, the female cuckoo quickly picks up one of the eggs in her beak, lays her own egg in the nest in a matter of seconds, and flies away. She eats the stolen egg, or simply drops it. In this manner the cuckoo can produce more young than she herself could feed. Interestingly, the cuckoo usually seeks out as surrogate parents the same species of songbird that raised it. Thus, over time, the cuckoo's eggs come to resemble those of the host bird more and more closely.

About eighty host bird species are known in Europe, but the cuckoo's egg is not very well adapted to all of them. If the host bird parents realize the trick, the cuckoo's egg will be expelled. If the stepparents are deceived, the cuckoo chick hatches along with the others, or somewhat earlier, and instinctively throws its stepsiblings out of the nest. A stressful four weeks are in store for the parents. The cuckoo chick grows very fast and is soon larger than they are.

Its appetite is barely satiable, and it constantly wants more insects and caterpillars. Cuckoos never take care of their own chicks. At the end of the summer they return to Africa. The chicks follow them somewhat later, on their own.

Message

If you have heard or seen a cuckoo, perhaps you immediately checked to see if you were carrying money on you. According to folklore, if you have money in your pocket when you hear the cuckoo's call, it foretells wealth, but if you have no money with you, you will stay poor. The cuckoo clock is also associated with money and prosperity. In fact, the cuckoo is associated with people's wealth and material possessions. The person who has everything he needs, or more, is rich. Unlike abundance relating to one's essence, this is a matter of material wealth.

Wealth grows and shrinks with wins and losses. Therefore, the cuckoo is not only the messenger of wealth but also tells us to examine our material situation. It urges us to consider what we spend money on and how much we are earning. Check to see if there is a cuckoo sitting somewhere in your material nest, suppressing your own individual truth and creativity and draining your energies like a bottomless barrel. It could be that you are expending a great material effort—after all, the life force is also a material energy—that only benefits other people. Be alert when the cuckoo calls to your consciousness, and guard your new plans especially well. We are often much like the host parents of the young cuckoo. It is very hard to escape from a pattern of loss that is already established.

Often there is nothing we can do but grit our teeth and change the situation as soon as possible. But it is advisable to get wise to the cunning of the brood parasite to prevent further exploitation. Wealth is a natural potential available to every person in the life plan. If this natural wealth is lacking in your life, it is due to lack of assertiveness and alertness, as well as feelings of low self-worth.

No matter how lovingly a cuckoo is raised by its surrogate parents, it remains a cuckoo. None of the good qualities and values the host parents try to instill in the adopted chick will bear any fruit. Just like its biological parents, it will do nothing for its own offspring. It will lay its egg in another bird pair's nest and destroy their eggs. Do not expect your parasites to change. The only help lies in experience and learning, which will allow you to protect yourself better.

DOVE

Peace

Among doves, the feral and domestic pigeon, the domestic dove, and the Eurasian collared dove are probably the most widespread. Somewhat more rarely encountered are the wood pigeon and the turtledove. In all, there are about 140 different dove species, all descended from the feral pigeon, which has been cultivated since antiquity. The domestic pigeon is originally descended from the rock dove and is hardly distinguishable from its feral counterpart. The feral pigeon, like its ancestors, nests in

hollows in rocks or niches in buildings. The wood pigeon and turtle-dove nest in trees and bushes.

In the wild, doves raise about two broods a year. The feral pigeon, however, raises up to four broods a year, sometimes even in the winter. Doves eat grains, seeds, and small snails. The feral pigeon has adapted itself to the food of human civilization and will even eat chocolate. Doves have become a major problem in cities. Not only do they dirty and damage buildings with their droppings, they also carry pests such as mites and ticks and transmit psittacosis. In many cities war has been declared on these messengers of peace. After public anger at the use of poisons and guns, birth control measures have been attempted, with little success.

Message

All types of doves signify peace. But they speak to this theme from various viewpoints. The theme of peace is very broad and is always connected with understanding, communication, and sympathy. Swarms of pigeons in cities remind people to come out of their isolation, take part in the life around them, and to let the processes in relationships happen. In this way one can grow into genuine contentment.

The hectic everyday city life, the grim daily rhythm that is imposed upon us, and the unconscious or partly conscious fear of crowds cause aggressive energy fields to appear, which make people anxious and force them into unnatural behavior patterns and life strategies. Thus, great mistrust emerges between individuals. Sympathy, communication, and understanding are only superficial and therefore lose their warmth.

Consequently, there is not only alienation on the individual level but also alienation from oneself. The idea of peace that the dove reminds us of has little to do with small, personal everyday quarrels and more with contentment, which can come out of deep exchanges between people. The solution to this problem is to not go out into the street to try to have deep conversations with whomever you meet. First, you would frighten most people by doing this, and second, much more importantly, you would overstrain your subconscious.

The feral pigeon wants to guide us to a long-term solution. This bird makes its medicine available to people every day, unavoidably, on every continent. For the individual person who is confronted by this bird again and again, it is recommended that one work consciously on oneself, strive toward contentment with oneself and one's own life, and thereby automatically become a life-affirming archetype for the people in one's surroundings. This could be viewed as sustainable work for the cause of peace, because peace is only effective if the deep-rooted mistrust is healed.

The wood pigeon and turtledove have fundamentally the same meaning as the feral pigeon. However, the turtledove speaks specifically to the topic of family and love relationships, while the wood pigeon speaks to creation in general.

DUCK, DIVING
Relationship to Oneself

The clearest characteristic distinguishing diving ducks from swimming ducks is their swimming behavior. Unlike the swimming duck, such as the common mallard, diving ducks sit much lower in the water. The tail is submerged. When leaving the water, diving ducks need a running start to get above the surface. They swim fast over the water, flapping their wings, until they have enough momentum to take off. Swimming

ducks, by contrast, fly directly from the water. Some of the best-known diving ducks are the common pochard, the red-crested pochard, the common goldeneye, and the tufted duck. Diving ducks dive under the water, submerging their whole bodies, and swim underwater. They dive mainly for mollusks, insect larvae, and water plants. They also dabble, but much less often than swimming ducks. Diving ducks brood in reeds on the edges of large lakes, and different species often crossbreed. They almost never go on land for food.

Message

Encounters with diving ducks are commonplace in summer on large lakes. If you especially notice an individual or group of these waterfowl, then you are advised to clarify your relationship with yourself. How do you handle yourself? Take a little step away from the outside world toward the inside. Now observe your own humanness. How much real, sensual, honest living are you allowing yourself to have at the moment? How much of your life energy is spent serving some external task, other people, or even some fictional story? Consider how everything you do is treating you. Does your life as it is give you energy, joy, and contentment, or are you just making investments in order to fulfill something? The diving duck wants to remind you that there is only one person on Earth who can adequately represent and protect the great asset that is your life, and that is you. It is important to be an attentive friend to yourself, to consider your own well-being as a best friend would, and to make sure that everything is going well for this person, who is you. This is not a recommendation for any ascetic health practices or rigorous restructuring in your life, in order to make you into an inviolable god. No, life is the way it is! But to support what is there through all the highs and lows and to appreciate the knowledge you have gained through the life you have lived, you must make careful use of your own life force and happiness. And no one other than you is responsible for that, no matter how close they are to you.

DUCK, MALLARD

Polarity of Emotions

The mallard is a widespread wild duck. Domestic ducks are descended from it. The male has brightly colored plumage, while the female wears dull brown all year, thus remaining well camouflaged. Ducks are very often seen by park ponds and lakeshores. They are also found on other bodies of water. Because they are not very shy around people, they perform their mating rituals in the open—usually unnoticed by humans.

They often fly to meadows, fields, or the edges of woods, where they look for food such as grains, acorns, and seeds. On the water they eat water plants, worms, snails, insects, and other small animals. They return to the water in the morning to rest, sleep, and preen their feathers.

Their nests are often built on riverbanks in the reeds but can be built up to 1½ miles inland from the water. Although the actual breeding starts in the spring, the choice of partners begins in the fall. The female builds the nest. To line it, she plucks downy feathers from her breast. About three weeks after mating, the ducklings hatch. They are precocial. Just after hatching they leave the nest and can swim right away.

For safety, the mother often leads them on the open water. The mother alone is responsible for raising the eight to twelve ducklings. Only a quarter of them live to be more than a year old; many are lost to cold, predators, and the fall hunting season.

Message

We encounter ducks very often. As waterfowl, ducks speak to the domain of human emotions: the world of feelings, perceptions, and impressions. Because male and female ducks are easy to tell apart, it is important to consider the sex of the duck you encountered. Often, however, these birds are encountered in pairs or in flocks.

The duck stands for the relationship between our emotional poles. The human world of feelings is composed of positive and negative fields. Joy and sorrow, happiness and unhappiness belong together. To have experiences, tension between the poles is needed. Painful experiences are often on the negative poles. So we are anxious to blot out the shadows, the negative sides, and turn only to the positive. This gives us the possibility to enrich our lives through experience, and the experiences—negative and positive—repeat themselves endlessly.

The male duck, with its colorful plumage, symbolizes joy and happiness. The female duck, on the other hand, symbolizes sadness and sorrow. If the two poles of the ducks were separated, they would soon vanish from this planet. Only the equilibrium of yin and yang makes creation possible. Thus, the duck urges us to find loving joy with our two poles. Try to see your weaknesses, without judging yourself, and set up a corresponding joy across from each individual weakness. Make duck pairs out of your emotions, and allow them to live out their feelings on the wide waters and create new feelings continually.

EAGLE

Spirit

High above, between the sun and the clouds, the eagle circles majestically. Its raucous cries echo off steep, bare cliff sides. It is an acrobatic flier, a king of the air, with a majestic wingspan up to six feet. While sailing the skies it searches the ground for food, or else hunts from exposed locations. For this, it chooses a well-suited place from where it can view a large area. Its eyesight is outstanding; for example, it can spot a hare more than three thousand feet away.

The eagle's prey range up to the size of foxes and young sheep. In the winter it also eats carrion. By preying on domestic animals, the eagle has made itself the enemy of humans. Gruesome stories of child abductions have also contributed to driving the eagle to the brink of extinction. Today it is protected by law.

Eagle pairs conduct their mating dance in the open skies. They are faithful to each other for life. Together, in a high place, they build their aerie, or else refurbish an old aerie with new greenery. The female, more than four inches taller than the male, incubates the eggs, but the male helps to feed the chicks.

Message

The eagle is a mystic bird. People have always marveled at it. Attitudes range from worship, awe, and fear. Many stories revolve around these secretive, noble birds. To encounter an eagle, one must usually get away from dense civilization into the quiet of the mountains. The eagle signifies the spirit, and just as you must leave thickly settled areas to meet the eagle, so you must leave the external world to meet the spirit. It is this part of yourself that has gone through tough schools of initiation, passed trials, and come close to truth, purity, and light.

The eagle flies in a circle and oversees the whole pattern of the world. If you encounter an eagle, it is inviting you to rise up for a moment above the earthly world, spread your spiritual wings, and look at the pattern of your life from above. Have the courage to recognize or perhaps test your connections. For this moment, completely let go of the world of emotions and duties. From the eagle's perspective, problems are small and inconsequential, solutions easy to see. But it is up to you to decide on these solutions and take action. Think of how precisely the eagle focuses on the goal, for when it swoops down, it cannot afford to take its eyes off the goal even for a second.

Contact with the human spiritual principle is a wonderful thing. But in life, this principle can only be effective if one knows all one's abilities, strengths, and weaknesses, accepts them, and works with them. An encounter with an eagle foretells a contact with the spiritual principle, and this contact will always end with the fulfillment of an inner experience. But enlightenment is never a gift. There will be trials in your life through which you will gain valuable experiences and take great steps forward. But you will only pass the trials if you first walk through all the stadiums where they are to take place.

This means that experiences and insights turn into physical reality. During the time of the trial, try to remain mostly alone. Practice inner communication with your spirit, and go along your way carefully, step by step. Again and again, raise your eyes to the heavens, let go of your fears for the future, let go of the Earth, and devote yourself to your truth. You can now take your time in spotting your "prey" from high above. Circle quietly, but when you have decided to take a real step, there can be no more hesitation, no affected, unauthentic behavior, no uncertainty, and no wavering. A flubbed dive has consequences.

The eagle also tells you not to clothe yourself in false feathers, especially not spiritual ones. To live your spirituality, you must find your own way to express it. True spirituality is born of the spirit, and every ray from the spirit that falls upon a person's consciousness is entirely unique. If you are truly connected to your spiritual principle, your spiritual expression will be deserving of this uniqueness, and thus you will do your part in the development of humankind. It may be that you will receive an eagle feather as a gift; this is one of the most holy totems. The Native Americans protect these feathers, and today it is no longer permitted to bring an eagle feather out of the country. Simply buying an eagle feather does nothing for one's own spirituality.

FALCON, KESTREL

Communication, Message

The kestrel, hobby, peregrine falcon and red-footed falcon, and merlin all belong to this category. Falcons are birds of prey. Like all such birds, they are remarkably observant. Their eyes barely miss any movement, and their reactions are quick and certain. The falcon is an excellent flier, an acrobat of the air. Fast as an arrow, it appears in the heavens, plays calmly around the wind currents, and then suddenly disappears again.

The kestrel mainly hunts small mammals. The other falcon types prefer birds up to the size of a thrush, as well as field mice and large insects such as dragonflies, beetles, and bumblebees. In speed and accuracy, the peregrine falcon has no match. It dives to pursue its prey with speeds of up to 180 miles per hour.

Message

In almost all cultures the falcon is seen as a messenger from another world. If you encounter a falcon, it is advising you to perceive life entirely consciously. Be open and awake, look at your life consciously, and be alert to all possible signs.

The falcon is a kind of "messenger of fate." It makes us aware of itself and shows us how it can deal loosely, easily, and playfully with the energies in its living space without ever losing its dignity. With its appearance, it reminds us to make use of the possibilities in life, to enjoy them, and to create from the fullness of things. To carry this message into our lives, we must learn to make exhaustive use of all the things that Mother Nature makes available to us in everyday life.

But the falcon is not an exploiter, quite the opposite—some species even place their abilities at humans' disposal. The message of the falcon is to pay attention to the available possibilities and make use of the existence of your surroundings with playful easiness. Train your ability to observe, your sensory perception, and your memory. Be aware that when the falcon crosses your path, fate has important suggestions and information for you. But these are exclusively in the present moment and relating to your life's true path. Do not expect any remarkable events. Could it be that you have become entangled in the details of your past? Have you lost your personal way of seeing through the powerful influences of your environment?

The falcon often appears in those moments when a higher way of seeing is needed. Thus, it is not a message of the future but rather some helpful orientation in the labyrinth of the present. Many everyday problems emerge when the structure of one's own life's narrative is too complex for one's comprehension. Connections get lost in human consciousness and decisions become almost impossible.

Thus one loses, on the one hand, the foundation under one's feet, and on the other hand, access to one's higher guidance as well. Almost helpless, one is left hanging in one's own life's narrative. Only by "climbing out of it" into a higher level of being is it possible to gain a new understanding of the structure of connections, to root oneself in the now, and to follow the straight path of determination with joy once again.

FINCH, CHAFFINCH
Annunciation

Finches are songbirds. The best known of them are the chaffinch, the greenfinch, and the goldfinch. As with many birds, the females are unremarkable looking and thus better concealed. The colorful males are striking and also accomplished singers.

The finch belts out its song in staccato notes, fast and loud.

Beginning high, it hurries to the "coda." To sing this song the male chooses the highest place possible. Besides their songs, finches have countless calls and other vocalizations. Finches are partial migrants. Some of them may stay for the winter around human settlements, often living off the food in bird feeders.

Message

We encounter finches almost every day, but they do not always come into our awareness. If a finch appears to you very obviously, then it has news to share with you. Or rather, it is making you aware that news is coming your way and that you yourself have news to share. Having a message to share always goes hand in hand with receiving a message.

Things will befall you from outside that will have some effect upon you internally. Whatever comes from outside, accept it without judgment. At the same time, formulate the statements inside yourself that you must broadcast to the outside world. Listen attentively inside yourself, without shutting yourself off externally, and try to hear the inner message. Cautiously let it grow louder and clearer within yourself, and open your consciousness like a barrel into which this inner message can be poured, unaltered. Then bring the message out, clear, straightforward, and obvious.

The finch improvises its song; that is to say, it varies it with its own creativity. Therefore, do not strike other people with your message as if it were a wet noodle upside the head, but decorate it so that it can be accepted. In the case of animals that are seen often, this message applies to life in general. Every person should say what she perceives, feels, and knows. Only when the encounter is very definite is there something unusual about this annunciation. If you are still not clear about what you have to share, or with whom, then seek out a quiet place, close your eyes, and imagine that you are a little bird sitting on a tree branch, formulating your message in your throat.

Pay attention to what you want to say, then you will know who to say it to. It is not enough to know it, you must act upon it. Sit down and write it out in the finest form possible, choosing words that you find pleasant. But make sure your message remains clear and explicit.

GOOSE

Belonging

Wild geese are good fliers. In the fall, they return from the northern regions to the Mediterranean. They fly very high on this journey. When flying, they form a line or a V shape. Males and females have the same coloring and mate for life. If one partner dies, the other usually remains alone. Geese are very social, whether nesting on thickly vegetated ponds and swamps or searching for food on lawns and meadows, where they eat only plants. Their alertness and their feeling of belonging to each other are exceptional.

The first creature that the gosling sees after it hatches remains imprinted in its brain for life. Intruders in such situations are loudly warned, hissed at, and chased away when necessary.

Message

The goose points to the belongingness of a person, family, or group. If you notice geese, you should connect your spiritual powers with your sexual powers and provide a foundation for something new to emerge and grow. Perhaps now it is time for you to enter a relationship, start a family. Perhaps raising a child is a project you need to do, requiring you to establish a working team.

In any case, the creative power that you now want to materialize in your life needs a stable foundation, a firm basis. Become a parent, choosing the right partner for it. What is created in your life will always remain a part of your life. The goose flies high in the heavens, reaching the greatest altitude possible, giving its whole commitment to the divine plan. Take seriously the command to let the creative powers work through you, and guide and protect the new life with all your love.

If a goose attacks you, it points to your restrictive ideas of possession. Could it be that you have held on too tightly to people, projects, and belongings, making it impossible for the divine plan to be freely fulfilled? Give change and the flow of life a chance. When life brings other people something new, it also holds something joyous for you. Let go, set things free, and be on the lookout for a new task to which you can turn your full attention. Especially in relationships, no ideas of possession should dominate. A person belongs only to himself or herself. Your inner voice tells you when it is time to restructure things. Perhaps you can join in this flight. But you must also be free in order to hear your inner command.

If you see geese flying in formation overhead it is time for you to set forth and search for new levels in your life. Your true soul family will join up with you. Perhaps you will leave behind everything that used to be important, and perhaps you will have to let go of everything that used to give you security. But you are not alone. Break loose with endurance and strength, and you will be led to your new purpose, your new relationship, or your new task.

GOSHAWK

Achievement

The goshawk lives mainly in forests bordering open lands and is therefore seldom seen. It has long tail feathers and shorter wings than the similar buzzard, which makes it exceptionally maneuverable. It uses all available coverage in bush or tree to surprise its prey with its swift

flight. It hunts other birds almost exclusively and only seldom preys on small mammals.

The female is considerably larger than the male. Together they defend a sizable territory against intruders. The best chance of observing goshawks is during their courtship rituals, when they circle and call high above their territory. With their flexible flying style, they fly far up, dive down hundreds of feet, then climb back up again immediately. The birds build their nest together in tall trees, often repairing a nest from a previous year.

The female and male raise the young together. The female feeds the young while they stay in the nest. Thereafter, the male takes over responsibility, luring them out of the nest with prey that he brings. Because the goshawk occasionally also preys on domestic birds, it has been intensively hunted. Poisoning by pesticides has also caused the population to decrease dramatically.

Message

If you encounter a goshawk, it appears that you are on the path to success. Fate means well for you. The goals you are striving for are attainable; your wishes can be realized. Remember the roots of your strength, focus your capabilities, and grab on to every chance you get.

Do not be afraid of losing your head in your success, because, like the goshawk, you must be able to recover from past failures and use them in such a way that your next attempt will bring you even higher. In this way your intuition becomes a part of you, and the steps that lead to the great goal become visible to you.

If a goshawk has stolen a chicken from you, it is a clear warning. Your social thinking is getting in your way. You will not have any lasting success if you cheat your way into gaining advantages through intrigue and psychological games. Pecking orders, such as chickens have, should not be the basis for a functioning human society. Consider honestly and precisely in what areas you want to achieve advantages through intrigue and where you are trying to gain success by dishonest means. What you are doing is dangerous, and you will reap what you sow.

GREBE, GREAT CRESTED

Motivation in Relationships

With its slender white-feathered neck, conspicuous head plumage, and long red beak, the great crested grebe is a real beauty. It is the largest member of the Grebe family and is found in almost all of Europe and many parts of Asia. Although it is so widely distributed, this beautiful

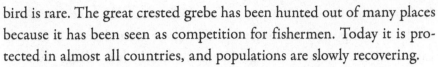

bird is rare. The great crested grebe has been hunted out of many places because it has been seen as competition for fishermen. Today it is protected in almost all countries, and populations are slowly recovering.

The great crested grebe mainly lives on minnows, insects, amphibians, and plants. It is ideally built for diving and swimming underwater. Its legs, set far back, make it an elegant swimmer. On land, however, it is ungainly. The courtship dance of the great crested grebe is very impressive. The pair always follows the same steps in this dance. The great crested grebe builds a floating nest of stacked plant matter, anchored to plants. Shortly after hatching, the approximately apple-size chicks, white and black striped on their cheeks, follow the parents into the water. At first swimming quickly exhausts the chicks. Also, their plumage is not sufficient against the damp and cold. So while swimming they climb onto the mother's back, where they rest and warm themselves under her wings. It makes an observer smile to see a mother great crested grebe diving into the water with her chicks on her back. Soon enough, like corks pushed under the water, the young birds pop back up to the surface.

Message

The message of the great crested grebe, like other diving birds, is similar to that of diving ducks. Whereas the diving duck speaks clearly to one's relationship with oneself, the great crested grebe speaks to relationships in general. The great crested grebe has come into your consciousness in order to remind you that you are a person who is connected inseparably to other people. It urges you to step back for a moment and thoroughly consider your network of relationships. Ask your heart who is important in your life. You are a person and should make the list of people who are most important to you. Who do you want to spend your time with? Who do you want to tell about yourself? Whose life would you like to be part of? Who would you like to exert energy for, and who does that for you? Closely examine the interplay of relationships in your life. Above all, consider your motivation for wanting to do something for or with someone. Consider whether what you see there really corresponds to what you want to see. Quietly interrogate your conscience.

Is there someone to whom you pay too little attention, who you always let down and put off meeting with? The great crested grebe is not telling you that you should change that immediately. It is telling you to be clear about your motivation in the relationship. Why do you spend a lot of time with one person and not with another? There may be relationships in your life that you can simply let go.

The relationship is formed by the other person. So you do not have to develop any of your own ideas. But you are responsible for deciding who you want to relate to and for how long. Consider your network of relationships and make sure that it is appropriate for you.

GROSBEAK
Primal Energy

The grosbeak is the largest of the finches. It stays in the same place all year and can often be seen at bird feeders in the depths of winter. Its large beak is a powerful tool for breaking up cherry stones, sloes, and plums. It lives in old orchards and in deciduous and mixed forests, where it prefers to reside in the upper parts of the crowns of trees.

If grosbeaks are not in evidence at your bird feeder, you should direct your gaze upward to see if you can spot them high in the trees.

Message

The grosbeak reminds you of your own primal energy and heralds a powerful upheaval, a change that will come from your innermost center. The primal energy is a mighty power. Whether a volcanic eruption, nuclear energy, or solar power, it is the same "core power." This energy also lives in the center of seeds and kernels. It prepares new life, gathers itself in a way that is predetermined by the great plan, and then, when all is ready on the inside and the outside, it breaks forth.

After its emergence the primal energy follows a natural, planned program. In this program, as the shadow of growth, destruction is always an insurmountable truth. Black and white are visible on the wings of the grosbeak when it flies. Black and white, coming into existence and leaving it, life and death are part of every process of growth. It follows the plan of extreme expansion. The same energy is in the stone of a fruit. When it erupts it follows its plan with the same energy. It is only this plan that provides for a precise outcome and for exact processes.

The human heart is another such kernel. It contains this primordial energy. This is an energy that finds expression in the human life plan. In this case it is not so closely bound to time and space as the plant, but it is much freer. The body has its form, but feelings are freer in their expansion. The change, breakthrough, and upheaval that are announced through contact with the grosbeak should always be understood within the domain of feelings. In your heart an enormous force has gathered, an energy that will soon break loose. You must now give this energy a form.

Do not let yourself simply explode as an emotional supernova, but make plans. Follow through with your plans, and with them form a good, livable future.

GROUSE, HAZEL

Honest Action

The hazel grouse lives in thick woods with much undergrowth from lowlands to the edge of the woods. It lives on buds, young shoots,

berries, and in summer, insects. The hazel grouse is very secretive, and loyal to its home. With its spotted and dappled plumage it is optimally camouflaged, and when undercover it allows predators and people to come very close. Most of the time this allows it to remain undiscovered, and the danger passes. But if the distance becomes too small, it flies away making a loud ruckus, in which case hunters say it has been "rustled up." The cock and hen form a pair in the fall. They spend the winter together. Spring is mating season, and the hen builds her nest in a well-hidden depression. During mating season the drawn-out whistling tone of the cock can be heard. The hen protects her seven to eleven chicks very secretively. She continually takes the chicks under her outstretched wings so that she can warm them. The chicks can fly after two or three weeks, and they follow the mother into the trees. The hazel grouse is very sensitive to disturbances, so it disappears entirely in forests that are intensively used or inhabited. Because it lives so secretively, its absence is hardly noticed.

Message

If a hazel grouse has made you aware of itself, it is recommending a new beginning. You do not have to reconfigure your whole life, only the way you deal with yourself. Be honest with yourself and behave in an authentic and truthful way with your surroundings. The hazel grouse is not addressing the way you talk or how you present yourself, only what you do when you are entirely alone. It is time for you to understand that no one knows what you need and want better than you do. No one is in a better position than you are to evaluate your strengths, talents, or weaknesses. Now, discard any expectations you had about the behavior of others. You alone are the ideal advocate for yourself. Do not wait for the day when the people around you will honor your achievements, thank you for your sacrifices, or recognize how kind you always were or how often you were right. If you know who and what you are, what you can do, what you do for others, and why you do it, then you are recognizing it yourself. Praise yourself for it, appraise yourself. You will quickly see the things you did for others that were praise-seeking. If you do not expect any praise from others, and do what you do out of your own conviction because you want to do it, then perhaps you will do less, but what you do will be honest and will attract unexpected recognition. Start now. Act honestly and openly in a way that works for you and makes you contented. When recognition comes from outside, that is a beautiful thing, and it will make you truly happy.

GULL

Ebb and Flow of Feelings

The black-headed gull has a gray back, the wings are white in front and black in the back, and the beak and legs are red. For a few decades now gulls have sought out human settlements outside of the breeding season. During breeding season the gull has a chocolate-colored mask. Gulls mainly eat earthworms, but also snails, insects, larvae, and dead fish. In cities they also eat bread and garbage. They always nest near bodies of water.

Near human settlements they usually find enough food and do not have to fly south for the winter. Consequently, the population has increased sharply in several places. Both parents take part in building the nest, sitting on the eggs, and raising the young.

Message

The gull tells us of the tides of the sea, the ebb and flow. Just as the endless waters of the ocean move following the rhythm of the moon, so the element of Water in us also moves. In our human bodies the water moves with the sea of our feelings. Indeed, our feelings are closely connected to the water. They go through the same cycle of renewal and are subject to the same laws of flow and union as in the water cycle. They flow to the deeper whole and absolutely obey the laws of ebb and flow.

People who live by large bodies of water, especially the ocean, automatically devote themselves to this pulsation of the water. The ocean gives and takes. It comes and goes, making no concessions and never going away. The waters in us pulsate, flow, wave upon wave crashing on our consciousness, expanding like the incoming tide and contracting just as rhythmically. But they always come back. As humans the way we experience the waves of feelings is substantially influenced by what we contribute to the flow of feelings. If I contribute only rubbish, filth, garbage, and debris, then much later on the tides of the sea will wash up only garbage on my shores. Wave by wave, what I heedlessly threw into the water is returned to me.

The gull did not meet with you to make you aware of your behavior. No, it is there to remind you that life follows the pulse of the sea. Just as the gull lives with this rhythm, so must every being on this Earth find this pulse in itself and follow it. Perhaps you are currently experiencing emotional ups and downs in your life. Perhaps you have yearned for an answer to the question "What is wrong with me?" The gull is your simple, unerring answer. The law of the tides is washing your repressed, unresolved feelings onshore. These are not the events that have led to the feelings, but the emotions that emerged in you and for some reason were tossed out by the consciousness, the flow of the inner Water. These feelings have returned.

Whether these feelings are of sadness, joy, excitement, fear, anger, or love, take them and accept them. The gull also means for us: "Pay attention to what feelings you have thoughtlessly let disappear into your subconscious." Every day, while awake, we take up the impulses, and the flow of our feelings carries them along, and these form the basis for our daily perceptions.

HERON, GRAY
Waiting

The gray heron is a stately bird, about three feet tall. Its upper side is light gray, its pinion feathers dark gray. Its yellow lance-shaped beak is impressive. In flight its legs stretch out toward the back and its neck bends in. Gray herons are attentive parents. They nest mostly in trees and almost never leave their young alone during the juvenile stage.

This proud bird hunts almost all day. It mainly eats fish and mice, but also frogs, reptiles, earthworms, and snails. It can fly over a mile in search of food. If it likes the look of a place, it stands there for a long time, motionless, like a gray pillar, zooming in with lightning speed when prey shows itself. Gray herons had to be protected by law after they were hunted year round. This has ensured the bird's continued survival. Populations have recovered. It does some damage to stocked fish populations in artificial bodies of water and when water levels are low.

Message

If you encounter a gray heron, it is recommended that you turn inward and become conscious of what direction your expectations in your life are headed. Most people spend a great part of their lives waiting but are not at all conscious of what they are waiting for. They go around pregnant with an unconscious feeling, nourish it, let it grow, but at the moment of birth they become afraid of the fate they have created for themselves.

Everything that happens in life is, so to speak, the child of one's own thoughts and feelings. Usually it takes awhile for our thoughts and feelings to materialize as destiny. We have long since forgotten that we ourselves planted the seeds. The gray heron could therefore be described as a cenotaph, a command to take responsibility for one's own thoughts and feelings, and a reminder that everything that happens was born out of you yourself. Are you aware of what is growing in you? What causes have you set in motion, even a long time ago? What can you expect from your life as a result?

For sure, you are waiting for happiness, good fortune, and love. But is that what you have sown, and is that what you can expect to reap? You will have no choice but to accept what comes, take responsibility for it, and proceed more consciously and with more discipline with your new feelings and thoughts. The way in which the gray heron catches its prey signals a clear "Yes" to the observer regarding what will be dished up. The way the heron handles its prey—with no hesitation, no wavering, snapping it up and swallowing it without reserve—reminds us that we have no choice. Anyone who can observe this great, noble bird is receiving a great gift of medicine.

It is the medicine of waiting and seeing. It is the power of listening and understanding. This understanding makes possible the unquestioning acceptance of the life one has created for oneself and the lessons that will come from it. It is of no use to quarrel with yourself if you do not like what life offers you. Accept what comes to you, consciously learn from it, and grab the happy, joyous moments from the river of your life. Let yourself be inspired by your joy in your thoughts and feelings, and you will sow—and be able to harvest—joy and happiness for the future. Take the message of the gray heron in earnest.

It will want to advise you again and again; it will stand like a pillar by the river for you, appealing to your inner sincerity and thus, as a wise teacher, leading you to find your bliss.

JAYBIRD
Zest for Life

With its piercing squawk and splendid plumage, the jaybird stands out year round. It is capable of a wide range of vocalizations, and it appears to find it fun to imitate other birds' calls with deceptive similarity. It especially likes imitating the calls of buzzards. In the spring before nesting season, jays can often be seen engaging in playful games with one another.

The jay is a cautious, alert, and attentive bird. If something unusual happens in its territory, it utters loud warning calls. It prefers to live near large trees, and at nesting time it flits silently from branch to branch. The jay eats mainly acorns, beechnuts, other nuts, and berries, as well as eggs and freshly hatched young birds, insects, larvae, and, when it can catch them, lizards and mice. It buries acorns for the winter, performing its duty as an "oak planter."

Message

If a jaybird draws your attention it wishes to prompt you to consider the joy in your life. Fun, humor, and joy are some of the highest forms of gratitude toward creation. Let yourself smile, play, and celebrate; let yourself banter, rejoice, and be silly. Seek out your joyous mood and share it with the people on your life's path. Our creator cares for us daily with love and light, gives us love, and gives us the possibility to grow and learn.

It may be that you have gotten yourself into a situation that seems to have no way out, and now you are suffering. This is when the jay's message is most important. Seek reasons to rejoice, even when it is difficult to do so. Open your heart to life, and see how this makes your heart start to smile and jubilate. You do not need to repress your worries and sorrows. But if you contrast these sad feelings with genuine happiness, the stranglehold of sadness will soon release your heart. Things will immediately start going better for you. Perhaps your current problems are not actually all that bad, or you have simply had too little time and space for fun and joy.

Perhaps your inner child is too much oppressed with thoughts of responsibilities and duties. Decide where and in what parts of your life there should be more joy. Consider the fact that when you say you cannot experience any happiness due to external conditions, other people, or lack of time, you are always just making excuses.

Take yourself in hand, look inside yourself, and find your happy

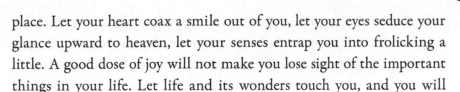

place. Let your heart coax a smile out of you, let your eyes seduce your glance upward to heaven, let your senses entrap you into frolicking a little. A good dose of joy will not make you lose sight of the important things in your life. Let life and its wonders touch you, and you will begin to radiate joy and touch others in turn.

KINGFISHER

Guardian of the Elements

The kingfisher seems to emerge from another world when it zips through the air, fast as an arrow. Right on target, it plunges into the water, grabs its prey, and easily flies back up with it. Small silver pearls of water fall from its colorful plumage as it finds a branch where it can perch and consume its prize. It lives by the river, where it digs holes in the riverbank in which to raise its young. From a high place on a tree above the water it watches for small fish. Flakes of dander falling from its feathers entice the fish, allowing this small hunter to dive for them with lightning speed.

It also eats dragonflies, beetles, and amphipods. The kingfisher often sits for half a day on its perch, absolutely motionless and always silent. Its gaze is fixed upon the water, and it calmly awaits its prey. It flies straight as an arrow, usually close over the water's surface. But sometimes it flies high over the water, fluttering or jiggling to hold still in the air for a moment, and plunging into the depths from this height. A nesting kingfisher will not be driven away from its nest by knocking or digging. With absolute strength of nerve, it stays with the eggs or young birds, moving only when practically tackled. The female broods alone but is fed and taken care of by the male during this time.

Message

The kingfisher is the guardian of the elements. It lives in harmony with them and in their flow. If you encounter this bird it is time to find the center of your life, your universe, and let it flow. Let things happen as they come. Go with the flow, and take part openly and perhaps with wonder in the world that you have created. Pay attention to the power of your thoughts and the flow of your feelings. Wind and water give life its form; send these two forces upward toward the light. Life wants to reward you richly, fulfill your wishes, and give you joy. If you align yourself properly, you can flow with the great stream of happiness. Riches will come your way on all levels of being.

The encounter with the protector of the elements can be the start of your entry into your own paradise. Accept this, and take the rudder. It is in your hands. It is rare to see one of these beautiful birds. But if it has shown itself to you, it is important to bow before your own life, set all ifs, ands, and buts aside, and give yourself over unquestioningly to fate. What wants to happen in your life now will happen, and it is no longer in your power to struggle against it. Consider how the truth in your own center feels; express this truth actively and consciously on all levels.

In this way you will return the energies to their origin, thus bringing great clarity to your life. Only in your own center can the messages of unified energy be heard. Now you will be guided and will always be conscious of the external steps you are taking. It may take some nerve, and sometimes you may believe that you are at the limits of your energies. You will need patience, but the way will finally lead you to your own new transformed greatness.

KITE

Expansion

Red kite: Expansion in relation to the world of feelings
Black kite: Expansion in the material world, in professional everyday life

Among kites, we distinguish the red kite and black kite. Both types favor
wide, flat land near water. They eat small mammals, birds, insects, carrion, and garbage. They often scrounge off other birds of prey and herons,
harassing them for so long that they drop the prey they have caught. The
black kite also eats dead and sick fish floating on the surface of the water.

Both types of kite return to warmer places in the winter; the black
kite is much more widespread and migrates much farther. Many older
red kites now stay for the winter at their nesting grounds. The red kite is
found mainly in Europe and the Mediterranean. The black kite migrates
as far as southern Africa and lives all over Asia and as far as Australia.

Kites are some of the largest birds of prey in Europe. In flight they
can be recognized by their forked tails and—compared to other birds of
prey—their thinner, angled wings. This form allows them to stay in the
air interminably without any great effort and to perform astonishing

acrobatics. Their everyday lives consist of flying far distances over land and water, at great heights, searching for prey.

Kites are not loners and are often seen circling in groups of four or five. Thanks to recovering populations throughout Europe, the black kite now breeds in loose colonies.

Message

Like all great birds of prey, the kite invites you to rise up. For the moment, leave your narrow everyday life and climb to a higher perspective. If you were restricted by ideas of your position in society, now you can see an endless distance, the many layers of truth, and the greatness of possibilities before you. What people think, believe, or expect is only a tiny spot in the great mosaic of the moment. Expand your consciousness. Let go of your behavior and your affectations and taste the power of the free soul. There are no burdens, no pressures, no expectations. How good!

But now the sharp glance of the bird of prey looks into your own self. Do I want this life, do I want to be what I see now, from the viewpoint of the kite? Yes? Then let loose, expand, break free of the self-imposed restrictions, shake off the rituals you have held on to in everyday public life, forget the ideas of the observer. Be limitless.

This means limitless love, limitless acceptance, and limitless openness for life—for your own and for all other beings. Expand your inner receptiveness so that the abundance thus created can also manifest in your external life. Only those who have great visions, who can free those great visions from limits (such as fears and dogma), and who can openly and curiously transform all that life offers into action and deed, will ultimately also be able to transform this inner expansion into the material world.

LARK

Prayer

The skylark is most widespread in Europe. In the spring it enchants people again and again with its jubilating song. It flies, singing, far up

into the sky, lingers whirring in the air, then brings its song back down again to Earth. In its incomparable song, stanzas, trills, warbling, and chirping segue seamlessly into one another.

The lark also unabashedly borrows phrases from other birds to incorporate in its songs. It is able to sing without a pause, almost entirely while flying, for five minutes or more. It sounds like a jubilant prayer.

Message

The lark is more likely to draw the attention of your ear than your eye. It is not so much urging you to pray as inviting you to do so. Try simply to rejoice at life with all your heart. You do not have to engage in dialogue with the divine. All that surrounds you, touches you, and moves you is divine presence. Call your god what you want to call it, but the important thing is: feel joy! Do you know the feeling of such great happiness that your voice rises and you begin to sing with all your heart? No matter what it sounds like, the important thing is that you feel it.

The highest form of prayer is deeply felt joy, which is also the highest form of gratitude. It does not matter what you are thankful for. A great event can move you to great gratitude, and an overpowering moment of beauty and contact can lead a human heart to jubilant prayer. We can all face the divine with the pure innocence of a child. Of course, we can also philosophize with God, criticize and advise him. But none of these prayers in the head are anything approaching the jubilation of the soul.

LINNET

Search for Consensus

The linnet is a member of the Finch family. Like all finches, it is a gifted singer. From high perches it sings entire melodies. This active bird also sings during its wave-formed flight and often forms "male choruses" of simultaneous song. The female linnet builds the nest relatively deep in low, thick bushes, lining it with wool and hair. Cuckoos often use the nests of finches, including linnets. However, because the linnet lives almost exclusively on seeds, the young cuckoos usually die. Only the green finch has as strong a preference for plant foods as the linnet. The common linnet is easily confused with the common redpoll, which is also a member of the Finch family.

Message
Like finches, the linnet has something to announce. It is telling you that there is currently a project, theme, or task in your life that you should review with a team. It will not be possible for you to achieve

consensus with all involved unless you discuss the topic with all partici-
pants, or with other people, and seek an open exchange of ideas. The
linnet indicates to you that as far as possible you should avoid including certain factors, from both your heart and your head, because you
are simply lacking the broadness of view necessary. Sometimes there are
tasks for which the optimal solution requires a kind of decision-making
or planning that is not part of your nature. But when it is the linnet
that has shown you this, it means that there is also a person involved
who has a command of the appropriate methods. Therefore, absolutely
seek out dialogue with people who are involved. Talk through possible
ways to proceed and give full consideration to others' approaches. You
will be able to tell what is right and how much of another person's style
you can and must accept.

MAGPIE

Stealing

The magpie is a member of the Raven family. It prefers animal food to
plant food. Besides all kinds of insects, it also eats amphibians, small
mammals, eggs, and young birds. It also will not turn down carrion and
garbage. It rounds off its diet with fruits and seeds. The natural drive

to collect provisions, common to all members of the Raven family, is very strong in the magpie. It not only gathers food but also colorful and shiny objects, which it collects in its nest and in other favorite storage places. Even valuable pieces of jewelry have been found in magpie nests.

The treasures that accumulate in a nest can be surprising: the magpie hoards glass and mirror shards, aluminum foil, nails, and all possible shiny knickknacks. This behavior has given it the reputation of a thief, but the collection of shiny objects is not the only reason. The magpie plunders the nests of songbirds, steals supplies gathered by other members of the Raven family, and will sometimes even steal spoons from café tables. The magpie does not need the food and objects it steals. It is simply following its instinct.

Message

It is no wonder that in animal symbolism, the magpie warns of exactly what it does. It is very important to know whether the magpie appeared to the left or the right of the observer and what direction your thoughts were taking when the encounter took place. On the left side, it is about your inner treasures, on the right side your outer ones. If you were thinking about yourself, your life, your perceptions, then it is about your capabilities, wisdom, and spiritual strengths. If you were directing your thoughts outward at the time of the encounter, thinking about your possessions or about other people, then the magpie's message relates to your material world.

The magpie to your left, as you think about yourself, signifies a warning. The magpie might say to you: "You have opened energy flows that invite thieves. Protect your treasures, your experience, collect your medicine. Only let very carefully chosen people near your inner jewels. Consider how the more shiny something is, the more thieves will be attracted. Do not set your powers against false energy fields. Think about whom you share your knowledge with and how you formulate it." The magpie thus advises you to consider exactly what internal things you show. Not all people are able to deal respectfully with their private truths. It may be that your knowledge stands upon a foundation that is not prepared for it. This often leads to misunderstandings. The magpie is not telling you to judge and condemn others but to take clear responsibility for your own words.

If the magpie appears from the left and you were contemplating external things, then it is telling you to be careful with your wisdom externally and adapt it to your own system of truth. When necessary, distance yourself from foreign thoughts. Perhaps at the moment you are in danger of taking the wrong direction, or simply of believing a bad rumor that you hear and thus contributing to damage done to some other person.

If the magpie appears from the right, and you are occupied with inner thoughts such as "Have I opened up the wrong energy streams, and will my treasures be plundered?" it is not your wisdom but your possessions and your power that are in danger. Watch where your time, money, and life force are disappearing to. You are obviously using valuable material energy through inattentiveness, false patterns you have been taught, gullibility, and so on. In other words, you are worn out. When someone else profits, materially or energetically, at your cost, you have unconsciously given them the possibility to do so. In this same way, you must not disregard your ideas. Stolen ideas are also lost energy.

If the magpie appears from the right and you are thinking about external things, then it is telling you to seriously examine your behavior with regard to material things. In what areas in the material world have you become a thief? You have let yourself be misled into misusing the ideas, materials, and life force of others. Even if this did not happen consciously or intentionally, take this warning seriously. Perhaps at first it feels fine to shore yourself up with foreign energies, but the price will be high, whether or not you were conscious of your own thieving. Ask your soul now to draw your attention to the misuse that has occurred, and remedy the situation as much as possible as soon as you can. You do not need to punish yourself, but it would be a good idea to interrogate yourself to discover what existential fears have led to this misuse.

MERGANSER, SMEW
Chance

Mergansers are members of the Duck family. They are distinguished by their bills, which are thin, straight, and hooked at the end. The edge of the beak is serrated, hence the term "sawbill." This well-adapted bill is excellent for catching and holding fish. Mergansers dive often and long. They live mainly on minnows, insects, and larvae. They will also eat larger fish when they can catch them. Mergansers search by sight for prey in the water, so these birds are drawn to clear waters with plenty of fish. Mergansers are typical residents of northern lands. Because they nest in hollow trees, they need forests with old trees that are within sight of clear bodies of water. If the nesting tree is too far from the water, many or even all of the chicks will fall victim to predators. Interestingly, a small independent merganser population has survived in the Alps, living there year round. Otherwise, mergansers are mostly just visitors in the north.

Message

The merganser has drawn your attention to advise you to utilize the grace of the moment. Events are under way in your life that will open up genuinely good possibilities for you. This could relate to business, bargains, the right relationship, your home, or finding the right job. Look around your world, recognize the things that life offers, and try to feel which of these possibilities you should accept and use. It should be a feeling like clear water when you choose from the possibilities and offerings. Then you can be sure that it is a genuine chance. Decide on it and take a step in this direction. If nothing else, it will bring you a step further and you will not only learn a great deal but also feel better about your life.

In the case of the smew, it is above all a matter of opportunity for partnership. Someone's heart is being offered to you, which you should absolutely consider. Offers of the heart are good offers that can only lead to win-win situations. It does not matter whether it ends in invitation or rejection, stimulation or disillusionment. In any case, it is a win for you. Offers of the heart are sometimes very secret: a nice gesture, a lingering glance, a small consideration. Be alert—if the rather rare smew has drawn your attention, it is because something special is in the air for you.

Life actually gives us opportunities fairly often. An opportunity lies in almost every encounter because we can draw knowledge from every encounter, even if it is meaningless knowledge. But the smew has not come into your life to indicate a meaningless opportunity; instead it indicates a distinct one. Examine yourself and enjoy this exciting time.

NIGHTINGALE

Yearning

The nightingale is one of the small thrushes. It lives mainly in shrubbery at the edge of the forest and prefers warmer climates. It is widespread in the Mediterranean area. Its nighttime song has always moved people. It is an exceptionally harmonious, musical, and elaborate song, somewhat melancholy and wistful. Although many people have heard of the nightingale, it is only rarely seen and recognized.

The nightingale is a rather inconspicuous bird with red-brown plumage on its back and belly and somewhat redder plumage on its rump and tail. It builds its nest from plant matter loosely woven together in thick undergrowth near the ground. Here it raises four or five chicks, which it feeds with insects, spiders, and worms. In the fall its diet also includes

berries. Around September the nightingales leave their breeding grounds in central and western Europe and migrate to Africa.

Message

Has the nightingale sung in your soul with its beautiful songs? Did it awaken in you a quiet feeling of wanderlust that felt like homesickness? Did you feel a yearning in yourself that was almost a little painful, telling of love, security, belongingness? The nightingale is a messenger of yearning.

It wants to touch you with its song, wants to remind you of your being. Its notes tie you to your soul. Your soul is your ancestry, your origin. We all yearn to be blessed. To be blessed is wonderful and slightly painful at the same time, because for our human consciousness there is a separation between the beings. In the consciousness of the soul, however, there is the all-embracing oneness of truth. In fact, our human consciousness consists of constant yearning. It yearns for unity, because separation is painful. This yearning lets us grow, allows us to search—to search for life, for light, for belonging, for a homeland, for understanding, for wisdom, for God. The nightingale motivates you, on the one hand, to open your heart to your yearning. But on the other hand, it also warns you not to make the yearning into an addiction. He who seeks will find; he who finds will seek further. The yearning addict does not know finding. The pain of separation becomes enormous agony.

Hear the song of this inconspicuous bird, silence your own sounds, and allow yourself to feel how everything you could have sought lies in this yearning, how in this instant yearning and finding have come together, formed a unity, and for a moment turned you inward toward your own soul. In this way the nightingale gives you the strength of memory and also the security that separation is illusory and that unity in God is the truth.

NUTHATCH

Withdrawal

This elegant bird has a broad range of vocal expressions at its command. It is the only bird in Europe that can climb down a tree head first. Its nesting hole, which it makes about six feet above the ground, is carefully closed off with mud so that the bird can only just fit in through the hole. In summer nuthatches live on insects and worms, which they find in the furrowed bark of trees. In fall and winter they eat nuts and seeds.

Nuthatches hold on to cracks in walls or tree bark and peck them open from above. The male performs a complex mating ritual. Once they have partnered for breeding, the pairs of birds are often seen flying together.

Message

If you notice a nuthatch it is time for you to withdraw in some way. Turn around, return to your roots, and barricade yourself in your private world. Let no one into the innermost realms of your private life. It seems you have ventured too far upward and outward.

You are unconsciously divulging too much, and the encounter with this singular bird is a warning to batten down your hatches. Holy areas are growing within you that will be put in danger if they are too open. Take this message in earnest and consider whether the important areas of your private world are protected and hidden from unauthorized intrusions. If you see a pair of nuthatches, the message clearly relates to your relationships. Do you give other people too much power over you in matters of the heart?

Perhaps, also, you have been too frivolous, not taking the sensitivity of love seriously enough, not protecting it. In the nest of a true couple, no one else is allowed to sneak in. Probably no great damage has been done, because the reason for the nuthatch's appearance is to prevent this from happening. But you must deal with it immediately. If you do not know exactly what you have to do, then think of your roots, your natural, real aspects, and make changes in your life in order to realize your own true norm. Come down from the treetops of purely spiritual explanations and create structures to shelter what heaven has made possible.

ORIOLE, OLD WORLD

Truth, Authenticity

This rare blackbird-size bird looks like a visitor from the tropics. The male, with his bright yellow feathers, is especially striking. The female looks like a green finch. In summer orioles live in dense deciduous, mixed, and alluvial forests. These shy birds are hardly ever seen, because they spend almost all their time in the high crowns of the trees. In the sunlight, between the sun-soaked uppermost leaves of the trees, the oriole's bright plumage is very well camouflaged. Their artfully woven

nests are built in the forks of branches. The oriole is not a very common bird, but it is found everywhere from Europe to India. It prefers temperate zones and areas near water. The oriole eats insects, caterpillars, butterflies, and also greatly enjoys berries. It has a liking for cherries and other fruit. It is a gifted singer with a broad repertoire of calls and tones. Some songs are reminiscent of the jaybird, others of the blackbird, and still others of the falcon. The name (*loriot* in French and *oriolus* in Latin) derives from a typical song.

Message

The oriole tells us to raise our feelings and thoughts to a high, pure level, free of judgment. The occurrence of feelings and thoughts should draw our attention to ourselves and not to the questions "What am I feeling?" and "What am I thinking?" Thinking and feeling are an expression of the way we have been shaped. Our experiences shape us; our surroundings and life events make their impressions upon us. These impressions are like windows through which the pure primordial energy streams into the consciousness. While streaming through the energy takes on these patterns and tones. The way you see things applies only to you. The oriole tells you to change your point of view and imagine someone else being shaped like you, having an experience in his or her life that arose from his or her own truths. Just as is the case for you, other people's perceptions are colored by their patterns, and they also experience this as the one and only truth.

If an oriole emerges from its hidden world and makes you aware of it, it wants to urge you to abandon these imprinted feelings and thoughts and rise to a plane where feeling means pure perception and thought, pure reflection. Perhaps at the moment of the encounter you were projecting things from your own truth onto other people. Based on feelings, you interpret the behavior of others with the assumption that they have the same fundamental feeling as you. Perhaps you consider yourself very intuitive and believe that you can tell how things are for others, but this idea blocks out the truth. Perhaps you love or hate someone and evaluate every positive or negative sign this person supposedly gives you on the basis of your feelings. It is rarely wise to seek the truth of others based on your own imprinted patterns. The oriole advises you urgently to rid yourself of the desire, or even the compulsion, to root others in your own feelings and thoughts. Grasp the reality behind your feelings and thoughts. If you recognize yourself in the above description, ask yourself why it is so important to know what others feel and think. What is the message in this wish, what do you want to achieve for yourself? When you observe how you fit in and perceive things in the world that surrounds you, what social place you really have there, you will have come closer to being fair to yourself. Feel things! But do not do so with any goal in mind. Feeling should be enrichment that deepens experience. Think! But do not try to figure out other people with your thoughts. Thinking should serve to draw knowledge out of your own actual experiences.

OWL

Wisdom

Owls are nocturnal birds of prey. They have exceptionally fine senses. No movement in the darkness escapes their sharp eyes. They are masters of concealment. Their coloring corresponds exactly to their favor-

ite habitats, and their silky feathers allow for completely silent flight. With its sharp claws, the owl grabs its prey tightly, then carries it in its sharp hooked beak to its accustomed perching place. After eating, the indigestible parts of the prey—hair, feathers, and bones—are regurgitated in what is known as an owl pellet.

Living in our region are various types of owls, such as the barn owls and the eared owls—a category to which the northern hawk-owl and Eurasian eagle-owl also belong—as well as the tawny owl, little owl, boreal owl, and Eurasian pygmy owl. Other species are spread throughout the world, even in the polar regions.

Message

In all cultures owls are often associated with wisdom. We seldom see them, but they can often be heard in the night. These secretive birds often retreat from civilization—which is too loud for them—into more silent areas. Therefore it is impressive to have a direct encounter with one of these birds. Whether an owl enters your awareness optically or acoustically, your attention is being drawn to its wisdom. But wisdom is mostly a treasure that lies buried deep within your own being.

From this wisdom, truth develops, for the latter lies at the root of the former, just as the nourishing earth lies at the root of a plant. The owl's wisdom makes aspects of your wisdom visible, just as the plant makes the nutrients in the soil visible. Thus, it is the potential of your wisdom that comes to light through truth when you live life as your true self. Your wisdom is an important key to your life. It will help you to make the right decisions. To live according to this wisdom means a life of happiness. However, this will not be achieved the moment you let your wisdom in and become conscious of it. Silently, with senses open, the owl glides through the darkness of the subconscious. It is able to perceive this world of your being, which is unreachable for you. And, of course, it is also able to remove "vermin" from this world.

The message of the owl tells you to accept your life as it currently is. Try not to embellish or dramatize anything. The owl tells you to let events happen. You should react to what is currently happening as authentically as possible and without any agenda. This message is especially clear when you encounter one of the owl species that have shorter stature and relatively larger heads. Often enough we only know in hindsight why things happen and how they happen. Thus, the owl bears a message to be taken seriously, telling you to relinquish immediately any involvement of your intellect in your life's narrative. This message is particularly strong in the case of a visual encounter with an owl, because obviously this means that an intensive process is taking place in your innermost self.

Learned and experienced knowledge is converted into wisdom, and thus the foundation for new life events is established. You can trust that the power of the owl knows the darkness, knows the hidden corners of the subconscious, and will oversee the process. Direct your attention upon every step of your life's path and make decisions carefully. Great things will happen in your life, but it will take awhile before your everyday consciousness perceives them. Such changes are also related to spiritual growth. If you have very frequent encounters with these nocturnal birds, or if one has taken up residence in our life, you can be sure that this is a matter of very strong spiritual (eagle-owl) or sensory (short-statured owl, barn owl) capabilities in your current development.

To develop wisdom, one needs great attentiveness. You are responsible for the effects of your truth. From a bright, pure wisdom, only light and purity can grow. Someone who uses his truth to interfere manipulatively in the lives of others is creating the foundation for black magic. If an owl attacks you, it is a very clear sign in this direction.

OYSTERCATCHER

Stability

Oystercatchers are large, black-and-white wading birds with a long red beak and red legs. The eyes are also reddish and red-ringed. Although their name suggests it, oystercatchers do not live on oysters. The lifestyles and diets of these birds have separated them into three easily identifiable species. One has a somewhat thinner and longer beak, ideal for digging out worms and snails from mud and sand. Another has a rather stronger beak, slightly pinched at the sides. These birds mainly specialize in eating mussels. The beak is used to pry open the shellfish. The third type has the strongest beak, which it uses like a hammer. It simply smashes the mussel shell to get at the flesh.

Oystercatchers live mainly on the northern coasts of Europe. They are seen only sporadically on the southern European coasts, and rarely spotted inland. In the spring mating season they form small groups. The female lays her eggs in low mounds, covering them with small stones and shells. In the winter these birds gather into large groups, and when conditions are bad they retreat to the coasts, lakes, and rivers of central and western Europe. The oystercatcher is a bird of character. Eye-catching and loud-voiced, it makes its territory known. It remains true to its breeding area for all its life, which can be as long as thirty-five years.

Message

Anyone who lives on the coast and goes walking there will often see these hardy birds, because the bird is not at all shy in its own territory. The oystercatcher is the messenger of stability. It tells you to stick with what fits in your life, what you like, and what works for you. Perhaps right now you want to turn your life around, because you see so much that is simply not fulfilling. There is nothing wrong about that. But the encounter with the oystercatcher reminds you to acknowledge everything first and accept what does fit. Make a list of what you want to hold on to. Look back at what moments, feelings, situations, functions, relationships, duties, and things you treasure. Once you know this—once you see what you want to keep from your current life—it will be decidedly easier to let go of what does not belong with this good foundation.

In short, don't throw the baby out with the bathwater. The oystercatcher may also have come because you are letting your current life control you too much. Is it possible that in your life you are conforming to a societal norm and doing nothing more than functioning? In this case, the external will has found a form and achieved its stability, but you have not. Perhaps the oystercatcher has drawn your attention to itself in order to wake you up. Stability in society quickly becomes an overly tight psychic-spiritual corset for the individual. It is very important for the individual person to define and establish her life, construct her own world, and always change it according to her own development. Then everything that fits and is right becomes the individual's structure. It is from this structure—of each individual—that societal norms should emerge. Then false ideas, rules of behavior, and restrictions will not be formed, either in your life or in the life of the group. Stick with those things that you find enriching, enjoyable, and affirming, and those things that are not can be changed.

PARTRIDGE

Custom, Tradition

The partridge's habitat is open agricultural land with hedges, margins, and various crops. They are exceptionally well adapted to nature's light and shadow games, and consequently they live a discreet life. If they are startled, they fly up in a panic. Intensive soil use, monocultures, and pesticides have seriously endangered the survival of the partridge.

In early spring the partridges flock together and form couples. Every couple has its own territory, defended aggressively against other partridges. Between twelve and twenty chicks are raised together by the cock and hen. In winter they form small flocks known as coveys. In these coveys, the birds stay close together to shelter from the cold. At this time lack of cover can make them easy prey for their enemies.

Message

The partridge tells you not to abandon your security. Perhaps something in your life is trying to frighten you; do not react with panic, but protect yourself by retreating deeper into your trusted world. The tradition of your family or culture originates from the needs of the people who have lived there. Traditions give people a societal framework for gaining experience and for trying out and establishing social affiliation.

Traditional behavior also gives people security. In times when there is much warmth and bright joy in life, it makes sense to loosen traditional customs a little and to learn and experience things on one's own. In current times, individuality—as a couple or a single person—is a positive power that contributes a great deal to development and spiritual growth. But when a cold wind blows through life and hard trials are to be undergone, it is very important to return to society and its traditions.

The partridge wants to remind you that, for the moment, it is important to check your social situation and cultivate your place in an appropriate social circle. It is not a warning of bad times but an admonition to recognize your own culture and traditions and conform to the requirements of the societal framework. Your place in a family or group must be cultivated during the good times. If one day you are in crisis mode and need people to keep you warm and support you, it will be too late to work on closeness with family and friends.

PEACOCK
Pride, Beauty, Art

Native to India and Sri Lanka, the peacock became known and admired worldwide as an ornamental bird more than four thousand years ago. In the Middle Ages it was a symbol of vanity as well as protection against the evil eye and lightning strikes. In certain religions this noble fowl is seen as an incarnation of a deity, and in the palace grounds of European princes and kings it represented the glamour of the current ruler. However, it was also often served up as a delicacy at banquets. The peacock's great reputation is due to the male's magnificent plumage, with which he impresses the more modestly colored peahen during courtship. The peacock spreads out his long tail feathers into a large fan. Over a hundred "eyes" decorate this display. The female often chooses the male with the most eyes. The peahen builds her nest in a well-hidden spot in a bush. Much like a hen, she leads three to five chicks watchfully

and carefully around her territory. In India peacocks are highly prized because they drive snakes out of their territory and eat the young snakes. They also warn insistently of approaching tigers and leopards, to which they often fall victim. The call of the peacock is loud and meow-like, for which reason it is rarely kept in densely populated areas.

Message

The peacock reminds you of your inner beauty. Are you aware that you are a divine creature, a divine creation? At the very center of your being, at the point in you from which your life energy, your life spirit, and your humanity radiate and are formatively fulfilled, that is where divine being transforms into human being. Like a spring, our life flows forth from the being of God then fulfills our inner self, creates our feelings and thoughts, and finally manifests our physical being. Just as the many eyes of the peacock's tail radiate upon the wooed peahen, so the divine being looks lovingly upon all that fulfills us and surrounds our human existence. It constantly fertilizes us with its absolute beauty and grace. What humans create is generated in our innermost selves by the divine being. Light and love, active and passive are the masculine and feminine creative energy, uniting to engender being. Light and shadow, corresponding to the peacock and peahen, are equally important for creation. The peacock tells you to be conscious of this inner beauty, to stand proud in your consciousness and express this inner divine potential in all ways possible. Let this divine beauty, this light and love, radiate in your eyes and underlie your voice and words. Let it flow into your actions, your movements, fulfilling your fertility. Everything that comes out of you is art and beauty. Only those who live up to their divinity, letting it into all areas of themselves, are authentic and touching in their creative power, their radiance, and their effectiveness. Then pride is not false vanity, but true venerability.

PEEWIT

Liberation

The peewit, or lapwing, is a member of the Plover family. Once a widespread bird living in large wetlands, the peewit population has declined very quickly as more and more of its habitat has been developed. Although the peewit has adapted to new landscapes, it has fewer and fewer successful broods. Its long legs and perky head feathers make it a striking bird.

During mating season the male performs midair acrobatics, accompanied acoustically by special resonant pinion feathers. After the male concludes his downward spinning swoops, he remains for a short time

with his wings spread wide open. If a female has noticed these hero-
ics, he digs a small pit in a chosen place and makes a seesawing motion
there to encourage his mate to build a nest.

Once the nesting place is chosen, it is vehemently defended against
all plunderers and birds of prey. In winter, like the golden plover and
the partridge, peewits gather into flocks.

Message

The peewit has entered your consciousness to charm you out of your
reserve. You are living with inner or outer constraints or feelings of duty.
True enough: whoever says A must also say B. But are you sure that for
each of the B's that you are now saying or having to live through, you also
said A's of your own free accord? Is it true that all the duties you are currently fulfilling, or should fulfill, are serving the goal that you originally
wanted to achieve?

If the peewit draws your attention to itself, it can be assumed that this
is not the case. At some point your active, male side did a courtship dance
and your feminine, intuitive side embraced the visions thus expressed.
From this gyrating courting of a possibility, a narrative emerged in which
you now play the main role. But was that really the original intent for this
narrative? Try to remember. How did you want to feel in all that you are
now living through? What did you expect for your being, and what did
you plan? Has this feeling and being come to pass? Has it been realized?

The peewit urges you to devote your whole attention to these issues.
Work on fulfilling your own visions and wishes, and make space for love
and for your being. You must not let yourself remain a slave to what you
have created in order to provide a foundation for your visions and your
space for love. Make a list and write down everything that works for
you as it is, what partly works, and what does not work. Now it is time
to change things. Restore the landscapes of your feelings. Remember
that this is about how you feel, not about what you do or have.

Release yourself from your constraints. Free yourself from duties
that only serve the ego and not the being. This does not mean, first
of all, to liberate yourself from relationships, friends, or your job. The

peewit is a clear bearer of the message that you should see yourself as the origin of the constraints. Once you have created a little more free space and can tell how your true nature would like to live, then you can look around at other people to see whether some are already waiting to share your newly liberated life with you.

PHEASANT
Religion

The pheasant was brought from Asia to Europe, where it became well established in the wild during the Middle Ages. Today it is still a popular hunting quarry. It lives in hollows and has a preference for lowland forests, reedy areas, and places near water, as well as for human-made environments. In these surroundings it finds plenty of nooks and crannies in which to hide. It is known as a sedentary bird, which means that it lives all its life in its carefully chosen territory.

The hen has a drab pattern and a short tail. The cock, on the other hand, has a red face mask, copper-colored plumage with dark spots, and a blue-green iridescent band on the neck. Its tail is very long and pointed. One cock leads a flock of hens.

The young birds can fly fourteen days after hatching. Pheasants live on seeds, fruits, and buds, and the chicks also eat insects. They are skilled at concealment, and when danger threatens they know how to make themselves almost invisible in the thick vegetation of their habitat.

But if hounded out, they fly up, making a loud ruckus. Giving space and distance, they can glide away with outstretched wings. Pheasants normally sleep perched in trees.

Message

The pheasant reminds us of our roots—the elementary roots in the divine. Are you aware that your origin lies in God? However we want to define God, there is a great, higher energy that pervades all things, a law that determines all processes. If you encounter a pheasant you should pause and consciously engage with this great energy. Certainly, we are individual beings, living according to an individual life plan, and we have all lived out our own stories. But there is another plane on which every individual being is absolutely connected to all other beings.

We all breathe the same air; we see the same sun, the same moon; we live according to the same laws of nature; we all long for love, light, and togetherness. Religion means connection to God. There are many gods in the human realm, and perhaps there are also some in the animal realm. We are all connected to the energy that stands behind these gods, the embodiment of light and love. The pheasant reminds you not of your traditional, instilled religion, but of your origin in God.

It may be that your true religion is suffocating from boredom, stuck under the religion you were instilled with. In that case, it is really time to nuzzle close to Mother Earth and plunge deep into the roots of your own energy. Here you will encounter this primal power, the fundamental divinity of the conscious. Accept yourself and carry it consciously into your life's narrative, into your traditions and structures. When the primal divine power flows through your life, everything is just right as it is.

PUFFIN

Control of Feelings

The puffin is probably the best-known member of the Auk family. Auks are seabirds that live almost all their lives on the water. They come to land only to nest. One might call them the penguins of the north. The auk's legs are far back on the body, and the wings are slender. Most auks, unlike penguins, are good fliers. They fly often, with swift wing beats, low over the waves. They make the same movements with their wings underwater as they do in the air. In fact, they almost fly under the water, steering with their feet. The outer plates on the beak are present only during breeding season. The beak has an important function in the bird's social behavior. During molting the outermost layer of the beak falls off. Auks brood in colonies. Coastal areas overgrown with grass are the preferred location for breeding colonies. Of all related species, the puffin is the one that spends the winter farthest from land.

Message

Puffins, or other members of the Auk family, are only encountered on the coast or at sea. Much like the penguin, the auk advises you to structure your feelings. You cannot simply drift in the endless world of feelings. You need reference points, rules, and guidance. Be aware that even when life seems difficult and harsh there is a powerful center inside you, a sun that warms and strengthens you from within. You are surrounded by the feelings and emotions of the world. But the way you perceive the world depends solely on your inner light. Your contentment, interpretation, and ability to love are the products of your inner attitude. This is how you create the truth of your world: magical and effective, but only for you. The world of others is not your responsibility. With your will, specify your feelings, the perceptions and emotions you wish to experience, and when you slip into old patterns, correct yourself continually, watchfully, with these specifications. Make your feelings as independent of your environment as possible. Then your life will hold a rich and pleasant world of feelings, a world that is not simply predicted by the external events that wash over it, but that—on the contrary—plays a significant role in shaping the external world.

QUAIL

Forgiveness, Renunciation

The quail is a member of the game fowl family. It is the smallest game fowl found in Europe and the only one that returns to the Southern

Hemisphere in winter. This is one of the reasons why quail are seldom encountered in the wild. In the southern Mediterranean they continue to be hunted as they have in past. Because the voyage over the sea is very strenuous for these birds, they often gather in flocks by the coasts, either wintering there or gathering strength for the flight onward across the Sahara. At these times the exhausted birds can even be caught by hand.

Quails prefer well-used meadows and agrarian lands offering plenty of cover. During the day they avoid flying as much as possible. They stay covered, and when disturbed try to run away on foot. Their plumage is adapted for camouflage. Quails are heard more often than they are seen. The well-known three-part quail call, "Pitch-wheeler," is often repeated. During an evening walk through the fields, if one listens carefully enough, one may discover a quail family and even see them flying. These small fowl live on seeds and insects. In potato fields quails help to eliminate potato bugs. They build their nests in hollows in the ground. The hen raises the chicks, which can fly after about three weeks. Quails have always been popular as domestic birds. Their eggs are low in cholesterol, and their meat is a delicacy. Domesticated breeds exist both with the coloring of wild quails and with diverse color variations.

Message

If you encounter a quail face-to-face and can observe it, take care to remember at what point in time the meeting took place. The quail tells you to forgive, in the sense of revoking a judgment. Thus a misdeed is forgiven. The two concepts, forgiveness and renunciation, have the same origin in that both mean letting go in the sense of dissociating. A meeting with a quail will motivate you to relinquish absolutely all judgments of guilt in regard to a given topic, as if it were correct and necessary to accept that topic and carry all the consequences yourself. Naturally, one could say that life might have gone differently had various things not happened in the past. But the past *has* happened. Whatever the motivation, whatever the mistakes made, what's done is done, and nothing can change that. Not only is it futile to contemplate how things would be if something had not happened, it is also wrong and dangerous. The things that happen in our lives do not follow what we consider the optimal path. They follow a great, all-embracing, truthful law. Your feelings, actions, thoughts, and ideas are unerring factors that have contributed to the development of your life's narrative and have at various points entered reality. Of course, it is not apparent to your intellect how and why these things have an effect. But this is no argument against the possibility that they will have an effect. What has happened in your life has happened because it was exactly appropriate for your development. Do not linger in the past and grumble about how good it would have been if such-and-such a thing hadn't happened. This behavior is self-destructive to the highest degree. It is often responsible for making a wound unable to heal and preventing positive things from being harvested from life's dramas.

RAVEN

Magic, Clairvoyance

Ravens live practically worldwide. In most cultures they are both respected and feared, and always viewed in connection with magic. For some it is a bird of death, for others a companion of witches and wizards. Secret powers are attributed to it, such as the ability to move back and forth between this world and the afterlife. Its blue-black plumage and guttural "caw" underscore the bad reputation it has in many places.

It is a carrion eater, and despite all encroachments it has maintained its population successfully. Ravens often play social games in the air, circling together, interlocking their talons, flying upside down, and performing wild chases involving nosedives. Young ravens raised by humans can not only become very tame but can also exhibit surprising intelligence in some regards.

Message

The raven foretells enchantment. Someone who encounters a raven has a mystical, magical experience in the works. Its appearance opens our bright eyes and gives our consciousness access to the inner void from which truth is born. This is a favorable opportunity to break out of the normal everyday framework and observe the world from the point of view of its mystical interconnections. Truly wonderful things will happen.

The medicine of the raven is magic. Magic is the primal creative power that follows its predetermined natural structure. The raven lives its life in this flow. It does not deceive, it does not keep secrets, it creates from the source of nature, and it symbolizes the flow of energetic currents. The raven is a social bird and can also be tamed by people. Many people are afraid of this bird because it represents something uncomfortable and threatening for them. It is there when life begins and ends. In folklore, some stories tell of the raven calling up the dead. Both death and life bring out fear in people. There is so much in them that is unexplainable, so many painful experiences.

But the raven reminds us not of external dangers but of the great inner void. Neither life nor death hurt us. We are hurt by our own lack of caution. We unconsciously play with the power of magic. Without realizing it, we turn this powerful tool over to our ego. The power of magic is nonpolar, meaning that nature and people themselves determine its purpose. There is no white or black magic, there is only positive or negative intent. It would be wrong to say that the human ego fosters negative intent. Much black magic arises from ignorance.

For most people, the intellect reaches into a void when we try to orient ourselves according to our purpose. This void appears because the connection between soul and intellect is being interrupted, but the interruption cannot be sensed. If a raven flies into your field of consciousness, it is reminding you of a pressing need to recognize your magical powers. Its intent is not to advise you to practice magic with your intellect but rather to give honest consideration to events in your life. Nothing happens to you that cannot also help you to find your divine path. The raven is a message from a world unknown to your intellect.

Anyone who wants to understand the raven's message has to learn to accept that the secrets of darkness must remain hidden from the consciousness of day. Perhaps you have tried to solve problems in your life with manipulative charm. But such an attempt to change the behavior of your environment through your own behavior is a frivolous misuse of magical energy. Do not be afraid, there is a possibility of learning here. Open yourself to the encounter with the raven. Allow the black messenger to dive in to your subconscious and make what you need visible to you. Stay calm, for the encounter with the raven presages enchantment.

ROBIN

Self-Expression

The European robin is a member of the family of small songbirds. It is widespread in Europe. It mainly inhabits forested areas with plenty of undergrowth, but in some places it lives in close association with humans. These small, pretty birds are seen very often in gardens and parks, trees and bushes. The robin is a songbird that delimits its territory by singing throughout the entire year. Unusually, the females also sing.

European robins are partial migrants, usually only departing in the winter from areas of high elevation. Their winter quarters extend to the northern edge of the Sahara. In winter they eat berries and seeds. Therefore, they are frequent guests at bird feeders.

Message

The significance of the robin is made apparent through its red breast. It has its heart in the right place and a voice to express itself. This is exactly what the robin means to tell you when it makes itself clearly apparent to you. Perhaps you should finally express what moves your heart. Perhaps it is time to show your true colors. Are you one of those people who live very much according to the expectations of others? Clearly state what you feel and think. Sometimes it is hard to know the motivation of the pure heart if its feelings have been too long suppressed and filtered through the head.

It often happens that simple feelings grow to great complaints in the discontent of the inner world. The robin is not telling you to denounce your surroundings but is motivating you to express simple sentiments. These can be a smile, sadness, joy, or sorrow. A sentiment is something that is your own, that arises in your innermost heart. You can sometimes perceive your own sentiments because we ourselves are reflected in the behavior of others. But it is never the other person who has created your sentiment.

The robin's message—to express yourself—is an important message for contemporary people. We can only perceive each other and interact attentively with one another when each of us has the courage to reveal the tender side of the inner self. No love can grow through mutual accusation.

SISKIN, REDPOLL

Family Ties

Siskins are part of the Finch family. We are most familiar with the Eurasian siskin and the common redpoll. The Eurasian siskin looks similar to the green finch but is smaller and more delicate with prominent black bands on the edges of the wings and the tail feathers. It is a social bird, gathering into loose flocks to search for food in birch trees and fields overgrown with weeds. In winter siskins migrate from the east into central and western Europe. They gather in large swarms that make quite a commotion. The common redpoll is somewhat larger than the Eurasian siskin and has a red cap; the male also has a red spot on his breast. The redpoll is the only type of finch that has a black spot under its beak. Siskins and redpolls can often be observed together in mixed flocks. These birds are also social during the breeding season, building their nests about twenty feet up in tall trees; siskins nest in spruce trees, redpolls in larch trees. The redpoll covers its nest to protect it from predators and late snow. Both species are good climbers. Siskins and redpolls, while looking for food on thin twigs, perform acrobatics reminiscent of titmice.

Message

If you see a siskin or redpoll, or a whole flock of them, there is a topic at hand in your life at the moment that is strongly connected to your family. The redpoll indicates the parental family that raised you, the siskin your current family that you have as an adult. If you do not have a biological family, it can indicate a family you have chosen. The parental family is clearly structured. There are the parents and siblings as the immediate family, and the grandparents, aunts, and uncles as the secondary family. The current family usually includes your spouse and children, and possibly the children's partners and your grandchildren. However, your current family can also include people who are like family to you, whom you care for, and with whom you make decisions together about your lives. The siskin or redpoll is telling you that in any decisions you make or think about today, you should think about your family and its needs and values. Include your family, plan for and with them, and discuss the steps you take with all the people who are close to you. Belonging to a family carries obligations with it, but it is also strengthening.

The siskin and redpoll also remind you that there are always topics in families that can be hurtful to individuals or are unresolved and painful. A wise family respects these things, behaves heedfully toward the individual in question, and tends to leave such topics untouched. This does not mean that a clear discussion should be avoided at all costs, but such discussions should only be approached very gently and lovingly. Often family members are our sharpest critics, and they often criticize things that are already long past. A family should be a vessel into which the individual can gladly step and feel supported and accepted as her whole self. If this is the case, a family can function as a source of advice for the steps the individual takes, knowing that she will be accompanied attentively. The siskin or redpoll has come to make you into the archetype for this truth in your family. You will see that if this vessel is harmonious and comfortable, life is much easier.

SPARROW

Simplicity

Is there anyone who does not know the lively sparrow? There is hardly any bird that has become so close to humans as this one. Traveling on ships, it has been spread throughout the whole world. The house sparrow lives with people. It finds food in the surplus we throw out, and uses niches and corners in human habitations for its nesting places. Two or three broods per year, with four to six chicks in each, is normal. As many as twelve pairs can live on the TV antenna of a single-family home. Males and females have different plumage.

These small tenants live on insects and their larvae, grains, weed seeds, fruit, berries, and young plants. In cities they live on bread and garbage. The field sparrow, the brother of the house sparrow, only follows people as far as the edges of their settlements and gardens. It prefers cultivated land, hedges, vegetable gardens, and orchards as residences, and breeds in simple hollows, free yet covered spaces, and especially birdhouses. The chicks are unceremoniously thrown out of the nest at a young age.

The only holes left for other, less robust hollow-nesting birds are those that are too small for the field sparrow to enter. Like the house sparrow, the field sparrow is also a prolific breeder. The two species are clearly different in their appearance. Importantly, however, only the house sparrow is sexually dimorphic.

Message

We encounter the sparrow on a daily basis. Its message is clear and simple. It urges us to practice simplicity. If you became conscious of this bird today, then use it as an opportunity to pursue thoughts on this subject. First let us consider our possessions. Do all the things in my life serve my well-being in various ways? This is not a matter of the great, ultimate well-being, but of the momentary flow of things. Simplicity means living in the flow, receiving and giving in harmony with the realms of nature.

What is important is not the masses of exchanged energies—material energies, as well as feelings, creativity, and thoughts—but rather, their flow. I can take in many energies from all planes as long as I can tolerate the exchange that results from this. Someone who sends out energy but does not want to react to the energies that flow back in return has broken the harmony. Blockages emerge, and the blockages of simplicity are poverty, deficiency, and privation on the one hand and excesses, pressure, and exhaustion on the other.

The sparrow lives around people, nourishes itself with our energetic garbage, and grows strong from its enormous multiplication of the disharmonies that arise around us from that garbage. Remember the saying "A bird in the hand is worth two in the bush." Herein lies its meaning. Live harmoniously with the energy that is actually available. You do not need a godsend of supplies to hoard, because the supplies are always there and you can reach into them at any time. The sparrow does not serve; on the contrary, it uses.

It exhausts the possibilities that life offers it. If our consumer behavior offers it a richly spread table, it expands limitlessly in number. It makes use of our living space so obviously that we almost trip over it. If we listen to its message, stem the flow, and reclaim our living space, then the sparrow will no longer find any holes or corners in which to settle and live off our garbage. Harmony with the flow of nature is a major requirement for true wealth. Simplicity is the basis for this harmony.

SPARROW HAWK

Clarification of Thoughts

An exceptional flier, extremely fast, the sparrow hawk shoots out of total hiding onto a flock of sparrows. Two or three small birds a day are needed for a sparrow hawk couple to feed their chicks. In nesting season the two parents raise four to six young birds together. The sparrow hawk population was mercilessly decimated during the 1950s. According to *Brehms Tierleben* (1934 edition), "This bird of prey deserves no protection, only the most unremitting and ruthless persecution."

Thanks to the timely knowledge that these birds of prey perform an important function in the food chain, they have been placed under protection in almost all of Europe. The population has been slowly recovering.

Message

Like a frightened flock of birds, thoughts chatter on all levels, mixing with impressions, thoughts, dogma, patterns, and fears, all assaulting the calm of your soul. They build nests and happily settle into your garden of feelings. Then suddenly, unforeseen, the sparrow hawk swoops down from its place of ambush and grabs one of these chatterers. The twittering, chirruping flock scatters in fright and flies away.

There is no reason for sadness, and also no reason for excessive joy. They will return, these phantasms, but for this moment, quiet clarity reigns in your system. Given a bit of courage, the things that you realize in such a moment of clarity will open a new perspective for your life. The sparrow hawk is not the messenger of action; it tells you to bring clarity to your feelings and thoughts.

With resoluteness, bring your inner world to rest. Take a conscious overview of the many voices in your inner self to know which ones you should really rely on. Consider which of your thoughts serve your own truth and which serve the convenience of other people. Every thought has the power to bring about an action. If you know your thoughts, you can steer your actions.

If the sparrow hawk shoots through your life like a flash of lightning, let your "sparrow flock" quietly flee. Immediately ask yourself: "What am I thinking and feeling in this moment?" Consider who this feeling or thought serves.

SPOONBILL

Connection to the Primal Poles

Broadly, the spoonbill is a member of the Ibis family. It is a wading bird that requires shallow, standing water. With pendulous movements, the spoonbill swings its unusual spoonlike bill back and forth through the water. In this manner it finds small animals in the water and mud. Once it has collected food, it tosses it back into its throat with an upward flick of the head and bill, and swallows it. Besides the characteristic head movements, another striking feature of the spoonbill is its long, tufted neck plumage, which fluffs out when it is excited. Due to the draining of wetlands and pollutants such as pesticides, hardly any spoonbills remain in Europe. Individuals and very small breeding colonies can be seen only on Lake Neusiedl and at a few locations in Germany. Spoonbills usually build their nests on the ground, in the reeds. Sometimes they also choose trees or rocky cliffs for nesting.

Spoonbills and ibises are very closely related, but their appearance is very different. Spoonbills can breed with the African holy ibis to produce viable, fertile offspring.

Message

The spoonbill reminds us of our connection to the primal poles. We are connected to the Earth; it is our nourishment and gives us strength and form. It gives us our footing. It is the love that surrounds us and accompanies our growth. But we are also connected to the light. The light is the energy, the motor that allows us to grow. Light fulfills form, light manifests itself in form. Light surrounds light, sets processes in motion, and these lead to transformation. Every person is made partly of light and partly of love. Individually, we connect these primal poles to our being. Every creature on Earth is a possible form of expression of this connection of the primal poles in time. The spoonbill tells us to revoke our judgment of ourselves and others. Creation is greater and more ingenious than we, with our human consciousness, could ever imagine. Whatever is, is complete. What takes place in the course of history depends on connections to individual completeness. Therefore, all dramatic human narratives emerge mainly from the created separation between the primal poles, and through the unconscious judgments we make.

STARLING

Opinion

Starlings are widespread social birds. Their black plumage, with purple, green, and blue iridescence and white spots, is somewhat reminiscent of the night sky. Like the alpine chough, the starling has a yellow beak and red feet. They are conspicuous birds, often seen traveling in very large groups.

When a great flock of starlings settles on a tree for the night, the branches bend under the weight. Outside breeding season, they gather in clamorous swarms upon orchards, to the distress of farmers, because they do a great deal of damage. The various measures taken to keep starlings away from orchards have not been very effective.

Message

If you have noticed a swarm of starlings, it is telling you to justify your opinion. It is hard to say what an opinion is, and equally hard to know which of your opinions is referred to. We encounter starlings when uncertainty is opening doors in our subconscious, so that other people may feel invited to tell us what to think. Have you somehow become exposed in society in a way that could be disadvantageous for you? Is it possible that others are secretly harvesting the fruits of your labors while you do not recognize your own talents and efforts? Then it is a good thing if the starlings have pointed clearly to your opinions. Consider your position in your family and in society.

Only take on as much responsibility as you can really handle. Carefully consider whether being too comfortable or neglectful has made you become a freeloader. Something in you is angry, some behavior of yours with respect to a group is inappropriate. It will be good if you can recognize and correct it yourself. Of course, not every individual starling carries such a massive sign for you.

The individual starling may be a sign of some bit of envy, a small grudge, or a slight infringement committed by you or by someone else. The more these birds come into your awareness, the closer they come, and the greater the damage they cause, the clearer is the message.

STORK

New Beginnings, Birth

The stork is white with black wings, long red legs, and a long red beak. The male is responsible for nest building. He inspects the old nest and builds a new one if necessary. Twigs and branches are used as the nest material. Stork nests are often found on roofs, towers, and chimneys. Nests are protected from rivals by the stork couple in fierce battles. The female then lays three to five eggs that are incubated by both partners. When the adult storks come into the nest, one can observe their famous bill-clapping, with their heads bent backward. This is how storks greet one another.

Storks eat mice, insects, frogs, earthworms, fish, snakes, and even the occasional mole. Storks are migrating birds. Between late July and September they fly via Gibraltar to tropical Africa; most of them return to their breeding grounds in March. Due to draining of swamps and wetlands, high voltage power lines, and pesticides, the white stork's populations have declined drastically in Europe.

In many places, thanks to environmental activists, storks have been able to return slowly to their original breeding places. Even today, some small children are told that the stork brought them. A stork nest on the roof has always been a symbol of good luck. Traditionally, it means the family will be blessed with many children, prosperity, and security.

Message

The stork shows us when it is time for a new beginning. New things must be painstakingly nurtured and encouraged, requiring your full attention. This may mean some intensive work for you, with sleepless nights and your full commitment. You do not have the choice of accepting or rejecting this. Compare it to a newborn child who is here now, and who you must raise. Indeed, the stork can presage the birth of a child.

Everything the stork indicates to you is something you have, at some point, eagerly wished for. Through your wishes, you have "engendered" the new thing. Thus, the stork's appearance can indicate that you have something new to expect, but also that you should be concrete enough in your wishes that you can fulfill them.

You cannot hope to win the lottery if you don't buy a ticket. So be ready to act to get your wishes, be open to the joy you want to experience, and be aware that the "newborn" in your life demands some things from you. Generally speaking, wishes that are nurtured with loving commitment will always lead to something beneficial.

SWALLOW

Happiness

Swallows announce the start of summer for us, and they live their lives mostly in the air. They are used to us, because they have lived in close association with people for centuries. They nest in barns, sheds, house roofs, under bridges, and on rock walls. Both sexes build the nest and raise the chicks. Two to six chicks are in each brood. At most, there are two broods per year.

When searching for food, swallows eat an enormous quantity of insects in flight. During their time in the nest, four young swallows consume about 150,000 insects, caught by their parents while flying.

Message

If you encounter a swallow, it is telling you to raise your view to a higher plane for a moment. The swallow is the medicine of happiness. All people, in their lives, are on the hunt for happiness. They fight for it, develop strategies and theories, work and put out effort—and sometime around the end of life, all that is left is the experience of life as a tough struggle. Happiness is not something that one can acquire.

Rather, it is a feeling that is present in people and that one needs to recognize, let in, and then project into one's own life. When someone avoids a storm or finds a treasure, she is happy. But this is not the happiness that the swallow makes known to you. The swallow encourages you to be happy. It lives a great part of its life in the air. There it is alone with itself, even when other swallows fly nearby. Being alone and living in the moment is the source of contentment, and from this contentment with oneself, happiness—whose messenger is the swallow—can grow.

From this contentment, in which all that exists can be accepted, you can rise with your senses into bliss. No "whens" or "buts" any longer hinder you from divining the wonder behind everything. You will not want to analyze anything to find a reason for your wonder. It is as if the heart begins to wonder and a comfortable feeling of happiness streams through you.

SWAN

Grace, Charm

The most common and best-known swan in Europe is the mute swan. Originally from northwestern Europe and Asia, it spread to many parts of Europe during the twentieth century. Like all members of the goose family, they live in long-term partnerships.

Outside of breeding season, swans are very social. In spring, however, the male vehemently defends his territory. This can lead to fierce battles. Swans are mostly nonmigratory, staying in the same locations for the winter. However, harsh winter weather in the north occasionally makes them retreat to the south or west. The young cygnets lose their dirty-gray plumage after their first winter.

Whether swimming or flying, resting or walking along the shore, all the swan's movements are graceful, dignified, and calm. For many people the swan is the epitome of beauty. Gray and unremarkable as a cygnet, its plumage appears to change to radiant white from one day to the next. It is as if the animal has begun to radiate from within, throwing its gray-brown feathers to the winds.

Message of the White Swan

If a swan has drawn your attention today, then your themes are charm, beauty, and maybe also grace. This is not a matter of outer beauty and charm but of the inner awakening of light.

One story tells of a young swan who flew up into the light and landed before the throne of God. The swan bowed his head humbly, and eternal happiness shone into his heart. He became whiter and more luminous, and his attention kept turning inward. He had reached the infinite grace of the highest place, and never again could this experience be lost from his heart. His appearance of charm and beauty was nourished by this inner happiness.

The swan advises you to rise up to the highest levels of your world of senses, open your bright eyes, and have courage for the highest spiritual experiences. In this way you will be able to kindle a light in your heart, let it grow, and wonder at this inner power and beauty. This experience will move you to bow your head. By listening inside yourself and wondering at your own inner light, this light will be turned outward. The outer shadows will dissolve, and the boundaries of your expression will vanish without your having to change anything externally. Your image will finally be graceful and beautiful.

Message of the Black Swan

If you encounter a black swan, the message is the same as with the white, except that it symbolizes the opposite divine polarity—namely, not light, but love—as a theme of grace.

TERN

Contentment

On the coasts, various types of terns can be seen, but inland, by far the most commonly observed is the black tern, on its way to or from the south. Others, such as the common tern, the little tern, and the whiskered tern, can be seen occasionally on lakes, but this is unusual. Terns live on the ocean or on big bodies of water, where they hunt fish. Many catch them by diving. Terns barely go on land except for mating and nesting. Their bodies are correspondingly adapted to this way of life. The thin, small wings, light body, and forked tail are adapted for long periods of flight and difficult maneuvers. Terns, especially the arctic tern, travel the farthest of all migrating birds. The arctic tern follows high noon around the world, so to speak. They probably see more sunlight than any other life-form on Earth. For about eight months out of the year, the sun never sets for the arctic tern.

Message

The tern is the symbol of contentment. It is the contentment felt when the day is done, one has found one's place, and when time simply flies. It is important to take life as it is. Much in a person's everyday life is not exactly likely to bring about ecstatic joy. But if you forget about the question of why you have to do these everyday things, if you simply do them and forget that you are doing them, then there is space for you to perceive life as a flow, to see the light in your being, and to feel your inner happiness. It is how it is. There are highs and lows, easy and difficult moments, sun and rain, day and night. The tern encourages you to deal immediately with everything that is hanging over you and not leave anything on the back burner. Do not wait until you want to do something—do it right away. Get the work off your plate as soon as you know it's there. Then there will not be much time left to ruin your mood by thinking about work. There will also be little time left to consider who could have done this work instead of you, and consequently no time for self-pity. Follow the light in your life, follow the being. Never let the mountain of work get so high that you can't conquer it without great strain.

If you encounter a tern and it leads you to realize that you no longer feel as light and in the flow as you used to, then this speedy bird is advising you, urgently, to simplify your life. Throw out everything that you don't really need and everything that doesn't really do anything for you. Perhaps you are one of those people who need three people to stand in for you whenever you can't be there. This is a sign that you are very productive, but it also means that you do not get anything out of your great productivity. Or are you also receiving a triple salary? Do you need that triple salary? Do what you can, and make sure it is done to a degree that is in harmony with your quality of life. Acquire luxuries only when you really have the time and inspiration to enjoy them. You cannot expect other people to do the same of their own accord.

THRUSH, SONG THRUSH

Life Plan, Life Phase

The song thrush is closely related to the blackbird. Thrushes are wide-spread songbirds. Their family also includes the blackbird, the fieldfare, the mistle thrush, and the redwing. Small thrushes include the common redstart, the black redstart, the European robin, and the nightingale. In folk tradition, however, "thrush" refers to the song thrush. Its dark-flecked white belly is distinctive.

Early in the year, often in February, the thrushes return from their winter homes in southwestern Europe and northern Africa. Thus, they are an early signal of spring. Song thrushes and mistle thrushes prefer to live in forests, where they can find enough space and food to raise their young. Thrushes are wary and always on the watch. They defend their territories aggressively, but like blackbirds, they define them with beautiful songs. Also like the blackbird, they are the messengers of boundaries.

Message

Encounters with thrushes indicate changes. Phases in life come to an end, then new ones begin. It is less about indicating your personal boundaries than about the natural rhythms, the time boundaries, the themes that

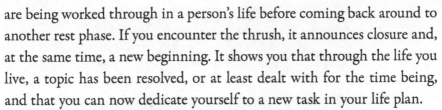

are being worked through in a person's life before coming back around to another rest phase. If you encounter the thrush, it announces closure and, at the same time, a new beginning. It shows you that through the life you live, a topic has been resolved, or at least dealt with for the time being, and that you can now dedicate yourself to a new task in your life plan.

It can also be an idea, or perhaps a fascination, indicating a new direction. Give this new energy some happy space, without holding it rigidly. But have the courage to take steps in a new direction, without knowing the goal. When the thrush announces a renewal, the cosmos is not expecting you to reach a definite, predefined goal. Rather, it is time to make your form of expression, whether it be professional or private, fit with this new stage in your development. It can be assumed that through your development, you have created or released new, beautiful, strong sides of yourself, which you should now allow to bloom on the outside. Often, there are old, established behavior patterns that stand in the way of this blooming. You probably already know how good you are—but do the people around you know it?

It is within your power to decide on joy or sorrow, happiness or heartache. Careful alertness to your own perceptions is now just as important as the taking of decisive external steps—as soon as these are recognizable. But consider that this is never about reaching a concrete goal. Each of these external steps will bring you new experiences. Do like the thrush, beginning this new step in life with joyous, love-filled inner songs. Seek joy and happiness in your everyday life, and radiate out some of the happiness that you have created.

TITMOUSE

Inner Child

There are many types of titmouse. The best known are probably the great tit, the Eurasian blue tit, and the coal tit. They share the common characteristics of nesting in holes and holding on to large pieces of food with their feet. The latter behavior can also be observed in ravens.

Titmice are very lively songbirds, dancing lithely up and down on branches. Some titmice store food for the winter, and when nourishment is scarce, these colorful birds can be quite resourceful.

Titmice are welcome guests at a bird feeder, partly due to their colorful plumage, but also due to their lively behavior. With their nimble feet, they can gain a good foothold on the wires on a block of suet and pick the seeds out of the fat while hanging on upside down. Titmice are very well-researched birds because they are so trusting. I personally observed how my son was able to stroke wild titmice at the bird feeder in front of the window. The small birds were not irritated by this touching. Titmice are distributed from lowlands to the edges of forests, depending on the species.

Because they nest in hollows and do not shy from people, titmice also gladly take up residence in garden birdhouses. Birdhouses should be in a location inaccessible to cats.

Message

In symbolic language the titmouse represents the inner child. It is light, lively, perky, comical, resourceful, and curious but easily startled and frightened away. The titmouse is a loving being, just like the human "inner child." Its safe world is delicate when it is not protected. For humans today, having a safe world is probably more important than it used to be. Turning to the world of the inner child, we are led to a place where we can still meet with our true nature.

In our culture, for hundreds of years, childhood did not even exist, and children could not be children in the way we take for granted today. Children are naturally curious, cheerful, and lively. It is obvious that children observe, imitate, and—in boisterous play—try out the effects of what they have perceived. In indigenous cultures children and youth learn and grow mostly without educational strategies on the part of adults. The child is the child and the adult is the adult. The one naturally provides the framework for the other. No artificial boundaries have to be erected, no overly high expectations fulfilled.

When I am entirely in my inner mother, my child can be in his whole inner child. It is a natural law that these two inner forms fulfill one another. But if someone's "inner child" is overwhelmed, neglected, and affronted, it can no longer recognize itself in its natural form. Such a person finds it hard to be a child, mother, or father. He will try to set everything right with his head, thus often hurting himself and others. For modern people it is very important to get a new grip on one's child-nature, to breathe in deeply and remember the naturalness of the child in the depths of one's own soul.

If you observe a titmouse, open your heart and deeply breathe in its lightness and liveliness. Venture to probe gradually deeper to find the hidden child within you, and if you have the courage to do so, live more often as that child. Children should also heal their child-nature, for the pain of a long tradition weighs upon their souls. Mutual tolerance and acceptance, understanding and love, will lead us back to our own nature more quickly than training, criticism, and judgments.

TURKEY
Giving Away

Turkeys are native to South America. They were brought to Europe by Columbus and have since spread all over the world as domestic birds.

Wild turkeys are not found in Europe. However, they are common domestic animals, and their meat is very popular. Their appearance, perhaps, takes some getting used to. With its naked, bluish head, long red wattles, red tassel over the beak, and intrusive voice, the turkey is rather strange. However, if one contemplates this bird a little more closely and observes its beautiful plumage, one will discover that it has its own type of beauty. The courtship ritual of these large fowl is impressive. A group of males dance together around the females. Bitter fights can take place, but they hardly ever lead to injury because the turkeys know their boundaries when it comes to biting. The dominant male gets his chance to mate while the other males protect the females from outside males. The hen lays her eggs in nests under thick trees and sits long and resolutely upon a clutch of up to fifteen eggs. When the chicks are hatched, the mother carefully guides and protects them. After fourteen days the chicks can already fly a little.

Message

The turkey tells you to give yourself, unquestioningly and boundlessly. Give yourself up, give in to life. Immerse yourself to the fullest in your life's narrative. Now is not the time for you to set boundaries and modify the events and relationships you live through, but to let them happen. In external self-abandonment, discover internal self-development. It will be a great experience for you, your fellow humans, and your environment. Giving yourself also means expecting things of yourself. If you want to have this life—and it wants to have you—then you should have it, all the way. The turkey does not tell you to give yourself like a lover, anxious to show her most beautiful and pleasant side. Give it all, your light and your shadows. With this giving, try not to seek affirmation or recognition, which do not matter at this time. Observe how you feel when you throw yourself into life so completely. The more you give of yourself, the more you let go of restrictive ideas about yourself, and by these means you can discover strengths, qualities, and possibilities that may have been long buried or lying idle. Give yourself entirely, and you will see that life begins to adjust to you, so that you can always experience things wholly and authentically.

VULTURE

Transience

This bird appears noble as it circles in a blue sky, looking for fallen, dying game. It is the messenger of death and transience. Many vulture species are found in Europe. They live mostly in warm mountainous regions but have more recently become established in the Alps. While the Egyptian vulture and the cinereous vulture are only found in southern places such as Spain, Greece, and Turkey, the griffon vulture can be seen in summer in the Alps, and the bearded vulture the whole year round. The Egyptian vulture, with its wingspan of up to six feet, is almost as large as a small eagle; the other species are larger, with wingspans up to ten feet.

Vultures need good thermal lift and a sufficiently high starting point to take off. Once the bird is in the air, it lets the rising winds carry it up and can glide in the air for hours without flapping its wings. Vultures live mainly on carrion. The vulture will tear open freshly dead wildlife and also domestic animals to get to the meat beneath the skin. Vultures will not even turn down bones. They carry them high into the air and let them fall on rocks. They then eat the bone fragments and marrow. Like all birds of prey, vultures have very good eyesight. If one of these large birds finds carrion or a dying animal, many others will soon gather to take part in the feast.

Message

If the vulture makes itself known to you, an important topic in your life has been exhausted. A pattern, behavior, belief, or action is dying, losing its form, and returning into the light. It will never come back, but its essence nourishes your life. Everything that makes up our lives is transient—even life itself. Death begins with birth. In every being the final goal is to cease to be. However, the vulture has not come to tell you this but to tell you that something is dead but is being artificially kept alive by you. What were you thinking of when you espied this mighty bird of death? Something in this theme is over. Could it be that you are paying homage to an image of yourself that no longer corresponds to the truth? Could it be that you are fooling yourself into thinking you are in a wonderful relationship when in reality there are no more living feelings there? Or are you relying on security that only appears to be secure, but in truth has no strength left? It is also possible that the vulture—especially if you see it gliding far overhead—is reminding you that it is now time to bury your old visions. What you have not fulfilled by now, you are not able to fulfill. Forget it and look for a new vision that is more fitting. Probe within yourself and your life to see what is no longer living, what has no more chances left, and separate yourself from it.

WARBLER

Revelation

The typical warbler, along with the Acrocephalus, grass warbler, tree warbler, and leaf warbler (to name the most common ones), belongs to the very large family of Old World warblers. The smallest birds, about the size of sparrows, are constantly in motion. They hop and fly, fast and lively, from one perch to another, feverishly flapping their wings or wiggling their tails. All warblers are good singers. After the garden warbler and common whitethroat, the Eurasian blackcap is the most widespread species in Europe. When one hears the characteristic song of the male warbler, it can sound as if the bird is packing all the emotions in his eventful life into a single verse. Warblers are not birds that one encounters consciously on a daily basis. They are too erratic, quick-moving, and lively. But in summer, they are among the songbirds that accompany us with their songs and make our gardens and parks alive with their assiduous fluttering.

Message

The warbler tells us to stay in the domain of perception and not slide into emotion. Express your perceptions without bringing them into connection with your environment. Emotions are polar feelings that supposedly originate from a situation in your environment. Emotions conceal the true reason for a situation and create complications.

Perceptions are neutral and nonpolar. Perceptions articulate a mood simply and clearly. Therefore, you should reveal whatever perceptions you sense in yourself, lovingly and without judgment. Above all, reveal your perceptions to your own consciousness. You must be the first to know what moves you. We live in a world in which most of our attention is directed outward, toward the events of life. Somewhere at the edges of this, we perceive our own needs, but our own perceptions very often remain hidden from us. This does not mean that when you stay hidden you do not have an effect on our lives. You make yourself noticeable in that your energy is reflected in external events and thus shines back on us. Now you are conscious of us, and you are connected with someone or something else. These reflections release emotions. These emotions often set whole sequences of events in motion, in which we participate, for good or ill. There is nothing wrong with this. But it would be much more pleasant if you knew what you were sending into that world of possibilities. When one shouts out in the forest it echoes right back. If you learn to recognize your perceptions, pay attention to them, and let them in, then life will not need to awaken any repressed feelings in you but will fit perfectly well with your own being. Reveal your being consciously, truthfully, and decisively so that you can experience whatever kind of narratives, encounters, and events you wish.

WARBLER, TREE; WARBLER, GRASS

Discussion

The tree warbler and grass warbler belong to the large family of Old World warblers. They are similar to the Acrocephalus and leaf warblers and are related to the typical warbler. There are five types of grass warblers in Europe, of which the common grasshopper warbler and Savi's warbler are most widespread. There are six types of tree warbler in Europe. The icterine warbler, and perhaps the melodious warbler, are found in the German-speaking countries. Like all warblers, the tree and grass warblers are true songbirds. They are lively and always mov-

ing around their habitat. They are all about the size of a sparrow and live on insects. Tree warblers live in trees and shrubbery. Grass warblers prefer ground level vegetation that provides sufficient cover, such as bushes and tall grass. While the grass warbler performs its monotone song best at night, the loud, long-lasting song of the tree warbler, sometimes melodic, sometimes grating, is heard only by day.

Message

It is rare to encounter either of these birds. Although they are present in the summer, and we can hear them singing and also hopping around, clear identification is difficult. Thus, an encounter with a tree warbler or grass warbler is a clear admonition. Whereas the Acrocephalus warbler tells you to speak, the tree and grass warbler tell you to be attentive. Discussions and rumors are afoot. Could it be that you have adopted idiosyncrasies that seem somewhat strange in your surroundings? Is it possible that you no longer even recognize yourself completely and therefore exhibit an outward behavior that you yourself would not find acceptable? People always talk; this encounter is not about that fact. It is not a matter of anything in your life of which you are conscious. This is about the things that you yourself do not notice. Perhaps your tongue has become too sharp and you are unwittingly striking out at people with your words. Perhaps you have been so long accustomed to some out-of-style fashion that you do not realize your appearance is somewhat bedraggled. Perhaps, when lost in thought, you stare at people in a way that is perceived as unsettling. Or could it be that out of boredom with your own life you ask others too many intimate and personal questions? Whatever it is, something is eluding you, and it will not be especially comfortable when you figure it out. Try to observe yourself closely. Consider the reactions of your environment carefully and sensitively, and if you observe some sort of typical unsettledness in other people, try to determine its cause. Perhaps it would also be good to discuss it directly with a good friend. Simply say that you have the feeling that you may have slipped into behavior patterns that can be unsettling to others. Ask for honest feedback. Ask to hear everything the other person thinks that you cannot see in yourself. Look at yourself to see what the other person says, and try to change it. However, if the answer is simply that you are fine and nothing is wrong, then ask more insistently or ask someone else. It is hardly possible to have a definite encounter with a tree or grass warbler without any reason.

WAXWING
Upheaval

The waxwing is a handsome bird, usually appearing in flocks. This mostly fawn-brown bird has black markings over its eyes and on its neck and a striking cap. In flight it looks similar to the starling. Waxwings live mostly in northern birch and spruce forests, where they eat insects in the summer. In the winter their diet includes fruits and berries. If these are lacking in their winter quarters, they may migrate to the Mediterranean. In southern climes, every couple of years great influxes of these birds can be observed. In imposing swarms they plunder the berries and fruits of the mountain ash, viburnum, and other bushes, as

well as unharvested fruit. Waxwings have remarkable digestive abilities. Each bird eats up to twice its own body weight in food each day. The food passes through its digestive tract in no more than thirty minutes. They sudden arrival in great swarms was viewed as a bad omen in the Middle Ages. Their appearance may have occurred in connection with the plague, lending them the name "plague bird."

Message
There is a kernel of truth in such beliefs. During the winter of 2004–2005, when the great tsunami took the lives of thousands of people in Asia, gigantic swarms of waxwings were seen all over Europe. The waxwing heralds upheavals. It brings the message that what is on top will soon be on the bottom. The suppressed will be visible, the inner will become outer, the external will become internal, dreams may come true, reality may turn into a dream. Nothing that was sure and certain will remain so. Dependencies will be dissolved and infringements ended. All in all, such upheavals constitute a deep, far-reaching cleansing and can be viewed with joy. This spring cleaning will make space for your own light and your own strength to blossom and become effective. The waxwing's message can refer to all areas of life, touch all planes, and apply to every theme. It does not threaten; it informs. What is happening now is all your own truth and often the opposite of your own thoughts, feelings, and actions.

If you see an individual bird, it applies to a topic of which you are currently conscious. What you have to deal with is that there is an entirely different way of seeing this topic, and you would do well to search for it. What are your blind spots in this subject area? If your awareness is drawn to a whole flock of waxwings, then your whole life is about to undergo an upheaval. Seek out someone who is ready to give you honest, but also loving, critical feedback. Perhaps this should be someone who would not stand to gain any personal advantage from knowing your blind spots. Otherwise, your repressed side will finagle its way permanently into your life and force itself upon you.

WHITE WAGTAIL, YELLOW WAGTAIL

Balance, Equilibrium

The white wagtail is one of the partial migrants or short-distance migrants. In the fall it flies to the Mediterranean and North Africa. In March it returns. It is widespread and follows people to their towns and villages. The gray wagtail prefers to live near water, although its life is not directly connected to the water. The white wagtail often builds its nest in odd places, happily using niches and corners in human houses and vehicles. It reacts to disturbances bravely, almost aggressively. It lives mainly on insects and small amphipods.

The white wagtail is closely related to the yellow wagtail, the latter distinguishing itself by the yellow plumage on its belly. The constant wagging movement of the long, elegant tail is noticeable in both species. Both birds have a very similar significance, but the yellow wagtail relates much more to emotions than to action.

Message

The white wagtail reminds us that the task of our human existence is to create equilibrium between the soul's wisdom and human action. In our world of thought and feelings, the impulses of the soul long for expression. It is not enough only to know things; it is also not enough to talk about them. Only action in life connects the soul to the acting person.

Only this makes the person into a channel for his soul's great wisdom. Our human essence becomes a vessel into which our soul's wisdom can flow. Here, this psychic wisdom should be used in real life in accordance with the human perceptions that are already possible. In the plumage of the white wagtail, pure black and pure white are connected by a silver gray. The physical and spiritual worlds are also connected in precisely this way. Neither black nor white is stipulated, rather the equal mixture of these two colors.

If the white wagtail has made itself known to you, it is telling you to examine the equilibrium between your inner wisdom and your outward experiences. Perhaps there are fears that currently live in your consciousness and that you would like to eliminate because your inner voice tells of an easy, light world. Take the warnings of your fears seriously, but not so seriously that your longing for the world of the soul's voice is suppressed. Fear carries experiences within itself: it urges caution, alertness, and clear thought and action. The soul's voice indicates the way that you should cautiously and alertly follow. That is the balance that you need to achieve, between external human existence and the soul. The balance makes you able to learn and grow joyously and happily.

Both of these are very important: hearing the inner voice of the soul's dream, and also perceiving reality with its structures and dangers. Thus the spiritual and the physical are together in a partnership, an equal relationship, in which they both serve the development of a higher equilibrium.

WOODPECKER

Security

Who doesn't love to see these colorful master carpenters? Their pecking grabs the attention of the naturalist. The woodpecker has fascinated humans since time immemorial. Most commonly we encounter the European green woodpecker and the great spotted woodpecker. The former is one of the ground woodpeckers. It finds most of its food in the ground, where it digs holes in ant mounds up to three feet deep to get to its main dish: ants and their larvae.

The green woodpecker couple, like their relative the great spotted woodpecker, carve out their nesting room about ten feet above the ground in softwood trunks. The entrance to the nest hole is quite small. Inside the tree trunk, however, there is a pumpkin-size hole, lined with wood shavings. The great spotted woodpecker has a large repertoire of vocalizations, but it is not a singer. Its music is percussion. The woodpecker pecks not only when building its nest hole and looking for beetles and larvae in tree bark but also simply for fun. As a drum it uses not only tree trunks but also thin branches, house roofs, sheet metal, and so forth. It flies in a wave pattern that, just like its pecking, is reminiscent of a heartbeat. In the spring, when the sap rises up into the tree trunks, the great spotted woodpecker pecks at the bark around the trunk in a spiral form in order to drink the sap that comes out. Its Latin name, Picus, comes from a deity who refused to marry Circe in order to avoid having the sun god as his father-in-law. In revenge, she turned him into a woodpecker.

Message

Whether the woodpecker has flown across your path, pecked at your consciousness, or been observed by you engaged in some other activity, its message is of security, nesting, warmth, love, and also feminine powers. Consider how secure you feel in your current situation and how loved, supported, and protected you are in your life and your surroundings. Consider how warm and loving your feelings for yourself are. If the woodpecker is visible to you, the applicability to yourself is even clearer. There is a difference depending on whether you encounter a green woodpecker (i.e., a ground woodpecker), a black woodpecker, or a great spotted woodpecker.

The ground woodpecker (green woodpecker) tells you to create security through love and endurance before you implement your plans externally. It is possible that at the moment you are anticipating great changes; now the green woodpecker is asking you whether you have a good starting point for those changes. First, make your home into a place of comfortable security. It is important to make yourself a warm nest, a place where you can soak up the love of Mother Earth, where you can commune in quiet with your innermost consciousness.

It is also recommended to spend time with lovers and people you can rely on, and to spend time in an environment where you can be entirely sure of yourself without having to behave in a certain way or fulfill expectations. Think about whether your external plans are in line with your current domestic and interpersonal situation. If you need people around you in order to feel secure, then in order to survive an upheaval you may be better off living in a city than on a mountain.

Or are you a nature lover, finding answers in solitude, only letting a small handful of people close to you? Would it then be better for you to build your nest in the country? Build your base camp first, before the upheaval begins. It doesn't have to happen right away. Thus, the green woodpecker strongly represents the quality of patience. It lives mainly on ants, the messengers of patience. The woodpecker also tells you, with its appearance, that patience will be worthwhile for you. This bird draws its power of security from constant patience, which is what it advises you to exercise in your current situation.

All woodpeckers carry the symbol of the nest, the warm, motherly love and security of Mother Earth. The black woodpecker especially encourages you to plumb the depths and imagine how you were carried as an unborn child in your mother's belly, surrounded by comforting warmth and security. Listen, in this harmonic silence, for the rhythmic sound of the mother's heartbeat. With this security, you can go about your life. You need love! Warming, healing, comforting love. Perhaps you have built a comfortable nest for all your loved ones. Did you consider that it is you, above all, who deserve such a thing? Let your heart beat for yourself one again.

You are responsible for your own happiness and for making sure you feel secure. Regardless of what relationships you have in your life at this time, it is possible to feel—and consequently find—love, warmth, and security. The great Mother Earth has made a place for each of her children in which every one of us can find the security we need.

The great spotted woodpecker shows you exactly where you can find your emotional security. It builds its nest in the trunk of a tree. If the tree is considered a symbol for the flow of human energy, then the heart is in the trunk. This is where you should build your nest. When you have your own nest in your heart, then you will also have the power to let someone leave that nest to build a nest of his or her own. Consider who in your life is looking for a nest, and consider how you feel about them. Under no circumstances may anyone force you to give up your place.

This means that you are as you are, and anyone who feels comfortable with that can feel secure around you. Do not let yourself be instilled with the idea that others should offer you security. Someone who does not feel well in his heart, as it were, is in the wrong place. The woodpecker, with its appearance, is advising you to dive back entirely into the flow of your own heart's energy, accept the way you are, and radiate it out. You will discover that this makes you entirely independent and free. Your love, your security, and your nest all lie in your own strength.

WREN

Wishes

At just under four inches long, the wren is one of the smallest birds. Its small tail contributes to its diminutive size. It has the ideal body shape and size for hunting in the undergrowth for insects and spiders. Agile and flexible, it hunts them in the tightest corners. Because it can hide itself well, it leads a secretive life. Its actions are emphasized by loud calls, and it demarcates its territory from the highest tree branches.

The male wren is an ideal husband, letting his bride choose from multiple nests he has built. He also helps assiduously with the raising of the chicks, and in a good year a wren couple can raise several broods. In this case the male takes care of the older chicks independently while the female cares for the new brood. An experienced male wren can even charm multiple females and provide for the needs of multiple families.

Message

In animal symbolism the wren stands for everyday wishes. It tells you not to get lost in grand visions but to take care of your small needs and those of people close to you.

It is not enough to shoo away the small everyday wishes like irritating flies, or impatiently quell them in order to get quickly back to the big thoughts. Consider that most of your life consists of the everyday. Someone who fulfills the smallest wishes, or at least views them as important and worthy, will find herself imperceptibly on the way to the fulfillment of the grand visions.

Primarily, this is not a matter of your wishes but of taking loving care of your fellow humans. Fulfilling the small wishes means expanding true life. Friendship, love, and relationships become the strength that lies behind every great expression of life. The cosmic law, that the small is in the large and the large is in the small, is affirmed in a wondrous fashion.

PART 3

Reptiles, Fish, Amphibians

CARP

Originality

Carp are originally from Asia and were brought to Europe by the Romans. Here, at first, they were mainly cultivated in monasteries to provide food for monks. Today there are numerous breeds of carp, and they are present in almost all fresh waters. Carp are a popular food, supporting a whole branch of industry. They eat insect larvae, worms, snails, and tadpoles. Various fish belong to the Carp family. The koi, a colorful breed from Japan, is a variety of the common carp. During mating and spawning season, carp are adapted to relatively high temperatures. Their numbers multiply naturally near the edges of ponds, small lakes, and gently flowing rivers with temperatures between 64 and 68 degrees Fahrenheit. When mating, the male and female go at it until they are both exhausted. The male motivates the female to deposit her eggs by bumping her sides with his jaw. The female deposits about a million eggs, which are fertilized by the milt that the male releases into the water. After about a week the young fish hatch from the eggs. The carp is a calm, unhurried fish that explores its habitat with great deliberateness. An observer can sometimes see the carp's bent back rising above the surface of the water.

Message

If a carp appears before you, it is time to remember your innermost emotional values. Calm down and dive in. Behind all the events that make up your everyday life, there is an entirely normal, natural being, something inherently good, removed from all duties, strategies, purposes, and dependencies. This being is simply you, as a natural part of this world. This being is the basis for all your experiences and possibilities. It is the foundation upon which your external life is built, even when this external life appears to be very far from its origin. The carp tells you to devote a little extra time to this foundation of your being: "Back to the roots," as people sometimes say. This is best done in the quiet of natural surroundings, where most people loved to be during childhood. Perhaps then you snuck away with a book, or just ran aimlessly through the woods. Perhaps you were drawn to colorful gardens or cozy barns where you could find peace and quiet, or else attics full of junk. Wherever it was, it is part of the experience that your inner self needs in order to feel right. The carp has come into your consciousness in a moment when it is important for you to connect to this original state so that you may mobilize all your energy for the things that are important now in your life's narrative.

CRAYFISH
Thought Hygiene

The crayfish, or crawdad, is found all over Europe. In the past many of them could be found in slowly flowing rivers, brooks, lakes, ponds, and ditches. They require good water quality, and they live in hollows beneath the water. In the Middle Ages, crayfish were served at bishops' tables at fasting time and were very popular as a novelty in the diet. In the late nineteenth century a fungal disease practically exterminated them. Since then, they are rare. Surviving populations are found in isolated waters to which the crayfish plague has not spread. Out of economic necessity, as early as 1890, American crayfish—recognizable

by the red stripes on their abdomens—were imported to Berlin. The American crayfish is immune to the plague and can also live in polluted waters. Today the American crayfish lives all over Europe and has become a permanent part of our animal world. Crayfish are nocturnal, and they eat all the small animals they can catch, as well as carrion and plants. Crayfish hatch from eggs without going through a larval stage. After hatching, the front part of the body is still full of yolk. The young crayfish hold on tight to their mother until these supplies are consumed. Then they begin an independent life, which can last as long as twenty years.

Message

If you have encountered a crayfish, it is time for you to consider your social graces more carefully. However, do not begin right away with your environment. First, look at the inner atmosphere you have created for yourself. Is it possible that you are poisoning yourself with self-criticism, envy, spite, discontentment, or some similar negative feeling? How often do you catch your thoughts slipping into that same old negative pattern, singing the same sad song? The crayfish urges you to stop this, to pause and clarify your feelings and thoughts. How often we spoil the moment by poisoning ourselves with worries and dreadful ideas! This self-poisoning is not part of your personal history. It is like a traditional current into which one is pulled. An encounter with the European crayfish, above all, bears the message that you should be very conscious of these things and remain in clear water. Search in a disciplined manner for light, joyful feelings; seek inner clarity and outer peace; and avoid negative information, negative people, and stressful situations. Quietly become somewhat demure and sensitive. The American crayfish tells you to practice thought hygiene and always consciously separate yourself from those negative, self-critical thoughts and feelings that correspond to the current trend. For example, do not keep on making yourself sick with thoughts like "I am fat, I am ugly, I am dumb." Also, comparisons with so-called ideals are destructive, as is the criticism of your own hard work or self-expression. It makes no sense for a woman to put dinner on the table then immediately say that she cannot cook very well and it is only something simple; nor for a man to exert himself in a sport then immediately remark that he is not in top form. With such self-deprecation, one hurts oneself and allows others to assist in dealing the blows.

EEL

Legacy for the World

The eel is one of the bony fishes. The freshwater eel, native to Europe, can grow to more than three feet long, and resembles a snake in its form and movement. The European eel was once very common in our rivers. This thick-skinned, fatty fish is a popular food in many places. Eels eat small water animals such as crabs, worms, snails, and also fish spawn. For breeding, eels swim from inland waters out to the sea—to be exact, the Sargasso Sea in the Atlantic near the Bahamas. Practically all American and European eels spawn there. After hatching, the young eels go through four developmental stages. The first, the larval stage—known as the leptocephalus—lasts about three years. In this stage the young eels resemble in size and form a transparent willow leaf with a fish head in place of the stem. The Gulf Stream carries these plankton-eating larvae into the North Atlantic. They then develop into so-called glass eels. In this stage they are about three inches long and transparent, but otherwise have the appearance of an adult eel. In the spring, glass eels gather in large swarms around the mouths of rivers and begin to swim upstream to where they will live as mature eels. They grow steadily and gradually take on a yellow coloring. The females are sexually mature at twelve to fifteen years, the males at six to nine years. At this point, on their way back to their spawning grounds in the Sargasso Sea, the eels once again change drastically. The yellow belly becomes silver, the eyes grow larger, and the digestive tract diminishes. From now until the end of life, the eels no longer eat. They swim through the open sea to their spawning grounds and die after depositing fertilized eggs.

The electric eel, known for its ability to give electric shocks, lives in American waters. In Europe it is only seen in aquariums and a few zoos.

Message

In Europe you will encounter the eel in only three of its four developmental stages. However, unless you are a fisherman, it is unlikely that you will encounter an eel at all. The eel reminds us of our obligation to the world. As humans we also go through four important developmental stages. There is the time before and after life, which we call death. It corresponds to the larval stage. It is light, subtle, and takes place in another world. Next is the stage of childhood, corresponding to the glass eel. This is the time during which people slowly move from the afterlife into this life. At first, much of the light world is in us and with us, and only with years of experience do we begin to take on the earthly colors with which our life's narrative paints us. Then is the time of the adult person. He lives, gathers experiences, and grows from them. He is hardly ever really creative during this time. He is a part of his environment and contributes to the development of his environment by living and learning. He gathers energy, and unconsciously, all his life, he collects everything that will make his final great journey possible. In the last stage, that of dying, his external form changes again. He makes ready for the transition from the physically real world into the astral world, the world of pure perception. He opens his other eyes, again becomes a creature the color of moonlight that can have no more influence on life's events, and he follows his inner guidance through the astral world to the origin of his being. This is his goal; he is not drifting aimlessly in all the sea's currents, in all the possibilities of perception. No, he is traveling the great distance back to the origin. The eel returns to his birthplace and the human returns to the source of his being, where he gives back into the great consciousness everything he has experienced, learned, and known. Here, he fertilizes humanity, so to speak, with the light and love that he has generated during his life, passes on his true spiritual legacy, and then returns into the eternal light of the divine being.

The encounter with the eel is about precisely this legacy for humanity. You live your life for yourself. You learn for yourself, collect experiences for yourself, and change and grow as a result. But at some point, at the end of life, you must relinquish the world, humanity, your family, and your spiritual legacy. This is when you really contribute to the development of humanity and the world; what you have left behind will contain true results for the great whole. Thus, if you encounter an eel, remember that you can do more for humanity and the legacy that you are to leave behind. What counts is not what you achieve externally, nor what you do with others, but how much light, love, and joy you have had in yourself. If humans in the future are to become light-filled, joyous children of the Earth, our legacy in this world must change substantially.

FROG

Purification

Frogs are amphibians. They spend the first part of their lives as tadpoles, entirely in the water. Gradually their bodies metamorphose, making life on land possible. Every year, for nature's rebirth, frogs return to their place of origin. For this they travel enormous distances, often costing them their lives. They announce love with loud croaking. All their activities are adapted to the weather.

Because their skin is adapted for high humidity, frogs are found most often in the evenings, mornings, and when the air is very moist. Thus frogs were long viewed as weather predictors. It was also said that they had the ability to call up rain. When it rains they leave their hideouts in the ground or water and go hunting for worms, small snails, and insects.

Message

If a frog hops across your path it is reminding you of your world of Water. Our inner nature corresponds to the outer nature. Water is the world of feelings. Just like the frog, human feelings are very dependent on water and are influenced by the rhythms of weather. Who has not known cold and warm, stormy and mild feelings? The frog is not only reminding us of our feelings and drawing our attention to our inner moods; it also wants to teach us to blend with the powers of the weather.

For us, the rhythm between the elements is just as important as it is for nature. Our perceptions are the rain that purifies and waters our inner nature. On its journey through the world, water purifies the atmosphere, absorbs dust and dirt, and gathers in the oceans. Some of this water rises up from there, drawn by the sun, and it clarifies the atmosphere and absorbs light. Blown by the wind, the water gathers into clouds, which block the view of the sun. Then it falls to Earth in the form of raindrops, percolating down and leaving behind dust and dirt.

In a clear, pure spring, the water returns to the surface. When it goes back into the Earth it brings life and growth with it. There are many places on the planet where it only rains about once a year. In these places, the whole cycle of growth, life, and death must take place in a short amount of time, racing to stay ahead of the burning sun. In other places sensations are rigid and frozen when they fall to Earth. In order for growth to occur here, the living power of the sun is needed. Here also, life completes its natural cycle in only a short amount of time. The icy wind will soon freeze sensation once again. Thus, there are many different natural realms within our being, and all is ruled by the interplay between water, wind, and sun.

To understand the frog's message it is important to observe the time at which the frog was encountered. Note what things were lacking in nature at the time of the encounter. If the Earth is dry, the frog is speaking to those feelings in you that have been dried up through excessive heat—for example, activity. A frog in the spring, after the snow melts, tells you to rediscover your joy in life and thus give life new possibilities to sprout forth and bloom. With loving sun rays, thaw away your covering of ice. Winter often forces us to retreat into our houses and cease to take part in pulsating life. This resting period for the feelings is a good thing, because it gives us time for inner reflection and gives us the possibility to find harmony and peace.

However, harmony and peace are not life. Be aware of the conditions of your current life and try to identify the areas of feelings to which the frog speaks. Then follow the natural cycle of the water. Let your feelings flow in the way they currently are. Project the essential aspects from there in to the light, let the wind (creativity) bring you thoughts and ideas, and allow yourself to have an emotional downpour. This process will cleanse your body of feelings. You will depart from your frog perspective, and life-giving clarity will fill your world of thoughts.

Warming light will find its way to your soul, and many things will be good again. The message of the frog does not tell you to do anything but rather encourages you to recognize the natural flow and follow it without questioning. Thus your being will return more and more to its origin and create new life.

LIZARD
Dreams, Ideas

Lizards are most often encountered on warm sunny days on walls in meadows and gardens. They love to lie motionless in the sun, appearing to dream. When approached they vanish in a flash into the nearby shadows. The lizard is an animal that does not make any future plans. Resting, it soaks up the sun, staying limber and well rested in preparation for the strain of possible flight.

The lizard chooses its nighttime hiding places so it can evade nocturnal predators via a perpendicular wall or an alternate exit. Even while hunting, the lizard is always wisely cautious. It is a master at using its capabilities to its best advantage.

Message

If you encounter a lizard, it is most important to observe what the lizard is doing. Is it hunting, running away, lying in the sun, or in its hiding place? Its message always relates to the dreams and plans that are current and going through your head or touching your feelings at the moment of the encounter. It relates to that exact moment.

In your plans and dreams, wise caution is recommended, because you have not yet dreamed your dream to the end. The lizard appears as an adviser. It leads you with its message through the dream in its realization.

If you saw the lizard lying in the sun, it is a sign that you still need to think about the domain of material power and flexibility. Are you well enough prepared for the realization of your dream? Think back to the first steps, that first moment that gave your dream its desired form. Perhaps the lizard resting in the sun is also advising you not to give the vision such a material and visual aspect but to concentrate on the feelings behind it. Plan your personal life, but leave the planning of the form that will go with it in the material realm to fate.

If the lizard is hunting for prey when it slinks through your field of vision, then it could be an indication that you should leave more things up to your intuition in the realization of your dream; in other words, listen to your inner voice in order to use your capabilities properly and precisely at the right moment. Take your main focus somewhat away from the goal and turn it to your inner voice. The hunting lizard could be telling you that you give too much weight to your dream images. Consider that dreams and wishes are only a motor for propelling development. Inner images offer the possibility of preparing our narrow point of view for reality by means of examples.

If you saw a lizard running away, it is probably a sign that you should observe your dreams more objectively, with more distance. Ask yourself whether you are running away from your own problems through the realization of these dreams. Consider that the difficulties you have in your life are an expression of yourself. No problems can be solved by changing the external structures of life; at best, the problems are given a new field for expression. In addition, the fleeing lizard—especially if it is being chased by a predator—can indicate that you are being steered by foreign dreams. Carefully consider whether your wishes and visions are really your own.

Or perhaps you discovered the lizard in its hiding place. The message of this encounter could be that you should keep your dreams for yourself above all others. Whittle at them and play with them. Time will tell you when this dream is ripe for decision, if it is still there at all.

PIKE

Coming to Terms with the Past

The pike lives in clear, standing, or gently flowing bodies of water with plenty of vegetation. This noble predatory fish grows up to three feet long and can weigh up to eighty pounds. Its jaw, resembling a duck's bill, has razor-sharp teeth. Its eyes are large and its vision excellent. Its torpedo-shaped body is extremely strong. The pike is a dedicated hunter, pursuing its prey with great vigor, strength, endurance, and extraordinary agility for its size. If a small fish hides from it between loose stones, the pike will ram the blockade with its head. When the pike has prey in its view, it is a merciless hunter. Its aggressiveness sometimes puts it in danger. When launching an attack between stones on the riverbank it can sometimes get its head stuck. The voracity with which it snaps after its prey can also lead to the pike's doom if the prey happens to be a lure on a fish hook. Pikes, in their habitat, attack everything that moves. They even eat fish up to 70 percent of their own body weight. Even young ducks, frogs, mice, and rats are not safe if they come within reach of the pike. They do not even stop at eating their own kind. Therefore, a great number of young pikes fall prey to their own family members.

Message

The pike comes in to your life as, so to speak, an antagonist. This antagonist wants to show you areas in your life that urgently need your attention. In the endlessly wide waters of our feelings, events accumulate, along with the experiences and impressions they carry. Our personalities are built upon this. Most of the time one should concentrate on the emotions and events of the present and shape this present with care and attention. The pike has come into your life in order to lead you for a short time out of the present into the gray past. It is important to attend to the pain of an old wound, an unhealed injury. Perhaps you want to look back on something in the past that is sure to catch up to you. But perhaps it is also necessary to remove a past pattern through a change in your life. In this case it is not enough simply to look on in wonder. Fate is now forcing you to attack the problem mercilessly, with great endurance and dedication. These old wounds in nature can be excellent at hiding themselves from our consciousness. And so, if you encounter the pike and hear its message, it can be hard to find what it means. Be like the pike yourself: go attentively through the length of all your feelings. Analyze every feeling that cannot hide from this attentiveness. Question it and seek out its true origin and purpose. For example, consider whether and how you attack your own positivity and sensitivity. Consider whether you fail to notice repressed things, or lie to yourself about them. If this work seems hard, do not hesitate to get professional help. If you catch a pike while fishing, then it is likely that a long-lasting antagonism in you is now finally beginning to resolve itself.

SALAMANDER, NEWT

Elementary Powers from the Past

Fire salamander: Fire
Alpine salamander: Earth
Alpine newt, smooth newt: Water
Northern crested newt: Air

Eons ago, dragons lived upon Earth. Dragons were the living agents of the four elements. Untamed, they lived with the energy of those elements, and thereby set free energies for growth and the transformation of the realms of nature. As the Earth grew more compact, the Creator told the dragons to hide themselves, then to retreat slowly into the ethereal world. Time passed, and the realms of nature evolved and expanded. Yet, for a long time the dragons lived in their hideaways and ruled their kingdom.

Humans spread out and rooted these strong but shy beasts out of their hiding places. In their ignorance, they feared the massive animals and began to kill them. The dragons retreated to the astral ring around the Earth so that they might continue to discern their task for the planet.

The fire salamander is a member of the Salamander family and also a member of the family of true newts. They have naked skin with striking yellow spots. Because they have no tough outer layer on their skin they can breathe through their skin, both in water and in the air. This restricts their lives to moist, shadowy, hidden places. In spring they deposit up to seventy larvae in the shallow water of a stream, which, like tadpoles, go through an initial developmental stage before they take on the appearance of their parents. Amphibians are cold-blooded. Their body temperature fluctuates with the external temperature. At low temperatures they reduce their activity and go into winter dormancy.

Salamanders eat snails, earthworms, and insects. The fire salamander lives in thickly wooded, hilly landscapes with plenty of water. The alpine salamander is distinguished from the fire salamander by its smaller size and its black skin color. In addition, the female gives birth each year to two full-developed young. As the name suggests, it lives in the Alps.

Newts are adapted to the water, where they reproduce. In summer they leave the ponds and live, like salamanders, hidden on land.

Message

If you come upon a salamander or newt, it wants to remind you of your true, elementary primal strength. Primal strength is like a dragon. It is aggressive, wild, and deadly unless it is transformed multiple times before it comes into contact with life. Something in your life is now in the process of influencing your development in a wholly elementary fashion. Do not be afraid, it is not anything threatening. It is exactly what should happen. We encounter "dragons" when a very important destiny in our life's plan is playing out, when something friendly and elementary is taking place.

Do not puzzle over what exactly it is. It is not possible for our human consciousness to distinguish what is truly important from what is secondary. But sometimes, even when we have no idea of the great interconnected energy events around us, it is important to give in, have trust, and let things happen. What happens in this moment comes from a deep past in your soul that can no longer be manifested and flips a switch in your life with a small, probably unnoticeable signal.

Somehow or other, it is a correction, sending you in the right direction. Try to be motivated, through the encounter with the salamander or newt, simply to assume an inner positive attitude toward yourself and your life, only for today, only for the moment. That is all you need to do in order for what must be and will be to find good, positive ground on which to grow.

SALMON

Completion

The life of the salmon takes place in a closed cycle. It swims from its birthplace to the sea, where it learns and grows to full maturity. After years pass, near the end of its life, the salmon takes a long, hard journey to the place of its birth. Here it mates, spawns, and then dies.

The salmon is born in freshwater, spends its "childhood" en route to the sea, gathers experience and wisdom in the wide ocean, and ends its life at its birthplace, in freshwater once again. Shortly before completion, when all the trials of the return to the source have been passed, it becomes the creator of the new generation.

Message

The salmon reminds you that you are on a journey from the source of life, through learning and experience, back to the origin. This journey is your life. The meaning of life lies in your own process of maturation. The salmon lives in the element Water, and for humans, this element stands for the world of feelings and thoughts. Only in this realm can humans achieve maturity. We like to build monuments in life, especially in the material world (the element Earth); we want our deeds and actions to go down in human history; and we like to talk as if we are contributing something to the betterment of others.

These are the traps of the ego world. The salmon urges us to think only of our own growth, openly and heedfully, through constant learning. You are not the teacher of others; the environment of your life, with all the beings that are part of it, teaches you. Perhaps you met the salmon by chance, perhaps you sought it out. People usually encounter salmon on their journey back to the source, a moment at which their message is clearly emphasized. Maturity should be the foundation for the creation of posterity, not power or ability. Forget about leaving posterity a monument to yourself. If you really contribute something to humanity that is recognizable in society, your name will not be forgotten. Focus on the trials and learning steps that life requires of you. Dedicate all your energy, your knowledge, and your ability to being a complete, radiant person.

SLOWWORM

Deceit

The slowworm is a member of the Lizard family. It is legless and moves like a snake. Like the lizard, when faced with danger it can discard its tail, which grows back over time. Slowworms are widespread in areas that are bright but not too dry.

They lead a solitary life. Their diet consists of earthworms and slugs. In midsummer the slowworm gives birth to up to twenty-five young. In winter they gather in frost-free earth and holes in rocks, where they sometimes spend the winter in dormancy along with snakes and amphibians.

Message

If a slowworm slithers across your path, it is making you aware of deceptive feelings, thoughts, or life conditions. Like the lizard, the slowworm comes from the world of dreams. It has burrowed through your dream world and has happened upon dreams from which wishes arise. The slowworm is not telling you to let your dreams go but rather to dream your dreams on to the end, then compare them to the reality of your life.

Slowworms prefer to live in places that resemble a healthy world, where the four elements come together in harmonic composition. Such places are wonderful and very creative, but also often hinder one from recognizing and correcting disharmonies in real, everyday life. If you have created such a harmonious living space, you will encounter these animals again and again as a warning, urging you to test the truth of this harmony. Even if things feel harmonious, have the courage to keep on letting changes and corrections into your life.

Consider the natural, true harmony required by constant growth. It slumbers softly in the equilibrium of the elements, and disharmonies appear trivial for a long time. But at some point, you will wake up from the nice dream, and it will take a lot of energy and strength to restore harmony in the outside world. Therefore, if a slowworm has established itself in your personal living space, it is telling you always to be aware of external reality and always look for clarity. Then the harmony can expand almost infinitely, and the power of your dreams can influence the external world in a magical way.

If you encounter a slowworm outside of your own living space, then your thoughts and feelings at the moment seem to be flying deceptively high (see the Lizard entry on p. 206). Be realistic, and create the conditions for your dream in the real world first.

SNAIL, SLUG
Pattern

Snails prefer moist, calcium-rich soils with plenty of vegetation, where they can find food and shelter. The Roman snail is Europe's largest native snail, growing up to 1½ inches in diameter. Like most land snails, it is a hermaphrodite. To lay eggs, the snail digs a pit, which is then covered over. A few days later, the young snails hatch, already wearing shells with 1½ whorls.

The Roman snail has a large, round, light-brown shell. As with all snails, its body is divided into the head, foot, and a visceral sac that contains the internal organs and is protected by the shell. Snails have

four tentacles, two of which have eyes at the tips. As a plant eater, the Roman snail can have an enormous appetite, and in large numbers they can be pests. To hibernate the snail seals itself into its shell with its operculum to retain moisture and protect itself from predators. Snails move upon a layer of mucus that they exude. This serves as a lubricant between the snail and the surface beneath and significantly reduces abrasion.

Message

The snail and slug symbolize those domains in our energy field that are clogging up the harmonious flow. They also represent restrictions in general. Hardly anyone goes through life without encountering a snail. The snail does not show us an unknown pattern that we urgently need to work through but rather tells us to follow the path of a decision, carefully and precisely.

Speed is not the strength of the snail or slug. Likewise, our old ego patterns are almost immortal. The encounter with the snail may not be spectacular, and it often fails to catch the eye. But people who spend time in nature will encounter snails very often. They tell us of everyday problems and advise us to keep our patterns in mind while on our way to solving these problems. If you are under pressure to make a decision, give it time. Consider your situation thoroughly, keeping in mind all your possibilities. Do not expect a miracle, and do not expect that you will grow out of yourself. Even if our unresolved energy fields look ugly to us, they are still there and they merit consideration.

Any gardener will know the problem with this medicine. Rigorous methods are needed to silence these patterns and make it possible for the desired plants—that is, emotions—to grow. You can block out slugs and snails, poison them, crush them, or otherwise kill them, but they will always be there. This does not mean you should give up and not sow any more seeds. Wage the battle of life, but do so in a way that corresponds to your realistic possibilities, and build upon the success of experiences. Children love snails. Your soul knows that these little creatures symbolize your right to be as human as possible.

Snails

Snails, with their spiral shells, indicate particularly that the evolution of the spirit lies in the repetition of everyday problems.

Someone who keeps his distance from his everyday difficulties and allows his patterns to evolve is giving his spirit the possibility of gaining the experiences and knowledge that are necessary for development, without inviting pain in the greater existential sense. Thus, the snail that appears to you is saying that your established patterns should be respected. Be patient with your human nature. Consider whether you may have counted on some small miracle happening just for your own convenience. It could cost you dearly, and you will overstrain yourself for nothing.

Slugs

If a slug creeps across your path it is signaling to you that you are giving a great deal of space to your patterns for the sake of convenience and slowly destroying the goals you have achieved. Clandestine and silent, the slug devours young plants that have only just come to light. New knowledge and experience need your time to become effective in your life. Nurture these unprotected domains by keeping the old patterns at bay.

It is easy to rest on the first laurels you receive, but true development requires greater persistence, and the first decision is seldom right for all time. Only when your new knowledge has grown into a large, mature plant will you no longer need protection from slugs and snails. Then you can devote yourself to other tasks, namely new young plants. Someone who is faced with a long-term plague of slugs or snails should perhaps reduce the demands he makes on himself and enjoy existence with a bit more respect for the natural laws of development.

SNAKE

Metamorphosis

Snakes are reptiles. Their bodies are smooth, without limbs. They hatch from eggs, which are incubated by the sun. A few snake species incubate the eggs internally, then give birth to live young. The outermost layer of a snake's skin consists of scales. The scales on the underside can grip surfaces, facilitating movement. Lateral undulation, however, provides the main force of movement. Snakes can move forward effortlessly and astonishingly fast. They are excellent swimmers and climbers.

Many European snakes also hunt in the water. They prey on fish, frogs, mice, rats, and also rob birds' nests. The prey is swallowed whole.

For this purpose, snakes have a specially adapted lower jaw. The joint between the two jawbones can be opened very wide by means of the quadrate bone. Snakes grow throughout their lives. Consequently, they must shed their skin on a regular basis. After molting they are very vulnerable for a short period of time. Most European snakes are not poisonous. Poisonous snakes have two long, hollow fangs in their mouths. Venom, produced in glands in the upper jaw, is injected into the prey through these fangs.

The venom disables the prey, allowing the snake to swallow it more easily. Poisonous snakes only bite humans when threatened by them. The bite of a poisonous European snake is seldom deadly. However, it should be treated immediately by a doctor with antivenom to avoid damage to the heart and nerves.

Message

Snakes are among the animals that many people find very disconcerting. This is due in part to fear of the bite of a poisonous snake and also, probably in greater part, to the snake's message to our subconscious. The snake is the symbol of life, death and rebirth. Someone who encounters a snake is encountering death but also, at the same time, the eternalness of life, eternal growth and learning, and eternal change. The snake is the symbol of sexual power. Sexuality, the life-giving power, also ushers in the cycle of death. Since ancient times the snake has been worshipped and feared.

The deadly bite of the poisonous snake reminds one of death-bringing life. Everything that awakens to life is destined to die. The snake has slithered into your consciousness to advise you to let something die. Accept that life changes, that things must die, that situations grow too tight and must be shed to allow for your own growth. Do you have the courage to die now, in this moment? Do you have the courage once you become aware that in your next incarnation, by your twenty-first birthday, you will have again reached the same exact level of physical, spiritual, and psychic development at which you are now? Dying is only the shedding of a skin that has become too tight. The snake's skin symbolizes our life history.

The inner being keeps on going, eternally. But it does not change through death; it only changes through life. If you consider your life carefully now, where you currently stand, would you wish to transfer this state of things to a new life, would you like to build a whole new life upon the present moment? The snake may have especially scared you if you were unconsciously thinking that a great many things would be good to change. It is the messenger of death, and in this moment you must find out whether you can cross the barrier at which you now stand. Live in such a way that the snake's visit will not frighten you.

To live life in such a way that one is ready to die is an art generated from wisdom and godliness. If you are bitten by a snake, it means that the changes that are now taking place are no longer in harmony with your own being.

TOAD
Femininity, Healer

Toads live in damp areas. They are active at night, hunting snails and spiders. By day, they hide in holes in the ground, under stones and logs. Their backs are covered with wartlike bumps, which can exude a poisonous slime when necessary.

In spawning season they seek out puddles and ponds where they attach strings of eggs up to fifteen feet long onto water plants. The male midwife toad carries the string of eggs wrapped around his back legs until the tadpoles hatch, when he brings them into the water. Toads' bodies are tougher and more ungainly than those of frogs, and the back legs are less developed. Therefore, these amphibians move more slowly.

The toad has long been considered a symbol of femininity and the birth mother. Midwives and healers had a close relationship with these animals, often encountering them while searching for healing herbs. These women herbalists often worked near bodies of water and isolated swamps and had an extraordinary knowledge of these areas that were otherwise avoided. The paths that these witches used to travel through the swamps were known as toad paths, and the women could often elude their pursuers via these paths.

Message

When you encountered the toad, did you feel a light shiver going down your back? The toad wants to remind you of your hidden, perhaps somewhat execrated, sides of your femininity. Whether man or woman, every individual has feminine and masculine sides. The damp, highly intimate feminine domains often make us afraid of ourselves. Ponderous, dark, swampy, slimy, all these are attributes of the feminine medium—places where new things can find the right climate for growth. The toad meets you when you are consciously or unconsciously trying to deny or get rid of this secret domain that is so important for your growth. The deep feminine climate is also the inner place where healing power can become effective.

There are many healing practices, and they all have their validity. But like everything else in this polar world, the active side must work with the passive side to bear fruit. The art of healers and doctors expresses a male principle. The sick person must be fertile to the impulses of the healer. Only when you can open the deep, damp, slimy swamp of your soul will the healing impulse be able to reach you. The healing must find access at the same place where the sickness fertilized you. Whether you are sick or healthy, never shut yourself off from the deep domains of the feminine world. If you notice that the apparently ugly toad is looking at you with radiant golden eyes, you will perhaps get an idea of the beauty of this feminine plane.

It is not especially important which species of toad you encountered; what is important above all is that you recognize the wonder of fertility behind the apparent ugliness.

TROUT
Letting Go

The trout is a freshwater fish that lives in clean, flowing rivers and lakes. It shares common ancestors with the salmon. The best-known trout are the brown trout, brook trout, and rainbow trout. The native brown trout is especially delicious, smaller and thinner than the rainbow trout, which was introduced to Europe from California in 1882. The brown trout has an olive-colored back, the belly is light yellow to light gray, and the sides are mostly speckled with black and red spots. It lives mainly on insects, larvae, and young fish. In the eighteenth century the poet Christian Friedrich Daniel Schubart dedicated a poem to this speedy, shiny fish, which was set to music by Franz Schubert and became very well known as a song. It begins with the words *"In einem Bächlein helle"* ("In a bright little brook").

Message

Like all animals whose element of life is Water, the trout relates to the human body of feelings. The body of feelings, also called the astral body, is the place where the perception of human life takes place. Everything that comes into our consciousness—whether it be in the form of perception, ideas, contact, pain, or sensory perception of some sort—is transformed into images, feelings, thoughts, and experiences in the astral body. Like the hydrological cycle, the energies that flow though the astral body make a journey through all planes of the world of perception. Still new and undefined, the impulses rise to the surface of consciousness (the spring), where they follow the way through the patterns and dogma of people (stream- and riverbeds) out to the great whole (the ocean).

Through this network of the water cycle, through countless individual repetitions of the cycle, the whole planet is supplied with water. Together with light, supported by Earth, life and growth are made possible. The various types of trout advise you to remember the principal river, or in other words, to pay attention to your behavior patterns and dogmas. Earnestly consider why things always repeat themselves in your life. Ask yourself in what ways your dogma is standing in the way of change. Perhaps you have a deep yearning for something new in your professional life, your relationship, or your whole life situation.

It is possible that the desired miracle will happen when you are ready to leave your streambed. Become an observer in your life—*only* in your own life. How do you react emotionally, which emotional scripts keep repeating, how or where does the behavior—that is, the feelings generated artificially by the head—begin to articulate an internal or external demand? Trout are fish that are adapted to fresh, clear water. Your feelings are clear and fresh when they make the natural cycle possible for you and when they are able to forgive and forget all wounds and pain without question.

Do not ask yourself, "What behavior should I cease so that I can change such-and-such a thing?" Let go of all recognizable behavior. This will lead your way to a happier life.

TURTLE, TORTOISE
Mother Earth

Turtles are reptiles, their broad bodies covered by tough, hornlike armor. The head, legs, and tail can also be hidden inside this armor. The turtle's shell consists of a back plate and belly plate connected to one another on the sides. Under the hornlike plate on the turtle's back are bony plates that grow from the vertebrae and ribs. This produces the characteristic shell pattern. Turtles eat plants, mollusks such as snails, worms, and amphibians. They bury their eggs in holes in the ground, where they are incubated by the sun.

Turtles live primarily in warm regions, but if well supported they can live in northern regions. Turtles live to be very old, with the larger species living past two hundred years. There are sea turtles, freshwater turtles, and land-dwelling tortoises. In Europe the most common is Hermann's tortoise. It is found in the wild in the Mediterranean region. In the spring, when they emerge from their winter hiding places, they need to spend a couple of days in the warm sun.

In various swamps, ponds, and parks in Europe, Pacific pond turtles have been released into the wild. Although perhaps well intended by people, this has been disadvantageous to the ecological equilibrium of these places.

Message

The turtle represents Mother Earth. Its shell suggests a hemisphere, and the structure upon the shell, a mountain. Its movements are leisurely and calm. If you encounter a turtle it is time for a turnaround in your life. This animal is old and wise, and it lives the Earth's harmony and feels its pulse. If it happens to enter your life it is advising you to loosen your protective shell, in which you may be hiding.

Perhaps on the outside you seem to be a person who is not harmed by anything and who deals easily and prudently with blows from fate. But this is only half of the sphere, and at least you should know that deep inside the other half lies wriggling on its back. It is an unhappy position and takes a great deal of exertion to get back on one's legs. The harmony of Mother Earth requires that the light-filled half must have a corresponding side of shadow. The stronger the outer shell, the weaker, softer, and more helpless are the inside defenses.

You must admit at least to yourself that you have been hurt and formulate good arguments—at least before yourself—to present to others. When you have learned to handle sadness, anger, and pain inside yourself, to admit to it, and to understand your own pain, then you will see that your environment goes along with you lovingly. In the love of others you will find the protection that you wanted to achieve with your shell.

However, the turtle, as the messenger of Mother Earth, is also the messenger of love. Love is the power that nourishes all the beings on this planet. It is this power that gives your life new direction and makes new creation possible—but slowly. Consider how deliberate the steps of the turtle are. Do not rush into anything, do not let yourself be misled into spiritual time warps, and, above all, keep solid ground under your feet. If the turtle has become a permanent part of your life, that also means that Mother Earth is calling you. Make contact with her, and like a loving child nestle against her healing love and learn from her how to keep in step with the sacred rhythm between body and soul. This rhythm is the secret of a very long, and very happy, life of wisdom.

PART 4

Insects, Invertebrates

ANT

Patience

It may seem strange that the diligent, hardworking ant stands for patience. Is there anyone who has not watched them, enchanted, as they go about their brisk work on their anthill? With no apparent system, thousands of agile workers hurry around, carrying twigs, pine needles, and pieces of grass hither and thither. They bring their prey through the entrance into their storage chambers, they scramble in and out, up and down; in short, a great, apparently uncoordinated activity is taking place.

The activity in an ant mound must be observed from a higher level in order to see the connection to patience. Each individual ant follows its instinct, thoroughly scans its surroundings on its way, and reacts to familiar impulses. The workers, which do the building, check every pine needle and scrap of wood to make sure they are useful and often carry these for long distances. Hunters and gatherers follow the scent of prey and edible plants with their fine senses and often bring these painstakingly over long distances back to the nest. The individual ant acts according to its inner programming and directs its work accordingly. Each individual ant serves the colony and the queen unquestioningly.

The ant city grows and grows, the population increases, and additions to the colony spring up thanks to the labor of the diligent workers. If we watch the progress of one worker bringing a pine needle to the colony, we will see that she immediately receives help. The needle is carried by many helpers until it is placed upon the anthill so that it is no longer in anyone's way. Because each individual ant performs its work in the colony so diligently, there is a logical cycle of activity. The ants appear not to be hampered by any vision of a completed work.

The building and maintenance of the colony is the highest goal for every citizen. Because the ants are so hardworking, the whole anthill can change structure entirely, adapting to the growing population. If one wanted to wait for the building to be complete, this would be very taxing on one's patience, because it will never be complete. Even when small changes occur, the ants react spontaneously, set right to work, and continue their natural rhythm.

Message

The ant advises patience, meaning both great patience in all of life and patience in the small things. Your happiness and fulfillment are a construction project consisting of many individual parts, designed to have many different areas, the planning of which is far beyond possibility.

But if you patiently follow your life's flow, keenly intent on respecting the completeness of the moment, and if you are ready to gather the happiness, joy, knowledge, and impulses that lie along your path, then your inner life will work as a functioning center for you and your being. Thus, change and growth will be allowed and well-being made possible. Patience means more than just waiting. Patience is an all-embracing expression of one's own life in all domains. Patience is closely related to trust in the great destiny and requires that we follow destiny's plan with devotion. In doing so, however, we should deliberately disassociate from our task, observe the moment attentively, and keep our view away from the goal. If we, like the small, diligent ants, pursue our task with joy, then everything will be made ready for us in the right moment and in the appropriate way.

If you stumble upon an anthill, it is time to submit consciously to the great destiny. Trust that your happiness, and fulfillment will be built as you patiently devote yourself to the current task, seek fascination in it, and eagerly recognize and gather the small happiness of everyday life. The ant folk are not trying to put you off with a cheap "Be patient!" Rather, they are telling you that only the person who takes the individual steps can reach a goal, even though those steps may seem meaningless at the time.

If an ant scuttles across your path in a place where it does not belong—for example, in your car, on your desk, in a rubber boat—it could be that the building blocks of your happiness are seeking impossible places due to impatience. In this case the odd place where you discovered the ant is surely no coincidence. In any event, today it would be advisable for you to take care of the real task, to practice patience, and not to flee into revolutionary dreams. You run the risk of losing what you have built so far. Just like the small ant in the rubber boat, it would be very hard for you to find your own inner home again.

It is another matter if a line of marching ants has drawn your attention. Here it is advised that your patience should follow a clear straight line. Stay on the ball with regard to the question of patience. You are on the right track, and you just need to follow this path steadily and attentively. Everything that belongs to your happiness lies in this direction.

If you are confronted by an ant swarm that is ready to take flight, your patience may be at an end in certain areas of your life. Have the courage to seek a new horizon for your fascination with life. Your living space is exhausted, and everything that helped with happiness and growth is now superfluous. Make some space for yourself, draw away from your everyday routine a little bit, and consider without judgment what new things would fascinate you. Put your "feelers" out and let your intuition lead you. You can also ask yourself sufficient practical questions about new domains of life.

If you are bitten by one or many ants, it is a clear warning. Could it be that you are making others responsible for your happiness and letting all these people do the gathering? Or do you feel responsible for the happiness of other people, working only for their benefit? Be honest with yourself and remember the true laws of nature. You do not belong in another person's colony, nor do outsiders belong in your colony! Take back complete responsibility for your happiness in your life and your growth. Stop concerning yourself with other people's happiness.

Building happiness for another person is something that can happen only superficially. Ultimately, in reality, only your own steps count. Certainly most people have had the feeling that everything in their own lives is significantly harder and slower than it is for other people. But consider that with your destructive impatience, you are surely destroying your own happiness that you have only just built up. Perhaps you should scale down your high expectations of yourself, enjoy simplicity again, and get to know the wonderful treasures it contains.

APHID

Exhaustion, Robbing of Energy through Emotions

Aphids are probably the best-known and most widespread plant pests. Especially in damp weather, they attack all manner of crops and ornamental plants. With their sharp stylets, they bore holes between the cells of plants and suck out the sugar-rich juice. The plant gradually withers. There are many different types of aphids. Some have wings, some do not. Some use their secretions to create blisterlike galls on the undersides or stems of leaves. The life cycle of the aphid is complicated and would take too long to describe here. However, it is worth mentioning that especially in the spring, generations of females reproduce without the participation of males in a process known as parthenogenesis. Aphids can be enormously fertile, with one female able to give birth to several nymphs each day. Their sticky, honeylike excretions are used by certain ants; these ants keep colonies of aphids that they milk, as farmers do with cows.

Message

Aphids are always around us, especially those of us who have a close relationship with nature. If you have a plague of aphids—if these tiny plant-juice suckers have settled on your houseplants or window boxes—it should be understood as a sign worthy of interpretation. We encounter aphids when we are emotionally burned out. Perhaps it is your family, your neighborhood, or even some acquaintance. But there are some life events in which we participate, even quite actively, out of whatever motivation, which are actually not our own life events at all. Perhaps you want to help; perhaps you feel forced to listen out of politeness; or perhaps your patience is simply being abused, especially if the aphids are being cultivated by ants. In any case, your life energy is being tapped and you are exhausted. Consider which people tire you out when you interact with them. The message of the aphid relates very clearly to feelings and perceptions. Your health is not being attacked or weakened. This is about your emotional participation in a problem foreign to you, which weakens you. You are using up your energy on the growth process of another person, instead of on your own growth. It is good to participate, but only when other people's narratives give you knowledge that truly relates to you and your own life, and only when you are learning things about how destiny can unfold and what effects a given cause can have. Participation must always be enriching for you. Be cautious, for false participation also carries the danger of swiftly turning a person into a voyeur. Much of your own radiant strength and magnetism becomes lost when you linger in the gardens of others' souls, leaving your own untended. Such draining participation will not draw you away from your own truth, nor will it make you become a different person; still, save your time and energy for your own interests, your own development, and your own affairs.

BEE

Being

Like the silkworm, the bee is a small insect that humans have made useful as a domestic animal. Wild honeybees live in hollow tree trunks. Domestic bees live in beehives, where each population lives on its own level. Bees have highly developed senses. They have two compound eyes, and on the top of the head, three simple eyes, or ocelli, that probably serve for sensing light. They also remember landmarks for up to six miles as they travel in search of food.

For further orientation on their flights, bees use the sun, which they can also locate behind thick cloud cover. Bees also have a highly developed sense of time. Amazingly, they tell each other the locations of new feeding places by means of certain dances. Scents and sounds are also used for communication. A hive of bees is centered on a queen. She is fertilized by a male bee (a drone) at mating time, and then, throughout her life, lays over one thousand eggs a day each year in late spring. If a new queen hatches, the old queen leaves the hive with half of the workers, and they look for a new home. A well-established beehive has a queen, about one thousand drones (which only live from spring to summer), and between ten thousand and sixty thousand workers, depending on the time of year. The worker bee, which only lives about thirty days, begins as a cell cleaner, becomes a nurse on the third day, and from the tenth to eighteenth days transfers the incoming honey and pollen into the cells. After guarding the entrance, it begins with orientation flights and visits to flowers. After this, it is grown, and works for the rest of its life as a gathering bee. One collecting flight of one honeybee brings in forty milligrams of nectar (about one one-thousandth of an ounce), which produces ten milligrams of honey. In the process the bee fertilizes twenty to two hundred flowers. A kilogram (about 2.2 pounds) of honey requires four kilograms of nectar, corresponding to one thousand collecting flights. Only the female bees can sting. This defense, provided via a poison gland, is primarily used against hostile insects. But people and animals who threaten the beehive or the life of a bee can also be attacked. The stinger is barbed, so it sticks in the dense skin of humans and animals; the bee dies after such a sting, because the stinger is torn loose from its delicate body. When stinging less dense targets, the bee can pull its stinger loose.

Message

In symbolic language, the bee embodies the human essence. It is oriented toward the light, lives on nectar, and spends its whole life in submission to the laws of the whole. We encounter bees often in the spring, summer, and fall. With their humming, they tell us to seek the bright essence of our existence, orient ourselves toward joy, and let our life's path unfold in this way. Humans are beings of light, and our task is to make a celebration of our lives. Let yourself be carried away by the wonder of the moment, and taste the sweet things in life that come with joy. No true love, neither for another person nor for one's own life, can be built on ill humor and sorrow.

The laws the bee follows are the laws of life. The whole hive lives unquestioningly by these laws. All aspects life can offer are included in them. Learning and growing, separation, new amalgamation, birth, and death: all these are everyday things in the rhythm of a bee colony's life. Nothing is questioned or judged. You are also advised to direct your life toward the light of joy, to take part in society, and to look for new essences that may conceal new joy. Carry your joy in your external life and let the essence surround you. Human life consists of constant development. People only become radiant, sublime beings if they gather light and joy.

If a bee makes itself very noticeable in your life, you should consider whether your attention is really directed toward joy or whether you have directed your fascination toward weaknesses, illnesses, disasters, or crimes. Be alert, for fascination is the seed that bears experience as fruit.

BEETLE, DUNG

Cycle, Renewal

The dung beetle is a member of the Scarab family. Many different species belong to this family. The best known are the earth-boring scarab, the forest dung beetle, and the sacred scarab. Dung beetles are distinguished by their rounded shape, shiny outer wings, and hard breastplate. They dig long, branching tunnels underground. In side passages they store the dung of herbivores. The beetles and their grublike larvae live on these supplies. The female makes balls of the dung and deposits one egg in each. In ancient Egypt, and later in the eastern Mediterranean region, scarabs were greatly revered. They stood symbolically for the rising of the sun. The dung ball that the beetle rolls with its back legs was viewed as a symbol for the sun after it sets; the beetle rolls the sun back around the Earth to the East, where it rises again the next morning. In those days it was believed that all dung beetles were male. It was thought that they inserted their sperm into the dung ball and larvae emerged there as a consequence. Thus, enormous creative power was attributed to scarabs, and they were included as amulets in graves so that the dead could reincarnate. Over time the scarab became a symbol for renewal, creative power, and protection in general.

Message

We encounter dung beetles mainly in the spring. This is their breeding season, and on nice days they can be found hard at work. The dung beetle reminds us of our own strength—the strength that lies for all eternity at the root of every human. Like the sun, this strength radiates through our innermost worlds to the core of our conscious being. It is the source of our being, and it is always available for us to use. Around this power our outer self (which I call the ego) creates its worlds and manifests them by means of events. These ego-worlds and their events are the reality of our everyday consciousness. They surround the power of the source, and they transform, constantly bringing new facets of the eternal to light. The scarab scrabbles its way into your life to make you remember that your life story is only one of the possible forms of expression of your strength, and that it is possible—with your will and strength—to change this form of expression. Change is a flowing process, and it is necessary to respect the laws of the flow. Change follows our innermost will and beliefs, and life's narrative develops in keeping with these. Through our emotions, moods, fears, and fascinations, a midpoint between the poles comes into being, constantly undergoing slight change. This midpoint is the living core of our being, tasked with the expression of our life story. If the dung beetle comes into your consciousness, try to raise up this center. Lift your beliefs and feelings to the highest possible level of well-being. The reality of the world will work around this center with its events, and from this center narratives of light and shadow will emerge. The higher your center lives, the more full of light and joy your external life experience will be.

BEETLE, GOLDEN GROUND

Rich Harvest

When spring begins the golden ground beetles make their appearance once again. These beetles, some of the most beautiful in Europe, spend the winter hiding in rotten tree stumps. After this long time of fasting they can often be observed on the hunt. They eat worms, snails, larvae, and grubs. Ground beetles digest their prey from the outside, spitting stomach juices into the muscle tissue of their prey. This changes the muscle tissue into a liquid, which the beetle sucks up. This can cause the beetle's abdomen to expand considerably, so that it has hardly any room left under its wings. This noble predator can eat up to 1½ times its weight each day. Unlike other ground beetles, it is diurnal. If threatened by an enemy, it secretes an evil-smelling liquid. Ground beetle larvae are as predatory as the adults. In spring, shortly after the beetles dig their way out of their winter hiding places, they lay their eggs. The black larvae are considered beneficial by foresters and gardeners because they eat large quantities of the larvae of other insects. After shedding their skin twice, they pupate in late summer. Under good weather conditions they can even reproduce in the fall of that same year.

Message

The encounter with the golden ground beetle announces a rich harvest for you. The current projects and tasks in your life are destined for success. But for the success to set in, some effort from you will be necessary. In any case, the work will be rewarding. The golden ground beetle appearing before you is telling you to concentrate clearly on current tasks and put all your energy into them. This will not be a victory delivered on a silver platter; an extreme effort will be required of you. But the reward for this effort will greatly exceed your expectations. In earlier times it was considered a bad omen to step on a golden ground beetle. Bad weather, rain, and storms were expected as a result. It is unthinkable that such weather could have any connection to the death of a beetle. However, care is always recommended when you encounter these messengers from the animal world. You will have to plan and define your steps carefully and apportion your energy well to weather the storm of demands that is coming your way. In times when extreme physical, emotional, or mental efforts are required, there is the danger that neglected areas of our emotions may become embittered. Frustration and worry reduce our ability to handle life. Therefore, the message of the ground beetle should be seen as a warning to guard rigorously against possible disrupting factors and practice disciplined emotional hygiene.

BEETLE, MAY; JUNE BUG

Ensnarement

For many people the May beetle is the archetypal beetle. In *Max and Moritz* the bad boys deposit them in Uncle Fritz's bed. It is drawn and dissected in the school classroom, and for gardeners its larva, the white grub, is

a dreaded pest. The beetle is well protected with its many-layered chitinous carapace. Beneath its red-brown outer wings, transparent flying wings are folded. Before flight, the May beetle fills its breathing system with air by making pumping motions with its abdomen. It is a clumsy flier.

At dusk, with loud buzzing, the May beetle flies in search of food. With its mouth parts it eats pieces of young leaves and pine needles. The May beetle's main swarming and mating time is usually in late May and early June. The female lays sixty to eighty eggs the size of a hemp seed, burying them four to eight inches deep in the soil. After about six weeks small larvae hatch; they live on rotting plant matter until winter. The larvae are dormant through winter, and during the summer they eat plant roots. In this way they cause considerable damage. After 2½ to 3½ years they have developed into large eyeless white grubs about two inches long.

In autumn of the third year of life the white grubs pupate and emerge the following May as mature May beetles. The development of the May beetle is dependent on temperature. In colder areas it takes them four years to reach maturity, in warmers areas three years.

Message

The May beetle is only encountered in early summer. In some years they swarm in great numbers in the evenings. Although it is an agricultural pest, it also has great significance for us. It could almost be viewed as a messenger of hope. Consider the sayings "haste makes waste" or "good things come to those who wait." The message of the May beetle is similar. This insect develops in a long cycle, hidden in the darkness of Mother Earth. The grub lies in the soil like an embryo, receiving the sustenance it needs to grow through the tender roots of plants.

Your wishes in life are like so many larvae growing in the soil. Like the larvae, your wishes develop over time, in secrecy, according to the laws of matter, into the topics of grown-up life. During your growth, they are constantly nibbling on the tender roots of budding feelings. For us this means that hopeful plans, visions, and feelings can suddenly wither for unknown reasons. This often leads to despondency. We can hardly understand how something that felt so right can suddenly vanish.

To encounter a May beetle means that new themes are emerging on your life's path. You are growing out of the larvae you planted. Of course, you will probably also find themes that relate to your family roots. Everything that is a pertinent topic in those roots is also a pertinent topic in you. Your soul chooses the ideal ancestors for its life. Therefore you are not the victim of your forebears. The white grub shows that concealed ensnarements keep reemerging powerfully. Every gardener knows the experience of lovingly planting, watering, and tending fresh seedlings only to see them wilt, powerless. No amount of watering helps; the culprit is found only when the roots are dug up. The roots have been eaten by one or more white grubs.

If this happens to you often there is a hidden ensnarement at work. Something in the origin of your being is gnawing at your current development. White grubs show you that you are not just a nondescript leaf and that what you have sown must be harvested. You do not need to wait for the grub to become a May beetle. Learn to notice when your feelings, hopes, and visions are ailing. No matter how hard you try, fulfillment is absent after a certain point. Only disciplined self-observation in loving devotion to yourself can create the climate in which these soul-grubs can be made into visible creations.

It is no use to complain and ask "Why me?" For some reason you laid these eggs in the soil of your life's plan. In many cases it was done unconsciously, but never meaninglessly. People are here on Earth for development and growth, and themes in life are—like the May beetle—brief guests in our consciousness. The essence of your life story, however, grows like a grub in the soil, coming back at you as a new theme. So do not complain about your destiny but learn to view it as an interesting task.

BEETLE, STAG

Realization

At three inches the stag beetle is an imposing insect. Males and females are clearly distinguishable. While the male has the characteristic "antlers," the female is smaller, with much weaker mandibles. The male's mandibles are used solely for pushing and shoving rivals. Stag beetles are only encountered in the month of June. They live on the sweet sap that oozes from the injured bark of oak trees. The stag beetle's whole life cycle is dependent on the oak. After mating season in June, the female lays her eggs in the rotting wood of an old oak stump. Here the robust larvae develop for almost five years before pupating. In a hole about four inches deep, these larvae metamorphose into mature beetles, hatching out of their pupae in October. The adult beetles, however, spend the winter underground. They finally emerge in late May or early June, but only live for another month.

Message

The stag beetle has come into your life to give you a special task. This is the year of the whole. Your individual development serves something greater, and you are called upon to restrict your ego and bow patiently to the course of events. You are not required to have anything forced on you. On the contrary, you will thoughtfully consider everything that comes your way, weigh the possibilities, and when something seems achievable, you will take the steps. The stag beetle instructs you to put forth your greatest effort. Pursue whatever is pertinent in your life. Do not ask yourself about the meaning of a job, position, or fascination. Perhaps these things are not yet knowable. Just do what you can. The Earth—and with it, human development—is using your personal learning steps as tools to enrich the collective experience. Even when, from your point of view, you seem to be doing meaningless things and concerning yourself with entirely simple matters, it is as important for the great whole as a missing piece in a puzzle. If the stag beetle flies or crawls into your life, you should recall what ideas, plans, and projects you tossed around long ago. What did you always want to do? Now is the time for it. Do it, or at least take a significant step toward it. What things did you put off in the past five years, waiting for the right moment? Do them now, or at least begin to plan solidly for them. Or was there something you worked hard on but didn't properly finish? Now is the right time to bring it to completion. The stag beetle is a strong symbol, and its message should be followed absolutely. You will see it is almost astonishing how things fall into place.

BUMBLEBEE

Lightheartedness, Wonder

Bumblebees are furry insects that build their nests underground. Like other bees, they produce wax and construct honeycombs. They gather nectar and stock small supplies of honey for rainy days. Each colony lasts for only one summer. In late fall fertile males and females emerge

alongside the workers and mate. Then the whole colony dies except for the fertilized females, who shelter under moss for the winter.

In the spring each female establishes a new colony. As with wasps, it is mainly the queen who takes care of the offspring, feeding them with honey. The females can sting; their stingers are smooth, and they can sting multiple times. However, bumblebee stings are extremely rare. According to the laws of aerodynamics, given the bumblebee's body weight and wingspan, it should not be able to fly. Because the bees do not know this, they do so with a loud buzzing noise.

Message

The humming of the bumblebee belongs to the summer. It is part of the easiness and lightheartedness of that season. An encounter with a bumblebee reminds you of enjoyment. Let go of those demoralizing thoughts and try not to plan your life around what is possible and what is impossible. Unhindered by restrictive knowledge, the bumblebee buzzes from flower to flower and gathers the nectar of existence, even if its life only lasts for a summer. If you have a very overt encounter with a bumblebee, it could be a sign that something impossible for you will soon become possible.

In other words, a miracle will happen. Perhaps all the miracles of today will be explainable by the science of tomorrow, but that does not matter. Miracles are unimaginable processes: events that are not predictable by present knowledge. So turn off your mind, breathe the moment deep into your heart, and let great, contented joy into yourself. What miracle will happen to you? You will see.

BUTTERFLY

Transformation

The butterfly is one of those insects that undergoes a complete metamorphosis. First, caterpillars hatch from the butterfly eggs. These are true eating machines. They eat nonstop, devouring huge quantities of plants, and grow constantly. When they have reached their full body size and weight they look for a protected place, where they pupate. Inside the chrysalis, an intensive biological transformation process takes place.

This process depends on innate genetic signals, and when the process is complete the chrysalis opens and the adult butterfly emerges. Some time is required for the colorful wings to dry and straighten, then the butterfly is ready to fly. A whole new world awaits it. Its life as a caterpillar was one of ponderous crawling; now it lives a light life of elated flying. Its main tasks as a caterpillar were eating and growing, but now it flirts with the light. The butterfly's food is the nectar of flowers, and its stimulus is the light of the sun. Some butterfly species even fly south for the winter like birds.

Message

In becoming human you yourself have gone through a transformation. In your mother's womb you lived exclusively in water. Your body was nourished through your navel, and you did not breathe. Much like the chrysalis stage of the caterpillar, you were enclosed in a protective shell in which you could come into being. In birth your lungs unfolded. You came out of darkness into light, from water into air. You had to get used to breathing, eating, digesting, and freedom. The metamorphosis of the caterpillar into the butterfly is much more pronounced. Its whole being is transformed while it sleeps. But transformation underlies everything in the human being and in her world of experience. The butterfly flutters into your consciousness to remind you, amid your present topics of thought, of the stage of transformation and as a bearer of the hope that lightness is the goal of every transformation.

The butterfly means transformation. Your thoughts and feelings at the moment of the encounter should turn more toward the light, to airiness, to colorful and joyful things. Consider whether your problem of the moment is in the egg, caterpillar, or chrysalis phase. Whichever stage the transformation is currently in, joy and faith are the right nourishment. Transformations are part of the life cycle. One thing ends so that something new can begin. Closure means letting go. You do not need to be disdainful of your past or your past actions.

The butterfly hardly notices the caterpillars. They do not matter to it. If you look back on your life there will be moments in which you can hardly understand your past behavior from your present point of view. Such moments may be painful to you. But, lovingly let it go. It was the caterpillar stage, and time has brought you to lightness. The butterfly reminds us to let our wings grow so that we can flutter into the light, show our true colors openly, and nourish ourselves with the nectar of life.

CENTIPEDE
Doubt

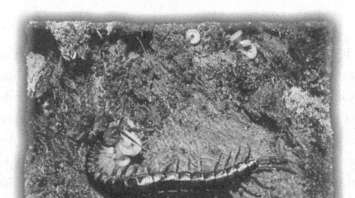

Centipedes are among the first land creatures to walk on Earth. There are countless species, and they are found throughout the world, including the north and south polar regions. In Europe the stone centipede is very widespread. All centipedes are predators. They lurk under rocks, in bark, and in other hiding places, waiting for prey. They are not picky. They eat practically all insects, spiders, woodlice, millipedes, and small worms. They will even prey on smaller members of their own species. Their pouncing reflex is activated by movement or chemical stimulation. With lightning speed the centipede jumps on its prey, grabs it with its claws, and kills it by injecting a poisonous substance from its front claws into its victim's body. It holds the prey still with its foremost four legs and eats out the body parts from inside the exoskeleton. The emptied exoskeleton is left behind. If a centipede is threatened, it usually flees. Only when this is not possible does it prepare to fight, lifting its front claws and also its elongated rear legs as a deterrent. As a further defense strategy, centipedes can pretend to be dead. In addition, some species have numerous poison glands on their back legs. By quickly wiggling its rear end back and forth, the centipede sprays a sticky, viscous secretion at its enemy. The attacker becomes stuck in the gluey mess, and the centipede can retreat to safety. For reproduction, the male produces a sperm packet. During this action, which the male performs with his rear legs, the two centipedes maintain constant contact with their feelers. After depositing the packet the male retreats, carefully leading the female over the sperm packet, which she takes up into her genital opening. The fertilized eggs are surrounded by a secretion and covered with soil through rotating movements. Then the female hides the eggs in the soil and leaves them. The young, in the larval stage, at first have only seven pairs of legs. Through several moltings during the first two years they grow into adult centipedes. A centipede can live to be five or six years old.

Message

The centipede is like a question mark in your life. Everything that you think, believe in, or consider real at the time of the encounter with this animal should be questioned. The centipede cannot be said to be a symbol for illusion; rather, its appearance interrupts your thoughts and whispers, between them, "Yes, but . . ." The centipede is not contradicting you. Actually, it is affirming your feelings or thoughts. However, it encourages you to consider further possibilities and thus expand your feelings and thoughts. The centipede is a reliable symbol when you analyze questions in your heart. You will encounter it when what you feel and think is fundamentally correct. But at the same time there is always still this "Yes, but . . ." There are always other viewpoints for your feelings and thoughts, and when you consider these, the feeling and thought pattern that led to the current conclusion will have considerably different implications. It is not obligatory for you to change your feelings and thoughts. With some centipede encounters, it is sufficient just to be aware that there are other viewpoints. If you have very frequent encounters with this ancient insect, it is recommended that you follow the call to self-reflection until you can see your original feelings and thoughts from the opposite side, just as well as from this side—just as a king may see a fool in the mirror, and the fool may see a king.

COCKROACH
Perceived Deficiencies

Cockroaches are very widespread. The European cockroach is smaller than its American counterpart, which has also been introduced to Europe. The cockroach is generally regarded as an unpleasant pest. It is a true survivor and eats almost anything it can find. It is found almost exclusively in houses and storage buildings, and on garbage dumps in the summer. With its long, backward-bending feelers it can perceive both obstacles and things to eat in the dark of night. Faced with danger, it can quickly scuttle to safety on its long, hairy legs. These shiny black insects, about 1½ inches long, have completely adapted themselves to living with humans. Always hungry and thirsty, the cockroach goes for anything edible or drinkable. In its short life of twelve to eighteen months, a single cockroach can theoretically have 1,500 direct descendants. Once the descendants begin having descendants, a cockroach family under optimal conditions can grow into the billions.

Message

The cockroach reminds us of inner deficiencies. Something in us is inexpressibly hungry for love. Love is people's nourishment. Water, plant-based food, and affection are all important "staples" associated with the element Water. Water is also emotion, and the deep roots of emotion lie in love. If you encounter a cockroach, it is telling you that you are hoping to remedy your lack of love through various games and tricks played on others. You are trying to demand, harvest, extort, and win from others the love that your own system is lacking. Or are you one of those people who flees into frustrated and depressed moods only to find that you cannot stay there because you are hungry for love? That too is a game! No one except you can remedy your lack of self-love. You will never be able to feel more love for yourself by tricking others into professing love for you. The feeling that you receive too little love will not go away. Seek inside yourself for reasons that will make it possible to love yourself. Fulfill yourself with love and learn to become secure in yourself through this love for yourself. Then the outside attention that you think you so desperately need will no longer matter. It will feel truly wonderful not to need it anymore.

CRANE FLY

Taking Responsibility

Crane flies have existed for more than two hundred million years. Of the three thousand species found worldwide, 180 live in central Europe. Although they are sometimes mistaken for mosquitoes, there are several differences. They are significantly larger and have no piercing mouth parts. With their mouth parts they drink water, easily accessible plant juices, and nectar. Thus it is understandable that they should often be found in damp, swampy areas. Depending on the species, the females lay their eggs in water, mud, or damp soil. In enclosed spaces, crane flies are awkward and somewhat gangly fliers. But in the open air they fly fast, legs pointed backward, straight to their goal.

Message

You encounter crane flies when it is time to retreat into your own energies and gain your own knowledge from your own experiences. In the recent past certain aspects of your being (but not you as a whole person) have put their trust in some external authority. You have bowed to popular or traditional ideas and directed yourself according to them without scrutinizing them. No wonder that so many encounters with these large insects take place in the late summer and early fall. In summer it is easy enough to surrender oneself to the light of day, enjoy the sun's warmth, and give in to the light easiness of nature. Love and light are almost like gifts from nature during the warm months. But in the fall the individual must focus heedfully and vigilantly on herself, strengthen her own light, tend her heart's warmth, and unfurl the lightness of her being. If you have a conscious encounter with a crane fly it is telling you to provide carefully and consciously for your current needs. You can no longer count on being so easily nourished with light and love. Be aware of your needs as a human and recognize what nourishment you have been receiving from others. Now it is important for you to give out the same leadership and energy that you have received from others, up until now, with such apparent ease.

CRICKET, FIELD CRICKET
Revelation

Who does not know the many-voiced summer concert of the crickets? It comes from the crickets' holes, where they sit making their music with the stridulatory organs on the undersides of their wings. This serrated vein has up to 150 teeth in the space of three millimeters. The cricket has a short, shiny, dark, cylindrical body with thin, shimmering, brownish wings, six hairy legs, and two long, fine feelers. Crickets eat mostly grass but will also eat animal flesh and plant juices. For building their holes they prefer dry, sloping meadows that face the sun. One cricket lives in each hole. There the males can be observed chirping.

The male plays his music to attract a mate or to display his prowess to the other males. His notes are very precise. He seems to be saying: "Look here, this is how I am. If you like my song, come closer, if not, go away!"

Message
The cricket's message to humans is that we should express ourselves just as strongly. Have the courage to display your art. Let your

humanness radiate and show the best, most beautiful external sides of yourself. Speak more for yourself and less about yourself. You do not need to say what you like. If what you have to say repels others, that is all right.

When you open up and offer your truth, you offer yourself up for judgment in a certain way. Let people decide whether they feel comfortable around you. But a cricket concert is also a collaborative work. It invites us to express ourselves and open ourselves. But just as strongly, it tells us to listen to what others have to say. Preserve your own tone, but also let the tones of others inspire you. In this way your self-expression will keep becoming stronger and more beautiful and will harmonize with the shared song of others in a wonderful concert on the psychic level. In this concert each individual creates his or her own space.

If you encounter a cricket in your home, it is especially important that you listen for the right cue, then express your personal truth and reveal your decisions unreservedly before the people who are close to you. In this way you will create the space in which your decision can play out, also giving others the possibility of reacting to it.

DRAGONFLY

Illusion

The dragonfly looks like a being from another dimension. Elfin, shimmering in the colors of the light, it flies fast as an arrow over the surface of the water. It is a skilled daytime hunter; not only do its four wings make it exceptionally fast and maneuverable, but it also has huge round eyes covering the entire front part of its head. Mating takes place in free flight. Dragonfly larvae are also hunters and live at the muddy bottoms of ponds. When ready, they climb up the stem of a water plant, break free of their larval skin, and fly away as adult dragonflies.

Dragonflies do not have a pupation stage. Like the kingfisher, the dragonfly is a messenger of the four elements and their natural spirits. Their development goes from Earth into Water, from there into Air,

and finally into light (Fire). Thus, they come in contact with all the elemental spirits.

Message

If a dragonfly zips into your life it brings a message from the elemental world. It is time, once again, to become aware that human reality is nothing other than sensory deception. There are many truths on this Earth, many possible truths. Consider your life entirely from the inside, from your own perspective. Seen from outside it could look entirely different. It is certainly right to form your life according to your own truth. The dragonfly advises you to expand this truth.

Maybe your worldview has become a fixed idea and all the in-between tones, the living games of light and color, nuance and shadow, have been forgotten. Do not let your world of feelings and fantasies become a garden without elves, fairies, and gnomes. Someone who wants to protect herself from sensory deception must train and expand her senses and perceptiveness. Have the courage to let change happen through constant reevaluation of your life.

Do not deceive yourself by narrowing your perceptions and becoming simply unable to sense the currents of change. Blocked perception always has its origin in fear. The dragonfly also always indicates fear.

Dive into the forgotten swamp of your subconscious and cautiously unmask the restrictive dogma. Your being will become brighter and shinier.

EARTHWORM

Security, Retreat

The earthworm is probably the archetypal worm for most people. Its long, thin body is composed of many equal segments from end to end. At the front end there is a sort of mouth opening, and at the rear end, the intestinal opening. The intestine runs the entire length of the body. If an earthworm is chopped in half, the two halves can sometimes regenerate completely.

The earthworm breathes oxygen through all its skin. However, this is only possible when its body is moist. If an earthworm dries out, it suffocates. When heavy rain falls the earthworms come out of the ground, because they would also drown in the water. They can sense light through their skin. Photosensitive cells are distributed all over their bodies. Earthworms convert decaying vegetable matter into humus, loosening the soil and making it fertile.

Message

Earthworms enter our consciousness when we return to the earth. Perhaps in recent times you had many emotions to work through. Perhaps your consciousness is longing for security, for a return to the Earth. Simply lie down on the ground and surrender yourself to the loving power that comes deep out of Mother Earth and turns your old, withered emotions into a new, fertile basis for life. There is no striving toward light and activity, no great fluctuation of feelings.

The earthworm does not gnaw at healthy, growing plants like the white grub; it is Mother Earth's helper, inviting us to relax and let go. It is probably time to give yourself, your body, and especially your digestive system a rest. A day of eating only raw food may be in order, or a diet; ask your heart what it wants—it will surely tell you. The earthworm reminds us that as humans, every day, we have an enormous amount to digest with our body, soul, and spirit.

Perhaps you would do well to retreat into silence, away from life's many impressions, expectations, and inspirations. Perhaps even when you encountered the worm you had already fled from everyday life and are now enjoying this silence and repose. Do not demand too much of yourself, and let your soul fly a little.

EARWIG

Conscience

Earwigs are elongated crawly creatures with pincerlike rear appendages. All species look fairly similar. Some of them have short forewings, under which delicate wings are folded. However, these wings are hardly used. Earwigs are primarily active at night. They live on the soft parts of plants and on soft-skinned insects such as aphids. Unusual among insects, the female exercises maternal care. In the winter she lays about fifty eggs in a hole in the soil and guards them until the young hatch. Initially the young earwigs are almost pigment-free. They leave the hole to look for food but return to their mother afterward. Only after

the second molting does the family slowly start to scatter. If an earwig feels threatened it raises its rear end and opens its pincers menacingly. Earwigs are welcomed in gardens and orchards. Many gardeners attract them with straw-filled clay pots placed upside down under trees. This insect's name probably comes from the rare occurrence of an earwig erroneously wandering into a human ear while on the search for a suitable hole. This is not believed to happen often.

Message

An encounter with an earwig is an admonition to remember to listen to your inner voice. This is not the voice with which you criticize, question, and reproach yourself but a gentle, melodious voice, deep in your inner self, that shows you the right way. It is the true voice of your conscience. It is not a voice that gives any commentary, but it is like a barometer, moving back and forth between "favorable" and "unfavorable." Conscience has its origin in knowledge. But this knowledge is not the kind of knowledge that is acquired in schools, jobs, or other external learning processes. It is much more closely connected to inner wisdom. It is a knowledge of cosmic laws, for example the law of cause and effect. If someone performs an action that, according to this natural law, has unpleasant consequences for the recipient, then bad conscience arises. It does not emerge as an advocate for those harmed but as a warning that if the deed is not immediately taken back or made right the consequences for the perpetrator will also be unpleasant. The earwig is a messenger of the conscience. It tells you to direct your life to this voice of knowledge and let yourself be led by it. And, guaranteed, this inward listening will make your external life significantly easier.

FLEA

Disturbance

Fleas are flightless insects, two to three millimeters long, more or less strongly dependent on their specific host animal. But if a flea has been hungry for a long time, it will readily jump to a different provider of blood. The flea's hind legs are relatively far forward on the body and are much larger than the other four legs. This gives fleas enormous jumping power; they are able to jump many times their own body length. The body, usually dark brown to black, is covered with bristly hairs. And anyone who has tried to crush one of these bothersome parasites knows how strong their bodies are. Fleas reside on host animals, or in their living space, and live on their blood. The abdomen is expandable and can take in an impressive quantity of fluid. Once the flea's belly is full, it waits in the cracks and hiding places of the host's habitat until it needs its next meal, when it jumps back onto the host at just the right moment. Fleas lay their porcelain-colored eggs in the sleeping quarters or nest of the host. In the larval stage they eat feces and other bodily waste, as well as remnants of blood left by the adult fleas.

Message

Encounters with fleas very often begin with uncomfortable itching. Often enough, one does not actually find the perpetrator, only its bite mark. Fleas are often brought into the vicinity of people by animals. Therefore, when interpreting the flea encounter, the message of the host is also to be noted. The flea tells us that something in life is disturbing our well-being. This mainly refers not to something foreign but something that is our own. Perhaps it is a pattern, some sort of conditioning, that makes us function according to traditional, instilled, imprinted requirements. This pattern hinders us from recognizing what really serves us and helps us. If your domestic cat brings home a flea, aspects of sensuality and fine perception should be considered. Perhaps your sensual needs are not being met because the pattern says that it is not right to be sensual, or else you are ignoring your fine perceptions because you have been taught that such perceptions simply do not and cannot exist. If the flea comes in with the dog, domains relating to loyalty and what belongs to you have been disturbed. Then, in many cases, you can ask yourself whether you are more loyal to others than you are to yourself or to what matters to you simply because good form seems to require it.

In the case of encounters with fleas, it is also advisable to consider whether anyone could have "put a flea in your ear." Did some other person say something that disturbed your serenity? Has this led to a new pattern? In this case you would do well to correct their statement vehemently and ignore it in the future. If the flea visited you for this reason it wants to tell you that this statement, idea, or advice is not to be taken seriously and only serves the comfort of the person who said it. If there is something in your life that makes you itch, disturbs you, and preoccupies you, then do not hound it out. Look at it and consider whether this topic can be cleaned up as quickly as possible.

FLY
Transformation

Awakened by light, the fly begins to buzz. It circles nervously in repeating patterns around the room, then lands and rubs its front legs together, preferably somewhere where it tickles and annoys you. Perhaps it simply likes the body warmth of humans and larger animals. It tickles our skin with its tiny legs, breaking our concentration. Our ears perceive its buzzing as bothersome and irritating. The fly is undoubtedly the insect with the largest population and the greatest range. Although persecuted mercilessly by humans, its numbers cannot be decimated. Its secret: astonishing fertility.

The female, during her two to three months of life, lays on average two thousand eggs. After less than twelve hours the eggs enter the larval stage, and after six to eight days, grown flies emerge. Theoretically, between May and September, one fly could be the starting point for four thousand trillion descendants.

Flies are an important link in the food chain. All insect-eating animals include them in their diet. There are many species of flies, and many of them carry dangerous diseases.

Message

In summer it is very unlikely that you will encounter no flies. So try not to interpret every single one of them. Flies like to be where decomposition—that is, transformation—is taking place. Dung, putrescent corpses, garbage dumps, cesspools, all these places hold a feast for the fly. If flies buzz around you it is because continuous change and transformation is also taking place in your energy fields. The transformation of organic matter produces waste material; so does the transformation of emotions. With their buzzing and their larvae, flies help the waste to decompose and go back into the earth. The larvae decompose the material plane, while the unnerving buzzing and tickling breaks down the emotional garbage.

Sometimes it is good to become annoyed and agitated in the process of emotional transformation. Anger and annoyance are Fire, and Fire element transforms. If a fly really drives you crazy, it appears that something in your system is rotten. So let yourself be bugged, be annoyed, but do not transfer the guilt on to anyone else; the process is taking place in you alone. Flies are a part of our life that we must simply come to terms with, and our hunting instinct is something the fly must come to terms with.

GLOWWORM, FIREFLY
Orientation

In the folk world both the lesser glowworm and the firefly are considered glowworms. Because their significance lies in their ability to produce light without heat, they are discussed together here. Both live mainly in deciduous forests. While the glowworm prefers damp forests, the firefly is found more often in dry places. The male glow-

worm is dark gray with normal wings. At the rear of his abdomen are two white rings that serve as light-emitting organs. The female glowworm has no wings and resembles a whitish larva with tiny wing stubs behind the head. The firefly looks very similar to the male glowworm. Like its smaller relative, it has a prominent pronotum, but the white rings are not present on the abdomen. The female firefly is dark gray or sometimes pinkish, and lacks wings. At twilight in June and July glowworms look for a suitable place for their nighttime mating dance. By climbing about six feet above the ground, the light organ is activated. They fly through the night like tiny lanterns. The flightless females sit on the ground and emit light as well. If a male spots a female, he circles around a few times to be sure he will land on a willing partner. Once mating has taken place successfully, the male dies. The female seeks out an appropriate place at the edge of the woods, where she deposits her fertilized eggs, then she also dies. Adult glowworms do not eat. The woodlouse-like larvae eat snails almost exclusively. The life cycle of the firefly is identical to that of the glowworm, except that mating occurs in July and August. Male fireflies that begin their search for a mate early in July are often erroneously attracted to male glowworms. Male fireflies have no light-emitting organ.

Message

An encounter with a firefly or a glowworm is a call to consider your orientation. For these insects it is very important that they find the right partners. Orientation, in this case, always relates to the person you were with when you encountered the insect. If you were alone at the time of the encounter, you are advised to consider your personal orientation, your ideal path of development that you plan for yourself. If you were in the company of one or more people, or your dog or horse, the encounter has to do with your relationship with them. An orientation is essentially understood as a clear concept that leads along a clear path to a clear, achievable goal. That is exactly what the encounter proposes. Clearly formulate the direction in which you want your development with the person in question, or with yourself, to go. Together, look for ideas that are realistically achievable. Try to make an approximate plan for the intermediate steps, and look for possible people to support, advise, or accompany you along your way. Set a definite time point at which you will consider together whether development is progressing within the desired framework. Normally, relationships can happen without orientation. In your case, however, it obviously makes sense to have a clear path mapped out, either for your whole relationship (with yourself or with other people) or for certain issues within the relationship. In this way a cosmic spark from the divine plan can light your way through the darkness of your subconscious so that you can seek your counterpart and then, almost as if by coincidence, trigger a meaningful act of creation.

GRASSHOPPER, LOCUST

Leap of Thought

Walking in a dry meadow in the summer you can see grasshoppers hopping before you with every step. There are various types, large and small. Locusts and crickets also belong to the same family. Cricket larvae differ from the adults in that they have no wings. The wings only become visible after the third of five moltings.

After the fifth molting the grasshoppers gather into small groups and eat to store up energy for reproducing. After mating and depositing eggs, the adults die. The back legs of the grasshopper are especially long, with strong muscles. With these legs, some varieties of grasshopper, such as the great green bush-cricket, can jump as far as ten feet. The males make music by rubbing their back legs. With these tones they attract the females, which do not make any sounds. Most grasshoppers are plant eaters. The large, bright green katydid, however, is a meat eater. Field grasshoppers go through two distinct phases: a sedentary phase, during which the individuals live on their own, without any social structure, and a wandering phase.

During the wandering phase the insects' coloring, body proportions, and behavior all change a great deal. As late as 1921 they were mistaken for two separate species.

Locusts, especially, bring about natural catastrophes in their social phase. Swarms of more than one hundred million insects can gather. According to the entomologist Jan Lhoste, one such swarm flew over Nebraska. The swarm was 2,500 feet high, 100 miles wide, and 300 miles long, containing 124 million insects. The damage done to crops was unspeakable. A similarly devastating locust invasion is described in Exodus as the eighth plague of Egypt. In 1867 a locust plague in Algeria led to the death of more than five hundred thousand people.

This phenomenon is entirely unpredictable. It occurs at irregular intervals, and when it does happen the mass gains insects like a rolling snowball. What starts it rolling is unknown. In Europe such plagues are rare.

Message

A person's thoughts balance as lightly upon his or her feelings as a grasshopper balancing on a pliable grass stem. The plant world corresponds to our developed perceptions. Perceptions are the basis for thought and serve as its nourishment, so to speak. Leaps of thought bring sensations together, fertilizing the senses. A summer meadow is a place full of harmony and beauty. The grasshopper reminds us of the lightness of thought, of those leaps of thought during which we unleash fantasies, pick up new impulses, and balance playfully upon our perceptions.

In the phase of solitary thought, leaps of thought are inspiring and creative. Later they come together into ideas that are fulfilled through action in a healthy, natural cycle. But when thoughts and ideas take on ever greater dimensions, rolling over the world of feelings like a swarm of locusts, it is a terrible catastrophe, for the individual as well as for society.

HARVESTMAN

Expansion

The harvestman, also known as the daddy longlegs, is an arachnid. "Daddy longlegs" may also refer to the crane fly and cellar spider. Worldwide, some four thousand species of harvestman are known. Due to intensive agriculture and exploitation of forests, many species are endangered. Harvestmen are very much tied to a particular place and live mainly on the ground. Unlike spiders, harvestmen do not weave webs. They can be easily distinguished from spiders because the harvestman's body consists of a single oval part onto which the eight legs are

attached. All spiders' bodies consist of two parts. The harvestman's diet consists of microscopically small creatures. After mating the female lays eggs in the soil. In some South American species the male builds a nest in which all the females he fertilizes deposit their eggs. After the young hatch, the father takes care of them. Harvestmen can often be found on house walls, where their long legs are especially noticeable. They look like little wheels on the wall. Interestingly, many people are not turned off by harvestmen the same way they are by spiders. The harvestman's senses play an important role in its life. Although its vision only serves to distinguish light from dark, its feelers have a special sensory ability that allows the harvestman to detect the chemical traces of its preferred prey as well as subtle changes in humidity and temperature.

Message

If your attention is drawn to a harvestman, something in your life is in the process of expanding on all levels of your being. Warily and gently, like a blooming flower, the deep inner soul powers of your life's destiny are unfolding. Energies that have always been yours but could not become effective in all domains will now be available for you. Do not expect anything from the outside. The source of this change is hidden in your own inner self. The unfolding of psychic energy into external life brings about harmony and equilibrium. The harvestman tells you to examine your own destiny with loving care and give up excesses of any kind immediately. All levels of your being—material, emotional, creative, and spiritual—should receive a gift from the great pure soul. It is important to open your heart wide for it. Your consciousness turns expectantly to your inner source in order to let this energy stream in with greater receptiveness. Trust in your plan, for the great soul in you knows what you need for happiness. The gift will strengthen this happiness to the greatest extent if your consciousness supports this unfolding within you. It can be helpful to learn to imagine, as you inhale, that you are drawing light into your heart from the innermost source of your being; and as you exhale, imagine that this light is shining out from your heart into your whole body.

HORSEFLY

Exploitation

Contact with horseflies is a part of summer and of being around water. About eighty native species are known, but not all are an annoyance to people. The common horsefly, about eight to eighteen millimeters long, is a particularly keen biter in hot, humid weather. Only the females bite. Their knifelike mandibles are used to inflict

fairly painful wounds. The bite of the twenty to twenty-five milli-
meter long dark giant horsefly can leave a wound that bleeds for a
relatively long time. If the horsefly is left on the skin and allowed to
bite, it becomes almost blind and can be crushed easily. Unlike the
smaller species, the dark giant horsefly makes a loud buzzing noise,
and many a horse owner or rider can relate what a strong reaction this
buzzing causes in otherwise calm horses. The female horsefly lays her
eggs in the soil or on blades of grass. The larvae are whitish and eat
rotting plant matter and small invertebrates. They kill their prey with
a poison secreted from the mouthparts.

Message

We probably notice horseflies most often when they are after our blood.
When you have an encounter with a horsefly—when it attacks and bites
you—the event is meant to tell you that there are certain things and talents in your possession, or in your life, that are coveted by other people.
This in itself is not unheard of and should pose no problem for you
However, the encounter with the horsefly warns you to be alert, because
it is very possible—especially if you are bitten often—that you are being
taken in by some sort of trick or underhandedness. If you are plagued
often by horseflies, then at least the intent to do this to you exists. The
horsefly relates less to specific topics and more to the idea that you are
predestined to attract the envy of others thanks to what you have, what
you are, and what you can do. Especially if a dark giant horsefly conspicuously attacks you or your horse, it is a clear order to handle your
energies, qualities, and rights with great care. Don't let yourself be bam-
boozled. Consider whether what you give to the people you know corresponds to what you receive. Protect yourself if you find that someone
wants to take uninvited advantage of your success or worldly possessions. Prevent any possibility of your being exploited if any kind of deal
is proposed to you with unclear intent. In projects, do not let your gifts
and talents be harnessed like a horse to a wagon while others take their
places on the wagon as drivers or passengers—perhaps even exclaiming
all the while what a great ride you're having together.

LACEWING

Bliss

The lacewing is a member of the Neuroptera family. These delicate-winged, green, elfin flies are about half an inch long with wings and feelers as long again as the body. Their prominent, shiny, gold, buttonlike eyes are striking. Lacewings are present throughout the world, except in Australia. They live in forests, gardens, parks, and towns. In winter they can be found in great numbers in attics and other places where they hibernate. They are active at twilight and night.

Lacewings are very useful insects. As one of the most important regulators of aphid populations in greenhouses, they are even cultivated. After mating, the female lays her stalked eggs on plants near aphid colonies. One larva eats between 120 and 150 aphids before pupating. Lacewings camouflage themselves from natural predators using empty aphid skins or pieces of bark. Larvae pupate in a cocoon. The life cycle of most lacewings lasts a year.

Message

Someone who observes a lacewing closely in the sunlight will agree: there is something fairylike about them. The light-green or yellow-brown filigreed body, the large, delicate, iridescent wings, the fine feelers, and especially the large golden eyes give it the appearance of a being that has come into our rough world from a light place between worlds; a visitor from the garden of souls whose real place is in a world made of the elementary powers. If your attention is drawn to this elf of the insect world, you should open your heart wide for a moment. Take in the light and beauty of the moment. Remember the bright, fragrant, enchanting soul's garden in your innermost being. Fill yourself with these beautiful images and the feelings that come from them. Feel how, behind your external form and role, you have great tenderness, lightness, and airiness. That is your bliss: a feeling that can be perceived from the garden of your soul. Your life story—with the roles you play in it, whatever they might be—is the wall that protectively surrounds this garden. Perhaps you play some grim roles in your external life. Perhaps not every role you find yourself in is the desired role that you would like to embrace. But this has nothing to do with your soul's garden. A wall is for protection, the garden is the important thing. The lacewing advises you to visit this garden more often, experience its inner existence again and again, and enjoy it entirely in private.

If you observe a lacewing preying on an aphid colony, it is a warning. Someone in your life is secretly using your energy. You are being depleted (see also the Aphid entry on p. 231). The lacewing advises you to arm yourself with your natural lightheartedness and airiness. Quite likely, your sympathy has awakened pity, which runs the risk of sucking you dry. Your lightheartedness must stem the flow from this sympathy channel.

LADYBUG

Luck

Ladybugs and their larvae are highly regarded by humans as voracious eaters of aphids and scale insects. Our fondness for them is reflected by the charming names they have in many languages. Their French name means "good God's animal," their Spanish name means "little Mary,"

in German they are called "Mary's beetle" and also "Lord God's beetle," and in English they are also called "ladybirds."

This red beetle, with black spots on its wings, is known everywhere as a symbol of good luck. However, not all ladybugs have this same coloration. Some are yellow with black spots, or black with red spots. The number of spots also varies. If the bug is disturbed, it plays dead by letting itself fall and folding up its legs. It also secretes a yellow liquid from its leg joints. In organic gardening, ladybugs are intentionally introduced for pest control.

Message

The ladybug is a bearer of good luck. To be precise, it announces a stroke of good fortune. It is a conspicuous message, displayed with warning colors: "Hey there! You're lucky now!" Good luck is like a happy destiny that seems to fall, unearned, into our hands.

The luck of which the ladybug speaks may refer to all domains of external and internal life. Perhaps you won the lottery or avoided falling in some pricker bushes. As noted, these are apparent coincidences. If you live devotedly, are close to nature, and stay alert, you will experience these coincidences more often; like little helpers in life, good things will come your way. Practically everyone rejoices at an encounter with a ladybug, and deep in their souls almost everyone knows that this lucky beetle bears a message of a special bonus.

LOUSE, HEAD LOUSE
Contemplation

This entry covers all lice that are parasites of humans, including pubic lice, body lice, and head lice. Head lice are parasites that normally live exclusively in human hair. Their legs are adapted so that they can cling fast to human hair and move around in it. The head louse is very stably built. Its body can withstand up to two pounds of pressure and temperatures down to fifteen degrees Fahrenheit. Its ideal temperature is around eighty-two degrees Fahrenheit, which is quite typical for a human head. It lives exclusively on human blood, of which it partakes about every three hours with its piercing and sucking mouth parts. It secretes an anticoagulant into the wound. This causes considerable itching. After every other blood meal the adult female louse lays an egg, which she sticks onto the hair roots. Head louse eggs are known as nits. Over the course of her life, a female louse can lay hundreds of eggs. The larvae hatch after about a week, and after another two weeks they are sexually mature. It is an incorrect belief that poor hygiene attracts head lice. The parasites are as happy in washed hair as in unwashed hair. Lice are transferred through direct head-to-head contact; sometimes nits and lice are transferred via things such as pillows. If the lice fall off their host they can live for about a day. During this time the female keeps laying her eggs, which hatch normally a week later.

Message

If head lice have come into your life there is no reason to panic. First, today there are good ways to be rid of these stubborn companions; second, these little pests have something to tell you. A person's hairs are like antennae. Everyone knows the expression "one's hair standing on end." Hairs transfer subtle signals and information to the nerves. This information cannot be formulated into sensations by the receiver. They are very subtle perceptions, causing a feeling of well-being or unease. Sometimes they are signals that are picked up and make sense as an afterthought. Scratching one's head when thinking is a very common gesture. If lice have made their home on you or on a member of your family, then there is something that you, or especially the afflicted person, must give great thought to. Usually is relates to circumstances that the afflicted person cannot identify. It is subtle and indefinable, but it robs one of one's inner peace.

Children are often affected by lice. Try to find out what could be unconsciously disturbing the child, or you yourself. Try to figure out what you are thinking and what is robbing you of your peace. The origin of the unpleasant feelings lies somewhere hidden inside you. Turning away from familiar things creates the conditions for the encounter with the louse. If your children have head lice, something is bothering them. But usually what children are thinking is obvious to adults. Try to be very clear with the affected child. Do not talk about the child with other people in a way he or she will not understand. Also try not to show the child a world that does not correspond to reality. The child has good antennae, and it is important for her to learn to use and trust what she senses with them. If you are the one affected by lice, treat yourself as you would treat the affected child. Take your perceptions seriously and do not mask them. Go to the root of the unsettling feelings, and try not to treat yourself as if you were stupid just because you believe something that may not really be the case. The louse has shown you that you are receptive to signals. If you observe and evaluate these signals, it will be harder for the head lice to bother you so much in the future.

MEAL MOTH, CLOTHING MOTH

Precision

Moths are known, feared, and persecuted in almost all countries as pests that ruin food and fabrics. The damage, however, is done only by their numerous larvae, which, after hatching from their eggs, voraciously eat the things humans consider their property. The clothing moth can even be found in winter in heated buildings. The clothing moth, the case-bearing clothes moth, and the tapestry moth can all do significant damage to wool, furs, pelts, rugs, and tapestries. The caterpillars use chewed-up fibers to make small tubular containers with which they cover themselves as they crawl around eating and constantly rebuild. After a major moth attack a nice sweater can turn out to be completely riddled with holes when it is brought out at the beginning of winter. The European grain moth, recognizable by its black and white mottled wings, lays its eggs in pantries and cupboards in packages of carbohydrate-rich foods. Food must be kept in tightly closed metal, glass, or hard plastic containers, or else the tiny caterpillars can gnaw their way through the packaging. The caterpillars spin small tube-shaped shelters with sticky threads made from their food. These threads, which are mostly attached to the sides of the container, will easily identify which food containers the moths have moved into. In the worst cases, the whole food supply becomes so infested that it must all be disposed of.

The moth has an exceptionally good sense of smell. Fertile females attract males with pheromones. This quality is helpful for attracting and destroying the pests. There are also many essential scents that repel moths, such as cedar wood, sandalwood, lavender, and lemon oil. In the past, camphor was widely used to combat clothing moths.

Message

There are two significant types of encounters with moths. One is with the moth itself, the other with its larvae. In the broadest sense, moths are members of the Butterfly family. They announce change, or even better, they advise you to change yourself. This message relates clearly to everyday life. If the moth enters your life very emphatically you should contemplate your everyday life and consider whether you are neglecting anything. There is obviously something in your life that needs your consideration, attention, or help. It is nothing big, but something that you once wished, something you were taken with, something you fostered. Perhaps it is a potted plant, perhaps a loose friendship, perhaps a forgotten promise. With your spiritual creative power you have supported the growth of something and then unwittingly drawn your energy back away from it. Now it is vegetating. As has been mentioned, this is not something big. Look for things that in some way depend on your care in order to flourish. Look for things that one could even describe as junk. Everything in your life that belongs to you also responds to your care.

If moths come into your life frequently, it is recommended that you thoroughly comb through the things in your personal life and keep only those things that you are happy to take care of, regularly need, or enjoy. You should do the same thing with friends. Take attentive and appropriate care of everything that is of value to you. Everything that means nothing to you is robbing you of energy and space. If the moths have attacked your food or fabrics then it is very likely that energy loss from the reasons mentioned above is already showing its consequences. Moth holes in clothes, fabrics, or food bags indicate holes in the realms of life energy, love, and finances. As that wonderful saying goes, a can of worms has been opened. Things that were once easy become messy, wobbly, and difficult. Decide right away to clean up your life. Reduce your possessions and pets to a quantity that is comfortable for you so that you can (and want to) perform their required maintenance with enjoyment. Give away those potted plants that you only water when they wilt; get rid of the furniture that you don't use or take care of. The moth is not telling you to be more diligent in the maintenance you perform. It is telling you that the personal environment you establish not only provides important protection for you but also is a vessel for joy and success. Having the wrong things in this vessel can lead to holes in your physical security.

MILLIPEDE

Tenderness

There are many species of millipedes. Their preferred habitats are damp deciduous forests, meadows, alluvial fields, and orchards. They eat rotting wood and leaves. Millipedes do not have a thousand feet, but some of the longer ones do have a couple of hundred. Each body segment has two hairlike pairs of feet. The body segments are made of chitin and form a relatively hard exoskeleton. The underbelly, however, is very soft and vulnerable. For this reason millipedes roll up into a spiral when danger threatens. They also have another form of self-defense. When attacked, they secrete a toxin from their sides. Some species can spray this secretion half an inch. The secretion is caustic to the mucous membranes.

Millipedes are very clean creatures. They spend a great amount of their time carefully cleaning themselves and smearing themselves with another secretion that protects against fungal infections. For mating, millipedes join together belly to belly for a long time, caressing each other, holding on tight with their many legs. They stroke each other constantly with their legs and feelers. Some time after successful fertilization, the female deposits the eggs in the soil. The larvae molt four times before becoming sexually mature adults. For molting, the millipede digs down into the ground, makes a small round chamber there, and remains until molting is complete and its armor is strong and stable again.

Message

If you encounter a millipede, it wants to let you know that there is a lack of tenderness in your life at the moment. It may be astonishing for such a tiny creature to be the messenger of tenderness. But the tenderness to which the millipede refers is something quite commonplace. It has to do with the consciousness with which you touch. Touching should be an alert encounter between your body and the body of another being. The millipede speaks not only to the tenderness that occurs between lovers but also to a sort of feeling in the fingertips when a person touches someone or something. Be alert in your touching; exercise a certain measure of care in your movements. Let your hands tenderly caress all the things you touch on a daily basis. A tender touch is also possible when you are gripping something firmly. Tenderness has a great deal more to do with consciousness than with the degree of pressure exerted.

It creates an empathetic relationship to the recipient of the touch and lets a connection grow that makes the being or thing one is touching understandable. These are important requirements to ensure that what is planned together, what will be carried out, will really work. Thus, if a millipede crawls into your life, it is telling you to feel very carefully with your fingertips—both physical and psychic—around your environment. You do not need to handle everything with kid gloves; but be tender, searching, and aware of the experience. Approach life with your heart wide open, your back strong and straight. Then life will be graspable for you and a great deal more things will be attainable. Those who move tenderly in their environment are accepted. Also—this may be something very important for you—you will attract plenty of attentiveness and tenderness to yourself as a consequence.

MOSQUITO
Relief

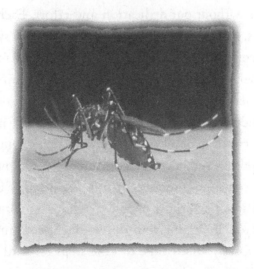

The mosquito is one of summer's great tormentors. It brings us infected bites, sleepless nights, and sometimes sickness and fever. It is only the females that cause such anguish. To produce their eggs they need blood. Males have no piercing mouth parts, live exclusively on plant juices, and are entirely harmless. The central European mosquito does not transmit any diseases.

The mosquito spends its larval and pupal stages in water. When the adult mosquito emerges from the pupa, delicate and iridescent on the surface of the water, it looks like the birth of a tiny angel. Mosquitoes, in water and air alike, are an important part of the food chain. Only in the developed world do people eliminate them with insecticides by the ton in order to get a good night's sleep. Sleeping under mosquito nets accomplishes the same thing in a harmless manner. However, the malaria mosquito is much more dangerous to humans. Malaria is a very widespread illness. About two hundred million people suffer from it worldwide. We not only encounter mosquitoes at night, when they are usually most noticeable, but also by day, in their habitat, when they swarm by the thousands.

Message

The mosquito is the symbol in our lives that tells us that no development can occur without our dedication and effort. Each step of development costs us, so to speak, a few drops of blood and sweat. If you are one of those people who get practically eaten alive by mosquitoes, you are probably making things too hard. It doesn't require blood by the quart; development is not a race.

You can endure a mosquito bite here and there, just as you can endure a step forward in development now and then. But whole swarms of female mosquitoes and developmental steps are too much for people. Oddly enough, some mosquitoes transmit diseases that lead to extreme lethargy. If you are one of those people to whom mosquitoes are greatly attracted, then you are letting your development consume too much of your life force. Give yourself time to take steps forward when you can, not when others expect it from you.

It is rare for the direct consciousness to say, "I have to develop." Much more often people sigh at the perceived burdens of life. If life is too hard it could be that your expectations of yourself, your visions of happiness, are set too high. Go easier on yourself and shrug off burdens that are too big or too difficult. Set priorities and live smaller. A little more permeability and transparency, a little more humming lightness over the habitat of your feelings, will not only protect you from many mosquito bites but also will give you a better feeling about life in general.

MOTH, NIGHT

Transformation of Hidden Sides, Hidden Dreams

There are countless large and small species of moths that fly in the night. Scientifically they are clearly distinguished and have different names. Moths live similarly to butterflies. Under ideal conditions eggs hatch into caterpillars or larvae, which then develop into adult moths. Unlike butterflies, moths are active at night. They are less strikingly colored, and some species are very plentiful. Because many of them are seen by day and by night, we will not distinguish the various species here. They all belong, in the broadest sense, to the Butterfly family, and the only difference relevant for symbol interpretation is that butterflies follow the light of the sun while moths follow the light of the moon. For the purposes of symbol interpretation, butterfly species that resemble moths can in fact be treated as moths.

Message

You encounter nocturnal moths when current events in your life have touched somewhere deep in your past. Normally past events are forgotten. They resolve themselves and disappear from the consciousness like fog beneath the sun. Only things that have not been worked through emotionally remain foggy within us. Remembering the past has a lot more to do with the present than most people believe. Facts are like ice: time changes their form. Light melts them and cold rebuilds them. The present always colors the memory. If things are going well, the subconscious releases only happy images from the past. If things are going badly, the memory focuses on negative events in the past. All people remember a long way back into the physical past, whether through genetically traditional images handed down by our ancestors or through psychic spiritual connections to a past form of existence. All these factors become intermixed in our subconscious and influence the present. The night moth flutters into your life to tell you that ingredients from this soup of memories are dissolving, and their essences are searching for your soul. You do not need to worry about the dissolution; you only need to let the light of your own being radiate so that the transformation of your feminine, sensual side can become effective. Let what happens happen. Examine your dreams and try to distinguish artificial light from natural light in all areas of your life.

SCORPION

Release from Trauma

An encounter with a scorpion causes mild terror in many people. We know from stories how dangerous, even deadly, their venom can be to humans. For European species, this fear is unfounded. They are hardly aggressive, and their sting is comparable to that of a bee. Scorpions are arachnids and are active at night. By day they hide in cracks under stones and in moist, dark places. Scorpions hunt at night for spiders,

millipedes, woodlice, and other insects. The sting is only used for very strong prey. Usually the scorpion grips and kills its victim with its pincers. If a scorpion is threatened, it raises its stinger and pincers. Scorpions are found all over southern Europe, from the southern Alps to the Mediterranean.

Scorpions are extremely robust, able to tolerate high heat and also cold without a problem. Some species can go for a year without eating. Others have been reported living up to half a mile underground. However, encounters between humans and these light-averse arachnids are rare. When mating, the male grips the female with his pincers and places a sperm packet on the ground. Then he dances with his partner and directs her to the place where she can take up the sperm packet into her genital opening. In the hottest days of summer the female gives birth to live young. At first the young scorpions are colorless. Until the first molting, they are carried on their mother's back.

Message

Scorpions remind us of our own personal hell. Deeply traumatic experiences are often the fundamental powers that lead to change in life. Much of human knowledge in the course of life is built upon hurtful experiences and painful knowledge. None of us remember how we burned a finger for the first time and thus learned not to trifle with fire and heat. In the moment the pain was a shock. From this shock, over the course of time, knowledge and experience grew. Hot remained hot, but we learned how to treat it and protect ourselves. If we were connected to the story and the pain connected to it, then dealing with hot things would always be hard. The scorpion comes into our lives to make us aware of the importance of traumatic experiences. Perhaps you have had a very hard experience in your life and as a consequence you are inhibited and irritated. You withdraw from certain areas of life and want nothing more to do with them. Now the scorpion is advising you to honor all difficult experiences and to draw knowledge from them. Only someone who can let things go and forget them is able to build upon the essence of the past. If I burn my finger it is not the fire's fault; the blame lies with my intent to do something that goes against the laws of nature. The same goes for experiences with other people. In this case it is often more complex. If you have been greatly hurt by another person, the scorpion is clearly telling you to bring the experience away from that person and to seek knowledge as to how you should conduct yourself in the future around such people in order to be protected by the laws of nature. Consider that your strengths also function according to the laws of nature. A mother scorpion with her young is telling you to pass on what you learn to other people to whom you are connected.

SILVERFISH

Baggage

Silverfish are light-averse, nocturnal, wingless primordial insects. As the name suggests, these half-inch-long creatures look like tiny fish, moving quickly and nimbly on land. Silverfish live mainly on substances containing cellulose, such as paper, wallpaper paste, and sugar, which they find in moist, cool, dark areas of houses and apartments. They fulfill their protein needs by eating the shed skin particles of their human landlords. In central Europe they are found only in human homes, especially in corners that are not often cleaned with chemical agents.

After external fertilization by means of a sperm packet, the females lay their eggs in cracks and crevices. Silverfish are essentially harmless in that they do not settle in libraries or file storage warehouses.

Message

Every person has baggage: conditioning that stands in the way of development; dogma that makes life hard; thought patterns that hinder one from taking the simplest and straightest way. Such things emerge, on the one hand, from one's own view and from the conclusions reached from past experiences; and on the other hand, from teachings imparted in schooling and the traditional worldview that our environment imprints on us. If silverfish start to be more present in your consciousness, your life should be examined with a great deal of attention and resolve. Shine some light into your accustomed emotional patterns, thought processes, and everyday routines. Ask yourself earnestly whether your feelings, thoughts, and deeds are just functions or whether they really come from a pure perception corresponding to the present. Do not let your life become stuffy and musty just because you have lost the courage to allow change to happen when necessary.

Not all patterns that people follow are baggage. Many patterns regulate our lives in sensible and useful ways and should remain in place. But the patterns that the silverfish points to are obsolete functions; for example, if as an adult you still behave like a small child whenever your mother is nearby, or if you have to speak loudly like a small child whenever you express your needs. Observe these behaviors with a great deal of love, and cease them, because now they only hinder you.

SPIDER

Fate

Not all spiders use their silk glands to spin webs, and not nearly all spiders spin such beautiful webs as the orb weaver. Most house spiders build messy webs, which can be found in stables, in the corners of rooms, and behind projections on walls. The body of the house spider is, as with all spiders, shaped like a figure eight. Instead of the cross pattern found on the orb weaver, it has a red stripe down the middle. Spiders eat insects, which they catch in their webs or hunt in various other ways.

The wolf spider, a well-known hunter, lives on the ground and is very fast. There are also spiders that live underwater. They build many-layered bell-shaped webs, which they fill with air. In these "diving bells," they create a tiny underwater world.

Message

The spider symbolizes infinite possibilities. With its eight legs it is anchored in every direction, and it weaves together the powers of the elements and their expression into a unified whole. The spider weaves webs of fate, in which we can get caught, and it encourages us to keep searching for new possibilities and explore the endless steps of our journey of learning. If your attention is drawn to a spider it wants to remind you that you are constantly building new webs with your own thoughts, feelings, actions, and visions that contain tasks you must solve and subjects you must deal with.

There is not any foreign being weaving your web of fate. You yourself are constantly weaving it with your conscious being, and probably much more often with your unconscious being. Every feeling, thought, action, and wish comes into reality over time and can be experienced. You can only determine good and bad for yourself. If your feelings are full of light, love, and vivacity, your life and your fate can be experienced with these qualities. It is exactly the same with negative feelings, thoughts, wishes, and actions. As you weave your "web," so your life will be formed.

You cannot change what is already woven and coming in the near future. But it is in your power to decide what will be woven from now on. The orb weaver, especially, advises you to make your great plans now. In a luminous and strong way, put feelings, thoughts, deeds, and wishes into the net. Someone who meets with a lot of orb weavers is being given the possibility of taking fate directly into her own hands. Be aware that you are an eternal creation, that the space you traverse is eternity, and that the possibilities within this space are limitless.

Everything you weave will bear fruit—really, everything—and it is up to you to sow only what you also want to harvest. Because every person has this possibility, you can renounce responsibility for others. If you encounter wolf spiders often, you are being told that your life and your destiny have been made too dependent on other people and their deeds, thoughts, feelings, and wishes. You are chasing after good luck, but it is often others who have the power to gain it for you or withhold it. Take this message seriously, for in the eternity of time only you can remedy this misunderstanding.

TICK

Encroachment

Ticks and mites are arachnids. They are mostly small, round, and have the eight legs typical of spiders. Hard ticks are among the most widespread. These creatures go through three developmental stages: larva, nymph, and adult. In all three stages the tick nourishes itself with the blood of animals and humans. Ticks live in meadows and damp forests. They lurk in opportune places, waiting for a host to brush by. On the host they seek out areas of the body with good circulation and cling fast with their sucking mouthparts. Left undisturbed, the tick will fill itself with blood and finally let itself fall off the host. An adult tick can grow from the size of a pinhead to the size of a small grape when engorged. Such a blood meal guarantees that the tick will be able to reproduce. After a blood meal, the male searches for a receptive female, fertilizes her, then dies. The female deposits a fertilized egg packet low down on a blade of grass. Up to three thousand eggs are placed in several such packets, then the female dies. The six-legged larvae hatch from the eggs and begin their search for a host. Their first meal usually comes from a smaller animal, such as a rodent. Over about three days, the larva sucks enough blood from the wound to live on until its first molt. After molting, the nymph, which now has eight legs, hibernates for the winter and looks for a bigger host in the spring to provide the next blood or lymph meal. After this meal the nymph molts again, reaches the adult stage, and searches to find a correspondingly larger host as soon as possible. Ticks are taken very seriously as disease carriers. The danger of acquiring diseases from them has grown considerably in recent years.

Message

The meaning of an encounter with a tick depends on who it has bitten. Fundamentally, it has to do with the listlessness of the inner energy. This means that when we have a lack of vision or a lack of joy in life, when we feel irreversibly trapped by a situation and resign ourselves to it, we are vulnerable and unprotected. The tick signals this weakness, indicating that you are being robbed of your life force and that all manner of parasites can feed on it. Depending on the tick's developmental stage, your weakness is of little, medium, or great significance. Wherever the life force is put to use, there are also weaknesses. Life is transient in the physical world. The life force is like a kind of raw material that gets used up. In reality the energy of the life force turns into experience and wisdom. Life force is available to people in limitless quantities. It is like gas in a car. Gas—at least currently—is available in enormous quantities. But this limitlessness does not apply to the gas tank. In order for your car to keep working you have to check and see whether the tank is sufficiently full. In the case of the human life force, this energy is distributed throughout many domains of life, and it is entirely possible for one domain to have very little energy while the others are brimming over with it. Ticks approach you, or come into your consciousness, either when the energy in your system is not equally distributed throughout the areas of your life—in which case you will encounter ticks searching for food—or else when you are paying too little attention to some area of your life and consequently putting it in danger of exploitation. Encounters with ticks on pets also indicate this. A third possibility is that your life force is being directly sapped by physical, psychic, or spiritual parasites in your environment. Even when such encroachments do not seem too significant, they can have fatal consequences for a system in the long term. If you are bitten by a tick, you should realize that inadequate self-protection, sooner or later, will make you into a parasite yourself, in some way or another. This vicious cycle is somewhat reminiscent of vampire stories. It is sensible not only to protect yourself and your pets from tick bites as much as possible but also to protect your life force from being wasted or stolen. Take the message of the tick seriously. Make sure there are no unprotected weaknesses in your system, and learn to oversee the boundaries of your energy and your possibilities.

TRUE BUG, STINK BUG

Protection of the Inner World

There are countless types of true bugs. Here the emphasis is on stink bugs. These are distinguished by their relatively large shield-shaped bodies and their flat body form, reminiscent of a small leaf. The shield is green in the spring and turns browner in the winter. In front of the shield is a small beaklike head with two large eyes and two feelers with five segments each. On the head there are also stabbing and sucking mouth parts, which are retracted under the body when not in use. Most stink bugs suck plant juices and live in meadows, gardens, and at the edges of forests. When disturbed they release an evil-smelling secretion. This is especially unpleasant when found on berries. The stink bug's development goes through five stages from egg to adult. The larvae look similar to the adult, except they are much smaller. The wings form the shield shape only in the adult phase.

Message

An encounter with a stink bug tells you to protect your inner health. One is healthy when everything in one's life is following the inner divine plan. Health also includes contentment, well-being, and being psychically and physically "in order." Health is more than just bodily health. Health is commonly understood to mean having a perfectly functioning body and a psyche that is well adapted to societal norms. But in the broadest sense, health means being connected with one's complete soul and being conscious of it. If this state endures one also experiences this higher form of health in one's life. If your attention is drawn to a stink bug, then in that moment you are losing light-filled and tender energy. Your connection to your inner flow is being disturbed, and the consequence will be that you will not be able to remain content and that not everything is in order for you. What is consuming you right now, what subject lingers in the background of your mind? It is now important to take on this subject consciously and deprive it of its lurking power. Perhaps worries are clouding the lightness of your life, and it is hard for you to stay in the present moment. The stink bug tells you not to let yourself be disturbed. With conscious love for your own being, you should protect a space that you can be in where, much like a child, you can believe only in light and good things. Even if a person cannot live solely in this healthy inner world, it is still true that this world is essential for a healthy life, and the overall assumption is that difficult times can be tolerated externally.

WASP, HORNET

Negligence

Superficially, wasps seem very similar to bees. They build colonies around a queen. Unlike bees, however, wasps and hornets build nests with material from their own bodies. They strip fibers from rotten wood with their sharp mouthparts and chew them to make a sticky pulp. They form this paperlike pulp into honeycomb structures. Each wasp and hornet colony lives for only one summer.

Wasps and hornets die at the first frost. Only the fertilized queen lives through the winter. She lays her eggs in the nest, and when the grubs hatch she feeds them with a pulp of chewed-up caterpillars and insect larvae. The young wasps soon help the queen with her work, taking care of newly hatched grubs. A breeding wasp colony consumes enormous numbers of other insects. However, the adults live mainly on rotten fruit and other sugary substances. In the fall a number of drones hatch. If these survive the winter, they found a new colony in the spring. The old queen dies during the first frosty nights. Female wasps have a smooth stinger that can be used to sting repeatedly, multiple times.

Wasps are easily provoked to sting. Hornets are the largest type of wasp. They are greatly feared due to their dangerous sting.

Message

Wasps and hornets remind us of negligence. If you have an encounter with one of these insects, you should pay more attention to your own self. How quickly we forget ourselves! It is not advisable to neglect one's own personality.

Do not nourish yourself on the apparent sweetness of rotten fruit. Nourish your being not with symbols of the past (grubs); live in the now. We are right to fear wasps, and especially hornets. Great and small negligence sows seeds for greater and smaller pain. During the good time—summer, when there is sun and ripe fruit—negligence often creeps in.

Do not neglect to be yourself, for it is not only your destiny but also your life's task.

WOODLOUSE

Radicalism, Discovery

Woodlice are crustaceans that have adapted, in the course of evolution, for life on land. Their bodies are covered with gray armor consisting of several plates. Underneath, there are seven pairs of legs. These gill-breathing arthropods are adapted to a damp, fairly cool habitat. Therefore they are often found under stones, in hidden cracks and corners, in the saucers underneath potted plants, and so forth. They are found throughout the whole world, living in colonies, and are mostly active at night. They live on decomposing plant matter. They chew up rotting leaves, grass, and even wood with their sharp mouthparts, thus making an important contribution to decomposition. Their feces are a significant fertilizer and also provide nourishment for many organisms involved in the conversion of plant matter into humus. Young woodlice hatch from eggs and molt about fourteen times before reaching sexual maturity at three months. After that they grow slowly and molt rarely. When in danger the woodlouse rolls up into a ball; in this body position it looks like a tiny armadillo.

Message

Anyone who works in a garden or cleans out a cellar will encounter these land crustaceans. Whole families of them often gather under a stone, flowerpot, or even under a damp towel. These shade-loving creatures, when disturbed, quickly look for something new to hide under. The woodlouse urges us to be radical, not so much in the work we are currently performing, but in the original sense of the word. It tells you always to go straight to the root of yourself. Ask yourself what your truth is at this moment. Who are you, and how do you feel? Who is this person with no makeup, stage, role, or mission? Confront yourself for a bit, honestly and radically. When you observe yourself in this way, you will see a completely normal woman or man. Normal is what grows out of people's traditions and background, with all sides of light and shadow. Go to the root of the realm corresponding to your most normal, natural self, so that you will be able to call up the memory for yourself, again and again, of the actual person who is really standing behind all the roles that you play. Everyone who meets the woodlouse meets with her own normal essence. You are no exception! And that is very, very important. Your image, your role in society, and the play of your life story can be something special, but a memory must remain in you of your human nature, your human norm. This is the root, the basis of which everything that exists is built. And as you know, a strong foundation is needed for a solid building. When you know your norm—when you have encountered this normal woman or man—then you can wink at yourself and let this normality sneak back into the play that you must put on for the world.

BIBLIOGRAPHY

Note: The following books are German editions used for the author's research. These books are not available in English, but translations of the titles are included here.

Bellmann, Heiko. *Der neue Kosmos Insektenführer* [The New Cosmos Insect Guide]. Stuttgart: Frankh-Kosmos-Verlag, 1999.

Chinery, Michael. *Pareys Buch der Insekten* [Parey's Book of Insects]. Stuttgart: Frankh-Kosmos-Verlag, 2004.

Dierl, Wolfgang. *Welcher Käfer ist das?* [Which Bug Is This?] 2nd edition. Stuttgart: Frankh-Kosmos-Verlag, 1974.

Eisenreich, Wilhelm. *Der neue BLV-Naturführer für unterwegs* [The New BLV Naturalists Guide], 4th edition. Munich, Vienna, Zurich: Sonderausgabe, 1998.

Heiligmann, Werner. *Das Tier* [The Animal], 2nd edition. Edited by Horst Janus and Helmut Länge. Stuttgart: Ernst-Klett-Verlag, 1983.

———. *Grzimeks Enzyklopädie: Säugetiere* [Grzimek's Encyclopedia: Mammals], vols. 1–5. Munich: Kindler-Verlag, 1988.

———. *Der Jugend-Brockhaus* [The Youth Brockhaus], 2nd edition, vol. 3. Edited by Eberhard Anger. Leipzig: Brockhaus Verlag, 1993.

Kahle, Dr. Walther. "Vögel." *Brehms Tierleben* ["Birds." Brehm's Life of Animals], vol. 3. Leipzig: Bibliographisches Institut, 1934.

———. *Die Vögel Europas* [European Birds]. Munich: Mosaik-Verlag, 2000.

———. *Die häufigsten Vogelarten der Schweiz* [The Most Common Bird Species in Switzerland]. Zurich: Verlag Das Beste, 1985.

———. *Schweizer Brutvogelatlas* [Swiss Breeding Bird Atlas]. Vogelwarte Sempach, Switzerland: Verlag schweizerische, 1998.

———. *Altentiere Kompass* [Old Animals Guidebook]. Innsbruck: Fleischmann and Mair, 1990.

Meier, Christoph. *Die Vögel Graubündens* [The Birds of Graubündens], 2nd edition. Disentis-Chur: Bündner Monatsbl, 1996.

Mermod-Gasser, Viviane. *Wunderwelt der Insekten* [The Wonderful World of Insects]. Lausanne: Mondo-Verlag, 1982.

———. *Pflanzen und Tiere Europas* [Plants and Animals of Europe]. Braunschweig: Westermann-Lexikon, 1995.

Svensson, Mullarney, and Grant Zetterström. *Der neue Kosmos Vogelführer* [The New Cosmos Bird Guide]. Stuttgart: Frankh-Kosmos-Verlag, 1999.

Urania Tierreich Enzyklopädie [The Urania Animal Kingdom Encyclopedia], vols. 1–8. Berlin: Urania Verlag, 2000.

Zahradník, Hísek. *Käfer* [Beetle]. Munich: Mosaik-Verl, 1976.

INDEX OF ANIMALS
AND THEIR MESSAGES

Animal	Message	Page
Hamster	Domestic balance, health	38
Hare	Fear	39
Harvestman	Expansion	264
Hazel Grouse	Honest action	121
Horse	Life force	41
Horsefly	Exploitation	266
Jaybird	Zest for life	127
Kingfisher	Guardian of the elements	129
Kite	Expansion	131
Lacewing	Bliss	268
Ladybug	Luck	269
Lark	Prayer	132
Linnet	Search for consensus	134
Lizard	Dreams, ideas	206
Louse, Head Louse	Contemplation	271
Lynx	Mystery, secrecy, concealment	44
Magpie	Stealing	135
Marmot	Modesty	46
May Beetle, June Bug	Ensnarement	238
Meal Moth, Clothing Moth	Precision	273
Merganser, Smew	Chance	138
Millipede	Tenderness	275
Mole	Action	48
Moose	Self-awareness	50
Mosquito	Relief	277
Mouse	Perfection	53
Muskrat	Settlement of feelings	55
Night Moth	Transformation of hidden sides, hidden dreams	279
Nightingale	Yearning	139
Nuthatch	Withdrawal	141
Old World Oriole	Truth, authenticity	142
Otter	Femininity, love	57
Owl	Wisdom	144
Oystercatcher	Stability	147
Partridge	Custom, tradition	149

INDEX OF
MESSAGES ASSOCIATED
WITH THE ANIMALS